# How Come I'm Dead?

# HOW COME? I'M DEAD?

by
**Glen McDonald**
with
**John Kirkwood**

hancock
house

ISBN 0-88839-187-0

Copyright © 1985 Glen McDonald with John Kirkwood

Canadian Cataloging in Publication Data

McDonald, Glen   1919-
How Come I'm Dead?

Includes index
ISBN 0-88839-187-0

1. McDonald, Glen, 1919-  2. Coroners — British Columbia —
Biography. 3. Vancouver (B.C.) — Biography.
I. Kirkwood, John, 1932-  II. Title.

RA1025.M29A34 1985   614'.1'0924   C85-091314-4

Edited by Betty Pembroke
Editorial assistance by Jerry Eberts and Dorothy Eberts
Typeset and paste-up by Hardip Johal
Design/Layout by Dorothy Forbes
Cover photo by Ralph Bower
Printed in Canada by Friesen Printers

Song *Those Were The Days.* Words and music by Gene Raskin.
Copyright © 1962, 1968, 1977 Essex Music, Inc.

Published simultaneously in Canada and the United States by

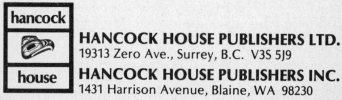

HANCOCK HOUSE PUBLISHERS LTD.
19313 Zero Ave., Surrey, B.C.  V3S 5J9
HANCOCK HOUSE PUBLISHERS INC.
1431 Harrison Avenue, Blaine, WA  98230

# Table of Contents

# *Prologue*

Oct. 6, 1969

Coroner,
Glen McDonald
Vancouver, B.C.

Sir,

The first thing that I must point out is that my failure to sign this letter is not from fear, but rather I would like you to appreciate the authenticity rather than from whence the letter came.

One of the most impressive moments of my life was when I sat in your courtroom and heard you say, "If Myrna Louise Inglis were here, she would probably say, 'Did you, my society, let me down?'" Then you carried on to discuss that nothing here would bring her back, but the purpose of this trial is to possibly prevent a reoccurence of the tragedy in the future.

This was possibly the most foresight used by any enforcement agency. It probably carried more weight than anything else done to educate the public of the possibility of a tragedy happening to them, rather than to somebody else.

Thank You Sir.

This anonymous handwritten letter was delivered to Judge Glen McDonald of the Vancouver Coroner's Court after he held an inquest into the stabbing death of a 26-year-old nurse as she walked home from St. Paul's Hospital in the city's West End.

Judge McDonald received many such grateful letters—some even written in Chinese—in the twenty-six years he served as Coroner. They gratified him because they showed that people were listening to what he and his inquest juries were saying.

He had decided when he started in the job in late 1953 that the Coroner was the *Ombudsman of the Dead.* His job was always positive, never negative. That job was to study the cause of death in order to protect the living.

Judge McDonald's morgue in Vancouver's seedy Skidroad district admitted an average of 1,100 bodies a year. Inquests averaged 1.5 per week: a traffic death every week, a homicide every two weeks, an industrial death every month, 75 deaths a year from suicidal or accidental domestic gas poisoning.

He and his staff investigated deaths by shooting, stabbing, strangulation, poisoning and bludgeoning. Deaths at sea and in the air. Deaths in the construction industry. Deaths on the railway tracks and on the streets and highways. Deaths by suicide. Drug overdose deaths. Deaths of the very young, the young, the middle-aged, the old, the very old.

The Coroner took pride in the fact that he never let himself become hardened and cynical in his years spent dealing with death. He never said, "Well, I've seen all this before—so what?"

Instead, he said, "The Coroner's Court is not a closure. Rather, it's an Open Sesame Court, a public forum where everything should come out. An inquest is the last hearing a deceased is going to have and all should be allowed to assemble and be present and all others will be duly informed by the media."

That was why Judge McDonald said to his inquest juries, "Ask of yourselves that one last question. How come I'm dead?"

The dead could not ask it.

The jurors could, on behalf of the deceased. Maybe they could also find the answer.

*A Coroner's duty is to warn*
*the populace of any pestilence*
*in the land.*

---

# *Dedication*

---

This book is dedicated to my staff who performed their duties faithfully and conscientiously during the twenty-six years I was Vancouver Coroner, and to the staff of the City Analyst's Office who always worked closely with us in a spirit of splendid cooperation.

It is also especially for the thousands of British Columbians who, as members of Coroner's juries, honestly and willingly discharged their sworn duties in my courtroom without fear, favor or affection. In this way they made the Coroner's forum work the way it should—in public and always with a view to protecting the living.

Thanks for the support of you all.
Glen McDonald
Crescent Beach
British Columbia
Summer, 1984

# Captain Blood's Last

# Hurrah

Vancouver is a good place to die, you
know. Texas Guinan died there.
*Errol Flynn* shortly before
he died in Vancouver.

It was eight o'clock in the evening of Wednesday, October 14, 1959 when Captain Blood arrived at the Vancouver City Morgue. The visitor was also Robin Hood, Don Juan, Gentleman Jim and The Master of Ballantrae.

It was Errol Flynn and he hadn't dropped in for a social chat. He lay on an ambulance stretcher under a grey blanket. For once, the Sultan of Suave wasn't acting.

Judge Glen McDonald of the Coroner's Court had been about to leave his office after a long day when the telephone rang.

"Glen McDonald."

It was the dispatcher from Metropolitan Ambulance.

"Mac, we've got a beauty for you."

"Who? What?"

"Did you hear Errol Flynn died?"

"No, I didn't hear."

"Well, he's dead and we're bringing him down to the morgue so don't go away. It's going to be a busy night."

"I'll be damned!"

* * *

So the famous Errol Flynn was coming down to Skidroad, not of his own choosing. How about that?

I'd been looking forward to a gin and tonic and dinner. Most everyone knew Flynn had been in Vancouver for several days visiting with a flamboyant businessman named Georgie Caldough. There'd been a lot of press. It had something to do with the buying of his yacht, the *Zaca,* by Mr. Caldough. Flynn was supposed to be financially strapped and needed the money. He was broke, I guess.

He was on his way back to Los Angeles with his young girlfriend, Beverly Aadland, and the Caldoughs. It turned out he hadn't been feeling well for several days up to this Wednesday and, on the way to the airport, had asked for a doctor. Caldough drove to the Sylvia Hotel on the English Bay waterfront to find the house doctor, Grant Gould. He wasn't there. He then phoned Dr. Gould at his office and told him what was what. Grant Gould said he was just leaving for home. Why not meet him at his apartment at 1310 Burnaby Street in the West End?

The visit turned into a bit of a party. Flynn was there for a few hours, talking about his swashbuckling life and his image as a matinee idol. Booze flowed. Everyone was having a great time but the star of the show was obviously suffering discomfort.

Flynn suffered severe back pain at one stage and excused himself. He went to Dr. Gould's bedroom and lay down on the floor and died. Dr. Gould and Caldough thumped on his chest, trying to revive him; Beverly Aadland desperately tried mouth-to-mouth resuscitation. The Fire Department Inhalator and an ambulance were called. Dr. Gould pronounced him dead and the ambulance crew took the body to Vancouver General Hospital where Flynn was further certified dead. He wasn't admitted, though. Instead, the body came down to the morgue.

* * *

The Vancouver City Police report, signed by PC 368 Marshall and PC 440 Johnston (who managed to spell the celluloid hero's name wrong) of Car 1, Squad 1, stated: "Sudden death; Flynn Erroll; 7047 Franklin Ave., Hollywood, Calif.; Nationality, Australian; Sex, male; Age, 50; Occupation, actor."

The report put the time of death at 6:35 p.m. and said the Fire Department Inhalator Squad and Dr. Grant Gould had tried unsuccessfully to revive Flynn. Others present at the apartment were Mr. and Mrs. George Caldough of West Vancouver, Beverly Aadland of Hollywood, and Mr. and Mrs. Art Cameron of the Sylvia Hotel.

* * *

At the Morgue things were going crazy even before the damn body arrived. The news media and everyone else were on the phone—the local media first, but it wasn't long before the international guys came on. And they came on strong! Was it true? What had happened? Had Flynn been murdered? Where was Beverly Aadland? Could they take pictures? At that stage I could say nothing. All I could do was stall, tell them to call back. I got hold of Dr. Tom Harmon, my Chief Pathologist. He said he could attend because he was just cleaning up the day's work. We were prepared, more or less, to receive the celebrated Mr. Flynn as a Coroner's case. Then he arrived—via the back alley. The name *E. FLYNN* was chalked on the morgue blackboard.

When a citizen of a foreign country, such as the United States, dies in Vancouver we are, of course, unable to find out the cause of death from a family physician. So, before the body can be removed in care of a funeral director or the next-of-kin, we have to have an acceptable cause of death. This is done by autopsy and it's standard procedure.

I'm talking about an ordinary guy—Joe Blow from Kokomo. But here we suddenly had the body of a man of international stature, a figure adulated around the world, the hero of millions. I knew damn well the cause of death was going to be positively and thoroughly ascertained by autopsy. I had a gut feeling that another autopsy would be done later, in California. We were on the hot seat.

The calls were even more fast and furious by now: from Toronto, Montreal, New York, Miami and, of course, Hollywood. But all I could say at this time was that, yes, we *did* have the body of Errol Flynn in the morgue; it had been positively identified. Four phone lines were jumping, non-stop. Even the night janitor was talking to *The New York Times.*

The autopsy was the important thing. Then there was the question of how the body was to be removed, where to and to whom. I called the American Consul to find out who Flynn's next-of-kin was and learned it was Patrice Wymore, the actress. Flynn had had two or three wives and I wasn't sure who the current one was, my theatrical expertise being somewhat wanting. Things were further complicated by the fact that the girl Beverly Aadland, who was only 17, was here with her late paramour. That didn't help.

Patrice Wymore's attorney phoned from California after a while and told me they would definitely do an autopsy in Los Angeles, as I had suspected. I told him we were about to start one here, that everything we did would be fully documented and all specimens we took would be sent south with the late Mr. Flynn. I said I'd let him know the minute I had a cause of death, give him all the details, sign the death certificate and a permit to remove the body would be issued by the provincial government Department of Vital Statistics. "Fine," he said.

The identification was easy. Who could possibly mistake Errol Flynn? We knew this unexpected guest couldn't be anybody *but* Errol

Flynn. But we did the routine photography and fingerprinting and so on as protection against questions that could be asked in the future. That's standard. You have to do that.

It was a sad and lonely final curtain to such a glamorous and magical career. It made me think of all of our frailties. Flynn was carried in by the ambulance guys, lying on a stretcher and covered with a blanket. He was all alone; none of the others from the party came, not even Beverly. He was wearing slacks and an open-necked shirt and a jacket.

He had certainly been certified dead enough times by now and, to all appearances, he *was* dead. However, he was still routinely tested for any signs of life. We used a stethoscope for pulse and heartbeat and we did a violent stimulation of the soles of the feet.

That's what happens to you when you come to the morgue. It's not nice but you aren't in a position to object. It's a routine job the technicians always do. If it isn't done, some smart lawyer may ask later: "Well, *why* wasn't it done?" The horror story could come up: "You mean to say you locked this person up in that refrigerated area in your bloody morgue and did not first ascertain that he was really dead? What do you think you're doing in this place?" No way a Coroner wants *that* question thrown at him.

Errol Flynn was stripped. All his clothes and personal possessions were noted and put in the old turkey bag and signed for and witnessed by the attending officers. This, by the way, is just a brown paper bag we put stuff in and staple shut. It's called a turkey bag because it's big enough to hold a turkey. Or maybe because the poor turkey whose stuff is in it is no longer in the land of the living.

We didn't find much in the way of personal effects. Not much money—a few bills, a few coins and a credit card. There was a ring. It was on, I believe, his left hand but it wasn't particularly noticeable, not a huge sparkler or anything. It looked pretty cheap to me, in fact, like a trinket from a five-and-dime store. Everything was itemized. If it was a penny, a diamond, a paper clip or a million bucks it had to be noted and signed for.

\* \* \*

The Vancouver City Police report of Wednesday, October 14, 1959 stated: "The deceased's body was searched and the following effects removed and tagged—1 cigarette lighter; 1 money clip contg follg denominations, Cdn money 1 x 20, 2 x 2, 1 x 1; American money 2 x 20, 1 x 10, 1 x 1. Total bills $76.00; silver, $3.70; 1 gold-plated men's w-watch with bracelet and band initialled 'E.F.' "

\* \* \*

Flynn's body was tagged, another routine procedure. We put a cardboard tag on the big toe and a grease pencil mark of the name and morgue number on the thigh. That mark stays on the remains until fingerprints and other means of identification either confirm or change it. It seemed, I thought at the time, an ignominious end for a famous movie star—lying in the morgue of a foreign city with a tag on his toe and a grease pencil mark on his thigh. But that's life. That's death.

There was no necklace around Errol Flynn's neck, or indeed, anything to indicate there ever had been one there. I mention this because a book has subsequently come out, written by a guy named Charles Higham, and called *Errol Flynn, The Untold Story.* In it, Higham writes that some people said Flynn was wearing a gold chain around his neck with a key attached to it, allegedly the key to a safety deposit box in Switzerland. When Flynn's body was returned to California, chain and key were missing.

That story sounds far-fetched to me. I certainly never saw a gold chain or a key of any kind when Mr. Flynn was a guest in my morgue. There was nothing around his neck except the collar of his shirt. Maybe a chain and a key had been there previously. Georgie Caldough could probably have confirmed or denied that but he's dead, too. Maybe Beverly Aadland had something to do with it. But had a chain and key been there when he came to the morgue, there would have been a notation of the fact signed by the attending officers and also by the next-of-kin is appointed funeral director when the personal possessions were claimed. There was nothing like that there that night. Curiously, though, our complete file on Errol Flynn, including photographs of him lying on a slab, mysteriously disappeared sometime later. Nobody knows who took it or why.

\* \* \*

Charles Higham wrote, in his book: "Up to the last moment of his life, Errol had worn around his neck the key to a safe-deposit box in Switzerland that contained numerous personal papers, stock certificates, bonds, and some half million dollars in cash. The key disappeared sometime between the apartment and the autopsy room. Nobody knows who stole it. Three weeks later, when Justin Golenbock (Flynn's attorney) authorized someone in Switzerland to open the box, it was empty. The mystery has never been solved."

As Judge McDonald says, the story sounds far-fetched. Nobody saw a chain or a key. And if Errol Leslie Thomson Flynn had half a million dollars stashed away in Switzerland, why would he have been trying to sell the yacht *Zaca* to George Caldough for $150,000?

\* \* \*

I couldn't help thinking that that remark Flynn made about Texas Guinan dying in Vancouver was terribly ironic because now here *he* was lying in our morgue. Somebody had asked him in Los Angeles why he was going up to Vancouver and he made the crack jokingly. Texas ("Hello Sucker") Guinan was one of the oldtime artistes, like Mae

West, and she was playing the old Beacon Theatre in 1933 when she suffered stomach pains, went to St. Paul's Hospital for an ulcer operation and died. Flynn had remembered that sad story.

I took a long look at the man lying there on the cold slab that night. After all, he was one of my heroes, too. I could relate to Captain Blood and Robin Hood and Don Juan. I recall Doc Harmon and one of the technicians taking a peek, too, and saying he looked like a man wasted away from fast and hard living. He was a tired old man; a man who had lived well and now was dead as a result. He sure as hell wasn't the dashing Captain Blood any longer.

His face was sallow and a bit puffy and he looked an awful lot older than his fifty years. He looked worn out, wasted. But you look a lot different in life than in death so comparisons aren't really fair. I felt sad because here was the end of an era, the end of a legend, the death of a hero. Now it was just another entry in the log. It was, indeed, Captain Blood's last hurrah. Alone in a morgue on Vancouver's Skidroad.

I told Dr. Harmon his autopsy would have to be dictated that night because of all the pressure from the news media. I also got Ted Fennell, the Chief City Analyst, to come down and run toxicology tests for alcohol, barbiturates and so forth as we proceeded with the autopsy.

*     *     *

The Coroner's subsequent Report of Inquiry into the death of Errol Leslie Flynn listed the autopsy findings as: myocardial infarction; coronary thrombosis; coronary atherosclerosis; fatty degeneration of the liver; portal cirrhosis of the liver and diverticulosis of the colon. The Coroner added: "I am, therefore, of the opinion that this death should be classified, in view of the above noted autopsy findings, as having been due to natural causes."

This finding would be released to the press. But I sure as hell didn't tell the press about what happened during the autopsy. That would have been a disaster! Before Tom Harmon started, we had made a complete examination of the remains. An observation Dr. Harmon made startled me. It concerned a number of VD warts on the end of Flynn's penis. Tom seemed fascinated.

"Well, Tom," I said, "they may be of clinical interest to you as a medical man, but there's going to be another autopsy done down in Los Angeles. I really don't think these warts are material to the case. Unless you disagree."

"Perhaps not," he said.

Then he added: "But, look, I'm going to be lecturing at the Institute of Pathology and I just thought it might be of interest if I could remove these things and fix them in formaldehyde and use them as a visual aid."

"No way!" I said. "We're not going to do that. I don't want

anything done that isn't relevant to this case because we're really in the limelight tonight. We're on the hot seat. How can we send Mr. Flynn back to his wife with part of his bloody endowment missing? That wouldn't be nice."

I also knew there was going to be a lot more publicity about the whole episode, including the treatment Dr. Gould had administered at the apartment. So I insisted on absolutely no change or variation of routine procedures. These are internationally recognized methods of determining a cause of death. They had to be followed meticulously. I left Doc Harmon and Errol Flynn alone in the autopsy room.

Meanwhile, the telephones were still ringing like mad and I went back to answering calls from Australia, London, Rome, Paris, New York. It seemed like it would never stop. The newsgathering agencies, Reuters and Associated Press and so on, were now wanting followups. Every branch of the media was in on the act. The night janitor had become an expert on evading questions. "No comment" was a phrase proudly added to his vocabulary.

After a while, Doc Harmon strolled casually into my office. "Well, I've finished," he said.

"Have you dictated it?"

"Yes."

"Good."

Now I at least had something written down as to cause of death which I could hand out to satisfy everyone that there had been no foul play or suicide. There was no reason to suspect anything like that. But when a man of Flynn's fame and flamboyance suddenly drops dead, all of these things rush forward and have to be answered. How did it happen? People wanted to know. I wanted to tell them. The autopsy findings would now get the bloody newshounds off my back for a while.

Tom and I went back to the autopsy room and the first thing I noticed was that the VD warts had gone—vanished from the end of Mr. Flynn's penis. Then I spotted a jar of formaldehyde on a shelf that looked suspiciously like it just might contain VD warts. It did.

Oh, God!

Tom had gone and done it.

Christ!

I sighed and asked the Doc: "Did you *have* to remove those bloody warts? Because I don't think you should have done that. We have nothing in the cause of death that indicates warts had anything to do with it. Did Errol Flynn expire because he had warts on his dong?"

Tom looked sheepish but we were both laughing at the utter silliness of the whole thing.

"Let's put them back," I said. "Right now!"

I should explain in passing that we do take specimens for analysis—blood, liver, kidney, brain and so on. But this was a different situation.

Maybe the Doc had never seen warts of that enormity. Maybe he wanted a souvenir. I never did figure out why but the temptation had been too great. I've since assumed that the warts—there was a circling of three or four—were the result of Flynn's carefree pursuit of the aboriginal women in Port Darwin, Australia in his youth before penicillin was discovered.

If it had been necessary to remove them for microscopic or histological examination, fair enough. That would have been correctly a part of the autopsy. But in my lay approach to the matter I couldn't see any need for it, particularly as we now had another message from the attorney who had phoned back to stress again that everything was to be sent to California for the second autopsy. The possibility had arisen that a double indemnity clause in Flynn's insurance might be applicable, this having been a sudden death. I wanted not only to cooperate but not to appear to have failed to cooperate.

So the bloody warts were fished out of the formaldehyde jar and, using the good offices of scotch tape, Doc Harmon and I stuck them back where they belonged. Everything was back to normal. And I was relieved to learn later, talking with the Chief Coroner in Los Angeles, that a further autopsy was performed and the results concurred in every respect with what we had found. The scotch tape was never mentioned. Odd, that. I thought somebody down there would have been curious.

And, while we're on the subject, I'll answer the eternal question: how big was Errol Flynn's penis? Looking at bodies over the years, I've learned that death has no compliments to hand out. Errol Flynn was no larger and no smaller in his stature, his jewels, his endowment, than any other man. So there may well be hope for the inferior feeling males of the world if, indeed, that's the sort of thing they're concerned about.

*　*　*

It had now been officially announced that Errol Flynn, the dashing hero of sixty not very good movies and single-handed winner of several celluloid wars, was dead. Vancouver buzzed deliciously with juicy rumours: women were pounding on the doors of the morgue, weeping and demanding to be let in; flowers were being delivered by the truckload; Flynn's penis, said to be fourteen inches long, had been cut off to be exhibited in a circus sideshow; Flynn had committed suicide; Flynn had been murdered.

All untrue.

*　*　*

Sure, we heard all these goofy stories. One radio report was that hundreds of hysterical girls were lining up outside the morgue to get in for a look, probably at his penis. Crazy stories like that were going around town by some sort of jungle telegraph. Another report was that we were allowing these gals in to put flowers on the corpse of their hero.

Well, I don't know what happened after I finally went home that night but if some folks did get in, I sure as hell hope my staff charged them admission and made a few bucks.

The true story of that night at the morgue is this: we had only a couple of policemen there for the identification and the witnessing of the taking of the clothing and personal effects. There were no outsiders, only the staff. The odd policewoman dropped in for a look, but what the hell! We certainly weren't going to turn this sad night into a Roman holiday or a circus. We would have been severely—and rightly—criticized if that had happened. It didn't.

*　*　*

The back of the morgue, where the bodies were admitted and taken up to the autopsy room in a slow hydraulic elevator, is in a lane that runs behind the police station. Years ago some wiseguys nicknamed it *McDonald Alley* because I had successfully petitioned the City Fathers to have it paved to get rid of the dust that floated into my office. That was where Errol Flynn was brought in and no one was there except the ambulance attendants and perhaps some passing cops. Maybe the odd drunk. It was that part of town.

People did take to walking down the back alley or along Cordova Street out front that night. They were staring up at the windows with lights on and asking anybody going in or coming out if it was true and could they, please, come in for a peek at the man from the movies? There weren't many, certainly not hundreds, and a lot of them were dear old gals from the Empress and Stratford beer parlors. I guess it was a bit of excitement for them; they didn't have much else to entertain them. But there was a genuine feeling of sadness. They had lost somebody, lost a hero. Part of the magic of the theatre or the movies is, of course, that people identify with the hero or the heroine and a lot of people had lost their hero that night. It was as simple as that.

I like to think Flynn had had good sport and a well-played game right to the end. People's reactions to his death were perfectly natural. They were interested, saddened and shocked. The one thing they all had in common was that their handsome, swashbuckling hero was gone forever. The patrons in the beer parlors felt honored perhaps to have in their midst—just across the lane—a man of Flynn's stature, even though he was dead. So their curiosity was natural. Why not troop and sometimes stagger down the alley to see what they could see and what they thought they might see and what they thought they had seen? Good on them. But we kept tight security that night. Our biggest damn headache came from the swarms of reporters and cameramen around.

*　*　*

Some months after that hectic night, the ghost of Errol Flynn walked into Judge Glen McDonald's life. The bizarre incident still puzzles him. Patrice Wymore, Flynn's widow, came to Vancouver to perform a nightclub act. The Coroner was seized with what he thought was a bright idea. Unfortunately, it backfired.

\*   \*   \*

She was booked into the Cave as a singer and dancer. There was a lot of publicity. Flynn's widow and all that. Well, it occurred to me that maybe she'd like to talk to me and Dr. Grant Gould, two people who had been intimately involved with the medical side of her husband's death. If she had any questions, we'd answer them, and maybe clear up some worries for her. I'd received absolutely nothing further from California; no further requests for information or anything. Not even about the scotch-taped warts. Dr. Gould and I met at the Cave and Ken Stauffer, who was co-owner, said he had arranged for us to see Miss Wymore backstage between sets. Fine. She was sitting in her dressing room, knitting.

Ken introduced us and I went quickly into my spiel. Obviously, we'd picked the wrong time or the wrong place or the wrong Goddamn something. Everything seemed to be wrong. She let go with an explosion of earthy, four-letter, longshoreman language to the effect that we were bloody murderers or had done something to cause her husband's death. We beat a hasty retreat in some confusion. It was my distinct impression, too, that a heavy and potentially injurious object was hurled in our direction as we fled. An ashtray, I think. It hit the door. So much for good intentions.

It was understandable, I suppose. Maybe sorrow had manifested itself in a sudden outburst of anger. We were just trying to be nice guys but she obviously had a few ideas of her own about what had happened the night Flynn died. The matter of his estate had apparently become very complicated and tangled and there was a lot of bad blood between various parties, including Beverly Aadland and her mother. So who knows what Miss Wymore had heard by way of nasty rumors and hearsay down in Hollywood? The lady had her problems and we weren't helping any by barging in on her. And, I guess, underneath it all was the presence of Beverly, Flynn's 17-year-old nymphet, nicknamed Woodsy. I always assumed that the gal was an intelligent and caring type because when Flynn had collapsed, she had immediately tried mouth-to-mouth resuscitation. By all accounts she'd behaved in a capable and adult manner.

\*   \*   \*

This was borne out by Vancouver businessman Ron Leggo, who had attended a party at George Caldough's lavish West Vancouver home the day before Flynn died. "I was very impressed by Beverly because of the mature way she behaved," Leggo recalls. "There were a hell of a lot of catty and cutting remarks being made about her by some of the females and the kid had the ability to take them without cutting the other gals down. She wasn't the scatterbrained gold digger many people made her out to be. Flynn, of course, was the magnet of the party. People gravitated to him and he was always in the middle of a group. He was wearing a mauve open-necked shirt and I do seem to remember seeing a chain around his neck."

\* \* \*

Speaking of Beverly, I still laugh about the outrageous remark Errol Flynn made when he arrived with her at his side at the Vancouver Airport. Ruth Pinkus, then a reporter with The Sun, asked him naively why he went around with such young girls. He looked her right in the eye and said, "Because they fuck so good!" Everyone blushed, except Flynn and Beverly. Jack Wasserman, also with The Sun at the time, was so shocked he vowed he would never mention Flynn's name in his column again. But Wass soon had to break his vow because a couple of days later Errol Flynn dropped dead and a gossip columnist sure as hell couldn't ignore that item.

To me, that blunt remark summed up the true nature of the man. He obviously said what he honestly felt. And he was famous enough to get away with it, whereas most of us aren't. I guess a lot of men envied him that special status—to be the swashbuckling celluloid hero who called things the way they were in real life. Certainly, his own life was scandalous and often mysterious.

Flynn's death certainly wasn't the most important or the busiest time in my 26 years as Coroner but it was one of the most publicized events. And I'm still damn proud of the way the staff handled such a delicate situation in the glare of worldwide publicity. The whole world had been aroused and there was enormous curiosity and interest. I felt the people had an absolute right to know all the details and exactly what happened that night. And they did. Except, of course, for the scotch tape.

\* \* \*

Errol Flynn stayed in the Vancouver City Morgue one night. The death certificate was issued the next morning, the permit to remove the body was granted and he left. Captain Blood, Robin Hood, Don Juan, Gentleman Jim and The Master of Ballantrae were trundled home to Hollywood by train, riding in a plain pine box marked "Please Handle Carefully." And not a question was asked about the clandestine scotch-taping of the world's most celebrated penis.

# Arsenic And Old Love

It was a serious dilemma. This was maybe a bloody awful investigation and a horrible mistake could be made. The prosecutor was probably afraid of this, too. I would have hated to have been wrong when capital punishment was involved.

* * *

The summer of 1965 found Judge Glen McDonald installed in the second floor Science section of the downtown public library.

He was reading everything he could find about arsenic poisoning because he had a strange feeling that one Rene Emile Castellani had been there some months before, doing exactly the same thing.

In one treatise Judge McDonald read: "Arsenicals have been known for centuries to be toxic to all forms of life. . .the use of arsenic trioxide as a poison prompted investigation into methods of its detection and determination in forensic situations."

In the *Encyclopaedia Britannica,* he read: "Arsenic poisoning in man most often results from the ingestion or inhalation of insecticides. . . individual susceptibility to arsenic poisoning varies widely; some persons have been known to develop a tolerance to doses that would kill others. Poisoning may result from a single large dose (acute poisoning) or from repeated small doses (chronic poisoning). . .

"With chronic exposure, the more common effects include gradual loss of strength; diarrhea or constipation; pigmentation and scaling of the skin, which may undergo malignant changes; nervous manifestations marked by paralysis and confusion; degeneration of fatty tissue; anemia; and the development of characteristic streaks across the fingernails.

"The criminal use of the colorless, tasteless compound arsenious oxide as a poison was common until chemical methods of detection were developed. Definitive diagnosis of arsenic poisoning is based on the finding of arsenic in the urine and in hair or nails."

Judge McDonald made a photocopy and carefully underlined the paragraph dealing with the effects of chronic exposure to arsenic poisoning. He sighed, walked down to the General Collection and checked out a book of infamous English poison murders. And he also took home with him a couple of Agatha Christie who-dun-its, just for good measure. One never knew.

The sudden interest in arsenic poisoning displayed that summer by the Coroner and his staff had been prompted by a disturbing report relayed by City Analyst Ted Fennell, whose laboratory was in the Coroner's Court building at 240 East Cordova Street.

This report was to lead both the Coroner's office investigators and homicide squad detectives on a twisting trail of investigation into a bizarre murder which, at times, seemed almost stranger than fiction and which culminated in two sensational murder trials.

*　*　*

Rene Castellani didn't come to our attention until after his wife, Esther, had been buried. It had been another death, another interment and then life went on. I was sitting at my desk one afternoon when Dr. Laurie (Lawrence) Ranta, who was then medical director of the Vancouver General Hospital, called to say he had just got a report from the City Analyst that arsenic had been found in samples taken from a patient who had died three or four weeks previously. Did I know anything about it?

Arsenic? I said I knew nothing about any case of suspected arsenic poisoning. We'd never had one during my years as Coroner. I asked Laurie how he had happened to get the analyst's report, which I knew nothing about, something which hadn't been done under my orders. What the hell was going on?

I got on the blower to Ted Fennell and he confirmed that he had indeed sent an arsenic report up to the VGH on a lady named Esther Castellani. The request for an analysis had been made by her doctor, Barney Moscovich, an internist at the hospital. He had sent tissue samples and Ted's staff had done a "general unknown," a test starting out with nothing specific to go by. They came up with arsenic.

Now, this seemed strange. Arsenic poisoning is something we rarely find today, although at the turn of the century there was frequent use of the poison in murders. It was used a lot for killing mice and rats, as well as humans, as many famous old Scotland Yard cases testify. This Castellani thing started to intrigue me.

I found that nobody at the hospital had a cause of death. The lady had been in the hospital for about seven weeks and during this time her condition had slowly worsened; she never seemed to improve. There had been a very bad period a while previously when the doctors thought they were going to lose her, in fact, but she weathered the storm. What was causing her illness? It was a bafflement and a mystery to everyone. The doctors had a case of heart condition and they had peripheral nephritis, meaning the extremities of the fingers and toes were numb—there was no feeling. The patient was unable to keep food down, of any kind, no matter what they fed her. It was an utter mystery.

Nobody ever suspected that a heavy metal, such as arsenic, was involved in Esther Castellani's case. The physicians never made such a diagnosis. They did not at that time—I think they do now—do a routine test for any metals in the body of a patient. So when death finally came on July 11, 1965, it was still just another death in another hospital. There was no reason to notify the Coroner. The body was removed and buried.

But Barney Moscovich was both intellectually and professionally curious as to what the cause of that death was. It stumped him and all the other doctors. I know it bothered Barney terribly that he had never been able to pinpoint exactly what was wrong with his patient. He didn't have an accidental death, he had a natural death. But he still didn't know from what causes. Damn!

Naturally, he wanted an autopsy. He went to Esther's husband, Rene, for permission. This he got, although it took Rene some time to finally give his consent. But, after the autopsy, there was still nothing from the hospital pathologist to confirm a cause of death. And at this stage Barney decided to send some specimens downtown to the city analyst's lab to see if the boys there could find anything. They had a lot of sophisticated equipment to do the required tests which the hospital didn't have at the time.

Sure enough, Ted Fennell came up with arsenic. And that was how the whole thing started.

Now, arsenic is a very interesting poison because you can live with it in your system. We all have it in our systems to one degree or another. And a lot of information on it comes right from old books dealing with true cases of murder by arsenic which Scotland Yard used to encounter frequently.

So I phoned a gal at the public library and told her, "Look, give us everything you have on file about arsenic poisoning." As a result, for a couple of weeks, my whole staff was boning up on what arsenic and old lace was all about. We didn't know at that time just what had been going on with the Castellanis, but we did know there was a big mystery here that had to be solved.

I got a lot of satisfaction going to fictional and non-fictional works whose authors were dandy experts on arsenic and its use in poisoning. As a matter of fact, there were so many arsenic poisonings in Britain at the turn of the century that the House of Commons passed an Act under which a person had to get a prescription to obtain arsenic and also had to sign what was known as the Poisons Book.

There was a famous case in England in 1910 in which a man gave his wife arsenic in her tea or a drink, three or four times a day, every day. But, cunningly, he also took it in his own tea. So, when it was found she had died of an overdose of arsenic and the finger of the law was pointed at him, he was able to say, "Well, take a sample of my blood, too. You'll find the same thing!"

The law then thought it was an accidental mixing of arsenic and sugar in the sugar bin. And he'd probably have gotten away with it except they discovered that a previous wife's body also had arsenic in it. That surely couldn't have been coincidence. So, clever as he had been by building up his own resistance to arsenic, he was caught. And, as it turned out, so was Rene Castellani in Vancouver—as clever as he had been.

It was a fact that Esther Castellani hadn't been anywhere for the last seven weeks of her life but in the Vancouver General Hospital. Dr. Ranta was certainly aware of the implications of that. If she had been accidentally getting arsenic in the hospital, how many other patients had been getting it as well? The mind boggled. The whole thing just raised my hackles the more I thought about it.

So, after talking to Ted Fennell and the lab technicians and to Barney Moscovich, I went back to Laurie Ranta and asked if I could have all the medical reports on Esther Castellani.

"It's a lot of paper, Mac," he said.

"I know," I said, "but we've got arsenic here and we've got a fairly high concentration of it. I hate to think this lady was accidentally being fed arsenic in your hospital. I also hate to think that somebody deliberately gave her arsenic in your hospital. I've got to investigate this as arsenic poisoning. In fact, Laurie, I'm just about ready to order her body disinterred. That's how damned important this is."

The case had now been going on for some time and there were complications that didn't make our job any easier. The autopsy done at the hospital showed that contributing factors in Esther Castellani's death were fluid in the lungs, infection of the heart lining, numbness of the extremities, and a kidney ailment.

The samples Barney Moscovich had sent to Fennell's lab were from her brain, liver, kidneys and heart. When the tests showed such high concentrations of arsenic, the matter of Esther Castellani had become a Coroner's case. My job now was to determine if her death was natural, accidental, suicide or homicide.

After reading all the reports, I decided to have the body exhumed, as was my power under the Cemeteries Act. I advised the Attorney General of my intentions and we went ahead.

*　*　*

On Tuesday, August 3, 1965, Jack Wasserman wrote in his widely-read column in *The Vancouver Sun*:

"Vancouver homicide detectives armed with an order from Coroner Glen McDonald today plan to exhume the body of a 40-year-old housewife who died in Vancouver General Hospital three weeks ago. Here's the background:

"The woman had been a patient in VGH for seven weeks when she died July 11. An autopsy was performed and death was diagnosed as due to an assortment of ailments including: acute pulmonary edema, acute infectious neuritis and nephritis.

"She was buried two days later. In the interim, her family doctor insisted on further tests and VGH authorities agreed to send specimens. . .to the city analyst. In due course the city analyst ran his tests, compiled the results and sent them to VGH by mail.

"The results arrived and police were informed. The tests indicated a high concentration of arsenic in her system: 2.6 milligrams in her kidneys; 0.07 mg. in her liver; and 0.76 in her brain. According to pathologists, .003 is the maximum a person's system can handle."

Early in the morning of that day, Judge McDonald, members of his staff and homicide detectives were busy doing exactly what Wasserman had reported. Armed with shovels and grub hoes, they gathered around the lonely grave in the Forest Lawn cemetery in suburban Burnaby.

It took only a short time to dig up the casket containing the remains of Esther Castellani. Heavy rain clouds massed threateningly overhead as the men stowed Mrs. Castellani in the back of the black morgue wagon and, in the finest tradition of Edgar Allan Poe, a sudden summer thunder and lightning storm ripped and crackled across the lowering sky.

*　*　*

We took the coffin back to the morgue and we opened it up and there we had Esther Castellani. She was, by this time, somewhat deteriorated. Maybe there was insufficient embalming fluid or formaldehyde used. We had found out what had been used because you've got to subtract that when you're running the toxicology tests so you don't get it mixed up with arsenic or other poisons and, as a result, get wrong readings. It's much easier to do toxicology on a body that hasn't been embalmed.

It had taken some time after death for the autopsy to be performed, the specimens tested in the analyst's lab and the results sent back to the hospital, the exhumation to be done, and then, of course, our tests on the body. Rumors were now flying, particularly in the Italian community. There were even suggestions and allegations that the body had been tampered with and the arsenic we found wasn't really from it.

Nonsense.

We were scrupulous to make sure there was no mismatching of samples and specimens. Every specimen was put in a jar and that jar was sealed tight and all details printed clearly on the label. Nothing is ever mixed up in such tests. It's all part of that old chain of evidence—if you lose one link, the whole damn thing falls apart.

Esther Castellani's hair and fingernails had arsenic in them and it was a considerable amount. It interested me that when we put the hair under the microscope, we saw there was a definite period in the hair growth during which there was no arsenic. Hair grows in a woman of Mrs. Castellani's age at a rate of one centimetre a month, or just over half an inch. It didn't occur to any of us at the time that this was of any significance. Why was there no arsenic during a particular phase of hair growth? The fact was duly noted, of course, but nobody realized just how important this question was going to prove in the end.

* * *

Rene Castellani, swarthily handsome, dapper and debonair and exuding swaggering self-confidence, was a born promoter. He thrived on and revelled in this role in the days when North American radio stations relied on gimmicks and zany promotional stunts to attract listeners and thereby sell advertisers' products.

One of Castellani's most publicized stunts, in June of 1965 when his wife lay dying in hospital, was to camp in a car on top of a 20-meter tower on the Bow Mac automobile sales lot on Vancouver's busy West Broadway. His pitch was that he would not come down to earth until every car on the lot was sold.

*Vancouver Sun* columnist Denny Boyd, in a column written after Castellani's death in 1982, quoted broadcasting executive Mel Cooper, who was with Radio Station CKNW during the time of the Bow Mac stunt:

"At the time of the promo, Rene's wife was in the hospital, terribly sick, and I begged him to scrap the promo, to spend his time with her. Rene said we had an obligation to the sponsor and that the show had to go on. I thought it was terribly callous, but most promo guys were a bit crazy."

So Rene Castellani roosted high in his perch for seven days, making friends with the seagulls and chattering cheerfully into his microphone to sell Bow Mac cars. From his aerie he had a commanding view of the Vancouver General Hospital, just a few blocks away, where his wife lay on her death bed.

It was this kind of supreme arrogance and egotism that led to the ultimate downfall of Rene Castellani, Canada's infamous Milkshake Murderer.

* * *

I got back to Ted Fennell and told him, "Look, you've got to be absolutely, positively, 100 percent sure that what we've got is arsenic in this body and to what extent it's there. How about sending some of these specimens back to the crime lab in Toronto where Lucas is the chemist, just to backstop us?"

Ted did this and, when we heard back two weeks later, we found Lucas and his boys had done an excellent job. They had actually plotted the ingestion of the arsenic on a chart—which was fascinating—covering the entire time Esther was in the hospital, and for a long time before that. The tests showed that, in fact, she had been ingesting arsenic for a period of six to 13 months before she died. It was possible, through examining hair samples, to chart the amount of arsenic she received day by day.

She had long, black hair and there was arsenic at the ends of the strands. Her symptoms throughout the hospitalization were absolutely consistent with the ingestion of arsenic on a regular basis, and even on a slowly increasing basis. She became unable to eat and developed the other symptoms as well. Christ, it was egg all over the face of the hospital staff and to this day it's a case they don't like to talk about. But at the time both Dr. Ranta and Dr. Moscovich did everything they could to help us. In fact it was Barney Moscovich who had started the ball rolling.

The next step was to call in the homicide guys. They immediately got down to a lot of serious investigation. Sergeant Bill Porteous was in charge and he had two detectives, Alex Reid and Archie McKay, working on it. The first thing they did was to set out to determine who Esther Castellani's friends were and who her enemies were. It turned out she didn't seem to have any enemies at all but she did have many, many good friends in Vancouver's large and close-knit Italian community. She was an immensely popular girl.

Naturally, all these people had been very concerned when she was in hospital. They thought maybe she didn't like the food so some of them took their own to her, even though the staff frowned on the practice. Esther's mother brought in homemade stews and favorite soups; hamburgers, sometimes; special things they thought she might like. And her husband, Rene, brought in vanilla milkshakes. Nobody suspected a thing.

What would our next step be? We had done all the tests and all the results were in. Esther Castellani had been put back to rest in her grave. Where did we go from here? It was up to the detectives.

Several weeks later I got a call from Bill Porteous and went to see him in the homicide division. He reported, "Well, we've been going around here, there and everywhere and, just by chance, we've discovered that Rene Castellani was friendly with a gal who used to be on the night switchboard at CKNW, the station where he worked. They've been seen together."

Rene drove a car at that time owned by the station and which carried its distinctive markings, so it was easy to spot. And it turned out it had been seen parked outside this switchboard girl's place a lot when Esther was sick in the hospital. Well, this wasn't necessarily out of line, I suppose, but it just didn't seem to me the sort of thing a concerned husband would do.

The homicide squad got more interested, too, when one of the boys happened to meet a Justice of the Peace and Notary Public he knew. During a social chat, the JP said Rene would probably be getting married soon.

"What do you mean?" the detective asked.

"Oh, they've been arranging to buy some property somewhere, a house."

"In whose name?"

"Might be a good idea for you to check that."

It transpired that the mortgage application was made by Adelaide Ann Miller, the telephone girl at CKNW, but was made out in the name of Adelaide Ann Castellani, with Rene Castellani as guarantor. It was dated July 10th, the day before Esther Castellani died.

All of a sudden, things seemed to be fitting into place. The penny had begun to drop. The cops started even more intensive investigation of Rene and of what he had been up to while Esther was in VGH. Something certainly looked wrong.

The boys questioned him about the big Bow Mac promotion. I remembered it because I'd listened to him on my car radio. The cops got the exact dates and these made me curious. Things were clicking now. Could it be simple coincidence that these were the dates when the arsenic had been missing from the hair? And were we absolutely sure the dates were the same? This required more intricate calculations by the chemists and a reference back to the lab in Toronto. And, by God, it did work right! The seven days when Rene was up on that tower selling his bloody cars corresponded exactly with the periods when Esther Castellani had not received arsenic. It all matched beautifully.

Mind you, we understood very well that circumstantial evidence must be consistent with guilt and inconsistent with any other rational conclusion. But, as well as these dates, we now also had the information about the mortgage application and the liaison with the switchboard gal.

Then things began to get even more interesting. Investigating Adelaide Ann Miller, who Rene called Lolly, we found out that a year or so before, she'd been out in a rowboat on Harrison Lake and her husband had somehow fallen into the drink and drowned. Lolly had inherited 25,000 dollars or so.

I immediately got hold of the Coroner in Harrison and asked if he had any more details. He said:

"Oh, yes, we know all about that case. It was an accidental drowning."

"Are you satisfied it was accidental?"

"Well, there were no witnesses except his wife. From what she told us, that was all we *could* suspect it was."

"Were you aware that she inherited some life insurance?"

"Well, yes. I had to sign the claim."

"Thanks ever so much."

Unfortunately, this Coroner died a few weeks later of a heart attack. But we had some more information for our puzzle.

Rene Castellani was a big spender of dollars, as all promoters seem to be. He spent way beyond his means, by many accounts. So where the hell did the money come from to buy property and get involved with mortgage payments and so on?

But the worst thing you can ever do in the Coroner's job is to be an investigator who thinks he has tracked down a culprit.

"Okay, I've solved it."

You haven't because something always goes wrong or new information turns up.

So I just said to the police, "It's up to you. It's clearly homicide. Let's find out more."

Then people began recalling these visits Rene had made to the hospital, the times he brought Esther the milkshakes. Was there something in them that shouldn't have been there?

There was one time when some visitors came into the room when Rene was there. He had brought some soup or stew or something and was trying to spoon-feed it to Esther. She didn't want it.

"Well, I'll have some of it," one of the visitors said. "It looks good."

Whereupon Rene snatched it away from this friend and hurriedly dumped it down the toilet. This was kind of silly—good stew is good stew. Why would he snatch it away like that? What was wrong with the stew? It meant nothing, but it meant a lot. Maybe.

We and the detectives had by now got a lot of information but we weren't able to do anything more. I said, "Well, I'd better go over and see the Chief Prosecutor and explain what's happening." I didn't really know what I was going to do. But if he did lay a charge, I wouldn't go ahead with an inquest.

Stewart McMorran looked at everything we had and then he shook his head and said, no, there wasn't enough evidence or sufficient cirumstantial evidence. He wouldn't lay a charge. I went back to my office wondering what to do next.

Then, for lack of a better idea, I said to one of the detectives, "Why don't you go out and take a look at Rene's place again?"

And that, it turned out, was the clincher.

Detective Reid found a tin of Ortho Triox under a sink in the basement of the Castellani home. This is a weed killer containing 53.5 percent arsenic. People used to buy the stuff at Esso gas stations and there was a poison warning clearly marked on the can. This tin was about half full and that was what interested us. Rene was many things but he sure as hell wasn't a gardener. He didn't give a damn about weeds.

Now what to do? Had we got to the source of the arsenic or not? So, one more time, I went to the Chief City Prosecutor.

"Look," I said, "We've got this, we've got that, and we've got that. We haven't got any other source for the arsenic. We haven't got anything else we can go by. What do you think?"

Again, Stewart McMorran shook his head, "No, not enough."

"All right," I said, "I'm going to order the inquest."

* * *

The inquest into the death of Esther Castellani opened on December 1, 1965, almost five months after her death. The little courtroom at 240 East Cordova Street was packed with relatives and friends of the deceased. In a row at the rear sat Rene Castellani, accompanied by a young woman.

The atmosphere was so tense and strained, in fact, that Judge McDonald felt compelled to advise the jurors at the start of the proceedings that, while they might find certain persons to blame for the death, nobody in his court was charged with any offence.

Much of the evidence was startling and, for Rene Castellani, damning.

Dr. James Foulks, head of the University of British Columbia's Department of Pharmacology, said Esther Castellani's ingestion of arsenic could be divided into three periods: an initial period of several months; two months with an increased dosage; the five weeks prior to death with a very greatly increased dosage.

Eldon Rideout, Assistant City Analyst, testified that three to five drops of the week killer Triox would be a lethal dose and that three fluid ounces were missing from the can found in the Castellani home, an amount more than corresponding to the traces found in Mrs. Castellani's body.

Warren Peterson, a builder, said he met both Adelaide Ann (Lolly) Miller and Rene Castellani early in June, that Lolly said she wanted to buy a house he owned and that she and Rene were to be married in two weeks.

Real estate salesman A.M. Gillis, contacted by Peterson to arrange a mortgage, said he advised Lolly and Rene to put the house in her married name and have Rene sign as guarantor. "I submitted an application for the mortgage as though they were married," he said.

Adelaide Ann (Lolly) Miller, the strawberry-blonde onetime switchboard girl at CKNW, denied she had ever had a romantic association with Rene Castellani before his wife died. She also denied telling Peterson and Gillis, shortly before Esther's death, that she and Rene planned to get married in two weeks' time.

But Lolly did confirm that, five days after Esther died, she and her six-year-old son and Rene and his daughter all went to Disneyland together for a 10-day vacation.

* * *

Well, pretty much everything was denied. The jurors were just like we all were. Who knew what was what, what was fact and what was fiction, what was right and what was wrong? We could deal with the question: Was this a natural death or an unnatural death? The pathologist's testimony concerning the second autopsy, together with the testimony of the pathologist who did the first autopsy, together with the toxicology evidence, was sufficient to determine that this was, indeed, an unnatural death.

So I said to the jury, "Now, if you are able, you should classify this death as being either accident, suicide or homicide. These are words with everyday meanings which you and I use freely in conversation. It could be that you are unable to so classify, and in that case, you might consider a word such as misadventure, or you might consider just leaving the verdict open. But that is entirely your decision alone. And if you need any further instructions from me or from any of the witnesses you have heard, please don't hesitate to let me know and I'll have them brought back and you can ask your questions directly of them."

That was it.

The jury was out for about three hours. The atmosphere in court was tense, suspenseful. The jurors sent out once for coffee and doughnuts and then they came back and the foreman stood up and said, "Homicide by person or persons unknown."

Well, there was only one person who *could* be known. Plenty could be unknown, I suppose. So then McMorran had to go ahead with it. A charge of capital murder was laid against Rene Castellani.

But I still feel this charge should have been laid in the first instance and all the evidence which came out at the inquest laid before a provincial court judge at a preliminary hearing. Then it would have been for him to decide, as the facts came out, if the charge should be proceeded with under the proper rules of evidence.

The Coroner's Court is not a criminal court and we allow hearsay and sometimes hearsay on hearsay evidence. It's really the only way we can find out anything. The only way we could have possibly known about the mortgage business was from what the Notary Public had said. It all tied together. It was the date that was so important. But it was still hearsay. At the same time, was it all a mistake? A coincidence, perhaps? The inquest had, of course, generated an awful lot of publicity. The public knew all about this case and had they already made up their mind? Had they already decided guilt? "It's *got* to be him"?

That's why, whenever a charge of murder is laid, or any criminal charge, most Coroners will waive the inquest and let the matter go directly to trial. Why have a sort of Kangaroo Court, just playing around wth things, with people whose minds are already made up?

Here was a well-known and well-liked radio promoter and funny guy. We had to be right; if we were wrong, we damned him. That's what I felt. Either be right or be damned! That simple and that awful to think about. It was such a classic case that sometimes, as it went along, I couldn't even believe it was happening. I'm certainly more confident now than ever that we were right in our convictions. But I would have hated to have been wrong when capital punishment was involved.

\*　\*　\*

On November 12, 1966 a jury in the British Columbia Supreme Court found Rene Castellani guilty of the capital murder of his wife, Esther. He was sentenced to be hanged by the neck until he was dead and may God have mercy upon his soul. The verdict was appealed, on a point of law, and a new trial ordered. There was much talk around town that, if he were acquitted, Castellani would be fed to the fishes, or at the most merciful, his testicles would be cut off and shoved down his throat. Esther had many good friends in the Italian community.

On October 6, 1967, the public gallery was packed with Castellani's female groupies. Mr. Justice Victor Dryer upheld the previous conviction and sentenced Castellani to be hanged on January 23, 1968.

Coolly, Castellani turned to the nine-man, three-woman jury and said in a low, flat voice, "May God have mercy on your souls." The man still had a flair for the dramatic.

His case was then appealed to the Supreme Court of Canada. Again, the conviction was upheld. The date with the gallows stood. But, two weeks before his final walk to the scaffold, Rene Castellani's life was spared when the federal government removed the death penalty for all but killers of policemen and prison guards. Castellani's sentence was commuted to life imprisonment.

The Milkshake Murderer was released on full parole in May, 1979, went to work for a radio station in British Columbia's Fraser Valley, married again, and then launched a station in Nanaimo on Vancouver Island. By that time Lolly Miller had also remarried.

Castellani, whose last promotional gimmick was to bill himself as *Rene the Roadrunner,* died of cancer in January, 1982, still claiming his innocence of Esther's murder. He was 56.

His obituary was written by *Vancouver Sun* columnist Denny Boyd, who quoted broadcasting executive Mel Cooper:

"All his life, Rene was in a dream world. The night his wife died, I went over to his house, just to be with him and give him my sympathy. I walked in and he had his feet up on the chesterfield, laughing at some comic on the Ed Sullivan show. Rene Castellani. Jeez."

# Go Tell It
# On The Mountain

AT THE BURIAL OF THEIR DEAD AT SEA
We therefore commit his body to the deep, to be turned
into corruption, looking for the resurrection of the body,
(when the Sea shall give up her dead,) and the life of the
world to come, through our Lord Jesus Christ; who at
His coming shall change our vile body, that it may be like
His glorious body, according to the mighty working,
whereby He is able to subdue all things to Himself.

*The Book of Common Prayer*
*The Church of England*

The evening of December 9, 1956 found British Columbia's weather
at its bleakest. Fierce gales howled and raged through the jagged
mountain ridges and passes strewn along the eastern end of the Fraser
Valley corridor. One of the peaks, towering Mount Slesse near the
village of Hope, lay silently in wait for a date with death.

Sheets of relentless rain lashed Vancouver and the surrounding
Lower Mainland. Far up the valley, lightning sparked and crackled and
thunderbolts cannonaded eerily off the yawning canyon walls.

It was not a night to be flying.

The passengers waiting in the terminal of the old Vancouver
International Airport were restless and irritable. Trans-Canada Airlines Flight 810, eastbound over the Rocky Mountains for Calgary and

points beyond, was behind schedule. The four-engine North Star had been delayed by bad weather in arriving from eastern Canada earlier in the day.

Among the passengers were four burly players of the Saskatchewan Roughriders football team who had played in the annual East-West Shrine all-star game at Empire Stadium the day before: centre Mel Becket, 27; guard Mario Demarco, 28; Gordie Sturtridge, 27, travelling with his wife; and guard Ray Srnyk, 23. A fifth ball player arrived minutes before takeoff and was assigned a seat usually reserved for a stewardess. Guard Calvin Jones, 23, of the Winnipeg Blue Bombers, had missed an earlier flight taken by his teammates because he had slept in. He thanked the TCA officials for their helpfulness in finding him a seat aboard Flight 810.

Captain Alan Clarke, 35, of Vancouver and First Officer John Boon, 26, of North Vancouver, arrived at the airport at 4:45 p.m. and attended a detailed meteorological briefing with forecaster D.M. McMullen. They also chatted with the flight crews of inbound planes. Despite the fierce weather, it was decided they should proceed routinely on the first leg to Calgary, 400 miles away.

Both pilots signed the flight plan at 5:14 p.m., and at 5:30 the fidgety passengers in the terminal at last heard the announcement they had been waiting for: "Trans-Canada Airlines Flight 810, North Star service for Calgary, Regina, Winnipeg, Toronto and Montreal, now boarding at Gate Five. . ."

TCA Flight 810 (North Star CF-TFD) lumbered down Runway 11 and lifted easily off into the lowering skies at 6:10 p.m. On board were 59 passengers, the two experienced pilots and a lone stewardess, 24-year-old Dorothy Bjornsson, of Swan River, Manitoba. The aircraft also carried 27 bags of mail, 1,000 pounds of freight and express, 500 pounds of fresh flowers and the passengers' own baggage, jewelry and cash, including $80,000 believed to have been tucked in the belt of a mysterious Chinese businessman named Kwan Song.

A few minutes later Capt. Clarke had a brief radio conversation with fellow TCA captain Jack Wright, bringing Super-Constellation Flight 7 into Vancouver from Toronto with 46 passengers aboard.

"We just yattered back and forth," Capt. Wright said later. "We usually do that. I've known Alan for a long time. I told him there was some icing around the Cascades and said if I was going back I'd fly at 19 or 20,000 feet. He was climbing then. He thanked me for the information and that was all there was to it. He gave no indication of any trouble."

But Flight 810 encountered increasingly stormy conditions, including severe turbulence, icing on the wings and fuselage, awesome cloud castles and jagged rips of lightning. She kept on course for Calgary, beyond the Rockies.

Then, at 6:52 p.m., Capt. Clarke radioed a terse message that plunged a dagger of fear into Vancouver Tower controllers, "It looks like we had a fire in Number Two engine. Shut down Number Two!"

One minute later the four-engine North Star—then 35 miles southeast of Hope, at the top of the Fraser Valley—turned back for Vancouver, one engine shut down, fuselage heavy with worsening ice, plowing and shuddering into 100 miles per hour headwinds, desperately fighting to maintain altitude but inexorably losing the battle. At 7:10 p.m., Capt. Clarke radioed Vancouver Tower and requested permission to drop from 19,000 to 8,000 feet. It was his last message.

Also at 7:10 p.m., operators at the NORAD radar station at Birch Bay, just south of the British Columbia-Washington state border, reported the blip of Flight 810 was at 10,000 feet—just 2,000 feet above the jagged mountain peaks—and descending. When they looked again it wasn't there. Astounded, the operators made three more radar sweeps of the scope. The blip was gone. A few minutes later a USAF Birch Bay operator called the Vancouver Tower with the chilling message, "Your Flight 810 has gone off our scope."

The TCA North Star had fulfilled its date with death, 7,970 feet up on the storm-lashed and snowy crags of Mount Slesse. Five agonizing and frustrating months were to pass before the first trace of the ill-starred airplane was found.

*    *    *

I remember that year's all-star game well because the players were at the Terminal City Club, downtown, afterwards to pick up their cheques at a special presentation. There were two eastbound flights on the Sunday. The players from the eastern team took the first one and got home safely. Some western players weren't so lucky.

I heard on the radio that the second plane had crashed somewhere near Hope. The meteorological reports we had at the time showed considerable turbulence over Hope, the turning-point for heading east to Calgary. It was a hell of a bad night for flying, with news of violent thunder and lightning storms, plus reports from people in the area who said they had heard explosions as well.

You know, I've often wondered about that NORAD radar tracking station. The operators had been plotting the course of the North Star and had even noted the turn the plane made before it suddenly vanished from their screen. But because of the top-secret military relationship existing between Canada and the United States, I just wonder how far up the ladder this information went.

There's no question in my mind that a lot of unnecessary searching could have been avoided had we been able to quickly pinpoint the precise area where the plane went down. No lives could have been saved, of course, but a lot of time, trouble and expense might have been avoided.

The Hope area has an infamous reputation as being as hazardous for airplanes as the Bermuda Triangle is for both planes and ships. It's all because of the tremendous winds coming into contact with the mountains, and the narrowness of the valley at this stage. You meet severe turbulence. And in 1956 we were using propeller-driven planes, not jets that fly much faster and up to 40,000 feet.

\* \* \*

The morning after Flight 810 vanished, 17 airplanes—mainly Royal Canadian Air Force CF-100 all-weather jet fighters—criss-crossed the angry skies in the Hope area. It was the largest search ever mounted by the RCAF and was joined by USAF planes from south of the border. The search went on for days and the days dragged into weeks. The weather remained the searchers' cruelest adversary. It was so violent, in fact, some air crews reported their safety belts snapped like cheap string.

"We were thrown around so much that our safety straps were breaking and our equipment was flying all over the place," said one fighter pilot.

An intrepid reporter from a New York newspaper hitched a ride in a search plane. He returned to base weak-kneed and trembling and told RCAF public relations man Sgt. Buzz Sawyer he was going home by train, never to fly again.

Canadian Army paratroops had been airlifted into Vancouver the day after the crash. They stood by ready to drop into the mountains the moment any wreckage was sighted.

But none was until five months later when, on May 14, 1957, a party of three climbers wading through waist-deep snow high on the slopes of Mt. Slesse found something that appeared to have come from an airplane.

\* \* \*

Let's digress for a moment. The Coroner's jurisdiction is prefaced by the fact that he has a dead body. And in this TCA case there was no jurisdiction under the Coroners Act because we had no bodies. Although, as days two, three, four and five passed there was no question in our minds that all aboard the plane had perished. That was a certainty. But at that stage I had no jurisdiction.

The search went on through December and January and February and we began to think nothing would ever be found. But, in May, these mountain-climbers were on Slesse—there was a girl among them—and they were well-known alpinists. They were near the top when they spotted what looked like a map lying in the snow. Elfrida Pigou picked it up and studied it. It was an airline transport map with beacons and so forth marked on it for approach to the airport at Sydney, Nova Scotia. It was turned in to the Mounties and subsequently identified as having almost certainly belonged to the flight crew of the missing North Star.

The climbers also found a small, jagged piece of metal with numbers and the letters TCA on it.

But where was the plane? No major wreckage and no bodies had been found. But the search area had now been narrowed to Mount Slesse alone. And, finally, the searchers spotted what looked like part of an aircraft's fuselage about 75 feet down from the mountain's peak. It was embedded there, stuck to the rock.

Now the snows were starting to avalanche down the slopes. As they melted, the friction between the snow and the rock became such that an avalanche would come without warning. It was simply too dangerous to even be in the area. So we knew we'd have to wait until the area was frozen over again and the dangers of avalanches gone.

I had to consider what to do. I got in touch with the Attorney General and asked him, since the International Airport is in Vancouver, what his instructions were on jurisdiction. He asked me to go into the area and open an inquest and just see how far I could go. This was done in Chilliwack, the center of the Fraser Valley. But we still had no bodies.

TCA had their own people and equipment in the area, along with the Alpine Club of Canada and the RCAF. So I was preparing for an inquest but knew we probably wouldn't finish it because the Minister of Transport had by now ordered a formal inquiry. But there was still a role for the Coroner to play in the areas of identification and the collection of any remains and the proper turning-over of these to the next-of-kin.

There was a hell of a lot of media interest all across North America while the search was going on. Paddy Sherman, who became publisher of *The Province* newspaper in Vancouver, and then *The Ottawa Citizen*, was then a *Province* reporter and enthusiastic alpinist with the Mountain Rescue Group. He was up and around the mountain all the time and had quite an edge for his paper. But as May and June came and went it became obvious we'd have to wait until the fall, until the mountain was stable.

There was a footing—a sort of step—about a thousand feet below the peak where the wreckage was. From it there was a drop of five or six thousand feet. This was a sheer drop and an avalanche would have been deadly. And one thing we had agreed on by now was that, whatever happened, no life was to be risked trying to recover dead people.

We had a passenger manifest and had also collected details of the clothes the people had been wearing. We had dental records and reports of surgical scars or excisions; all those little clues which might help us eventually to identify the bodies.

All this had been done with the help of the senior TCA vice-presidents, such as Norman Donnelly, who were in and out of the area throughout the search. Like us, they were waiting. There was nothing else to do. And another concern we had was the presence of bears and other animals in the area. We knew bears were common and they'd eat anything they came across. I didn't think we'd find any bodies at all.

We were months in the area. We used the Empress Hotel in Chilliwack and the courthouse as meeting places and every day picked up local gossip about what people had seen, or thought they had seen, and the latest weather conditions on the mountain. I had an inquest jury sworn in but it was still a matter of waiting until it was safe to go up the mountain.

There were two ways of doing this. One was to climb all the way up; the other was to go in by Bell helicopters which we had standing by in a farmer's field at the base of the mountain, by the river. The decision was made, mainly by the 'copter pilots themselves. They had spotted a little plateau on the mountain which they thought they could bring their choppers down on. We would fly in.

First, two helicopters went in, with Mounties and airline people aboard. One concern we had was the mail aboard the plane. Also, there was the rumor—which seemed to be endorsed by the Mounties and the FBI—that a Chinese passenger who had flown in from Hong Kong to board the flight had cash on his person totalling 80,000 dollars. His name was Kwan Song and, curiously, his address was listed on the manifest as The Bowery, New York City. This, obviously, was yet another reason for finding the bodies.

By August the search and rescue people had done three complete sweeps of the mountainside and we still didn't have a body. All we had was a foot in a shoe. Obviously, at impact, the foot must have been wedged between the passenger's seat and the seat next to it and was cleanly sheared off. It was the tibia and the fibula, standing there as if the foot had been cleanly chopped off by a guillotine. It was just one brown shoe lying there on the rock, clear from the wreckage. That was all the human remains we had found.

By this time the searchers had spotted a dark shadow against a 20-foot wall of snow which had broken away in an avalanche. It turned out to be part of a Merlin engine squashed against the mountain. It had rolled down several thousand feet but the men couldn't get to it, only observe and photograph it. The enormity and finality of the impact had been so great that a huge Merlin engine, about eight feet long and two or three feet in diameter, was now compressed into a chunk of twisted metal two feet in size. That impact, even with the plane flying on just three engines, was later estimated to have been at four or five hundred knots.

Obviously, the Captain was heading for disaster. He was off course, and with the loss of an engine, severe turbulence and heavy icing, the flight was mission impossible. And the terrible irony was that, had the pilot been just 75 feet to starboard or 75 feet higher, he would have missed the peak and been over the flats and fields of the Fraser Valley. It was that close.

What should we do next? Everyone regularly reported to the inquest, which adjourned every evening. We stayed on at the Empress but nothing much was happening. And, of course, the next-of-kin were always asking what was going on and hoping that, somehow, something more would be found.

The TCA people had taken their sacks up—plain old gunny sacks, potato sacks— and had collected all the mail and money they could find. The mysterious Mr. Kwan Song's 80,000 dollars was never found. Maybe it's still up there. Maybe it never existed. We also recovered the film clips of the football game. The cans had broken open and long streamers of film were strewn all over the ground.

It was impossible to get to what was left of the fuselage itself. This was literally hung up on a crag by the control wires, hanging there like some enormous dead bird. We could see a body in the nose area. It looked badly charred and mangled. We assumed it was a crew member, possibly the Captain. The climbers who did get to the top were able to look down on the wreck but they couldn't get to it, either. Our paramount rule still was—and still is—don't risk your own life to recover a dead person on a mountainside. It's a basic common sense rule.

One newspaper, *The Toronto Star* or perhaps the old *Telegram*, published a very gruesome story that the moutaineers had found half of the pilot's body leaning out of a window of the flight deck or something. Terribly dramatic. I don't know how the paper heard it but it wasn't true. Ultimately, the wreckage failed to hold up under the weather conditions and collapsed, fell apart.

Every day the searchers had to get out of the area by afternoon when the sun caused avalanches. These were awesome to experience, as I found out when I finally flew up. So the final decision was made. I said to the searchmaster, "Is there any chance I can go up there because I do have an obligation to say that, if there are any persons here, they're all dead and then get permission to sign any death certificates."

It was arranged that I would go up with one of my technicians, Bart Bastien. Meanwhile, Paddy Sherman was still climbing up and down the mountain and there was some jealousy on the part of Eddie Moyer, a hell of a good reporter and personal friend of mine, who was with the opposition paper. He wanted to go up in the 'copter with us but I said, "Eddie, you'll just have to study to be an alpine climber very quickly to qualify for a ride because at no time do we want anyone up there who isn't an expert. In fact, even an expert needs all the help he can get."

We landed by Bell 6-47 helicopter on a platform, a sort of floe, that looked down five thousand feet on one side and up fifteen hundred feet on the other. It was damn strange and frightening up there. Eerie. A small stone looked the size of a six-storey building; everything was all out of proportion; I was a pigmy in giant land.

Even then, some searchers were still picking up stray dollar bills and dimes and nickels and pennies and stowing them in their potato sacks. But it was obvious to me then and there that the official search had at last come to an end. I said to the searchmaster, "Well, is this our last trip as far as you're concerned?"

"Yes," he said. "That's it, Mac."

Besides the foot in the shoe and the busted-open cans of film, we found a piece of skull about the size of a teacup saucer. Bare. No hair. Just plain bone, part of the cranium. That was also put in a potato sack and taken back down. And that was the only other piece of human remains we ever found. What had happened to everyone?

The severe weather and, I don't like to say this but there were also the animals in the area—bears and eagles and coyotes and so on. Nature often works in its own way to put things back the way they were before humans arrived. Perhaps this was the case high on Mount Slesse. The searchers did find another Merlin engine which had rolled and bounced five thousand feet down into the valley, along with the wheels of the aircraft. They were all separated and disintegrated, strewn crazily about.

Flying in was scary. I've flown in many helicopters and was no stranger to the experience. But to fly that close to a mountain and then propose to land on it, that's something else. It's bad enough just looking between your toes and staring down four or five thousand feet. However, the pilots were confident by this time. They were real pros. They well knew that helicopters flying around mountains are often caught in downdrafts without warning. Or updrafts, and sometimes, drafts that go sideways. All these things were flashing through my mind that day. Talk about white-knuckle flying! I was laughing and chatting cheerfully on the outside but shaking like hell inside.

After we had looked one last time for any evidence of human remains, I went to the RCMP sergeant with us and said, "Is there anybody in your group who could help me with a burial service?"

I had prepared myself for this contingency and had slipped into my hip pocket a copy of the *Book of Common Prayer* with the Burial At Sea service in it. I just thought to myself, "Well, we've come this far so we might as well do the thing right."

One of the Mounties was Catholic, so I said to him, "Look, if you don't mind, you go over there and I'll go over here. I'm going to read the Burial At Sea and just convert it to the Burial On The Mountain. Perhaps you'd do whatever Catholics like to do."

I had taken the Captain's name and the names of the 61 others up with me, but I just used the Captain's name, the number of the flight and the date of the crash. And in this way, I committed them, not to the deep, but to the mountain. I'm not a particularly religious fellow but I do believe there's a Supreme Being and I did know that in this way we had at least done a little up there on Slesse that might mean something to the next-of-kin. I felt that perhaps it was something meaningful.

Then the Mountie and I found little bits of wood—a few scraggly things—and we tied them together with string and found stones and erected a crude cross on the spot where we had said our prayers. I don't think the cross lasted even a day the way the snows were coming down but there was nothing more we could do. It was a gesture, at least.

And even while I was reading the burial service another avalanche started. The mountain was warming up again, and it was a terrifying sight. Maybe God was adding His amen to the prayers on the mountain. Understandably, one doesn't feel like scampering back to the helicopter in such dicey conditions, so we walked very, very carefully. One wrong step could have meant drifting over the edge and falling into space.

The TCA men with their gunny sacks would be the last to leave. I said that was sure all right with me. I was in dire need of a stiff gin and tonic. I went in the second helicopter. But when I saw the first one lift off safely I wished I had gone in that.

Back at the hotel, we had a debriefing and I told the inquest jury all I had found and done on the mountain. The jurors eventually returned a verdict of accidental death as a result of instant and multiple injuries sustained when Trans-Canada Airlines Flight 810 was lost on the evening of December 9, 1956 near the top of Mt. Slesse in the province of British Columbia. That was that.

Later, we were sitting in the Empress beer parlor, relaxing and waiting for the last helicopter to get back with the airline people and their gunny sacks. They came in at last.

"Well, it's finished. That's it!" someone said.

There was a feeling of letdown but also accomplishment. And then somebody, offhandedly, asked, "Where did you put your bags—your sacks?"

I'll never forget the expressions on the faces of those three men. They had worked up there on this final trip collecting everything they could possibly find and then they'd forgotten the bloody sacks. They'd been in a hurry to get out to safety. It was so tragic and yet so humorous that all we could do was laugh and say, "Oh, well, maybe TCA will send you in again or promote you or just say goodbye to the bags." I don't think they ever did go back.

When the inquest and search were over, I got onto the Attorney General and explained all that had happened. Then I made the suggestion that perhaps—and I had already suggested this to the TCA officials—he could order that the mountain be made a memorial for the victims. The Minister of Forests could proclaim the area a provincial cemetery so climbers and, possibly, fortune hunters looking for the reported 80,000 dollars would be prohibited.

This would keep out the curious and the morbid because we knew that if inexperienced people got in there they'd get into trouble and Search and Rescue and the RCMP would have to go in and get them out. The government put this through by Order-In-Council.

Even though it happened so long ago, the memories stay with me vividly. That scene of absolute, total destruction and desolation just won't go away. It proved, to me, that the might of nature is such that it can erase all the damage and insults man can do; that those things nature constructed and maintained must, in the long run, prevail and ultimately destroy the human and the inventions he makes in the name of Progress.

*   *   *

On December 9, 1957, one year to the day after the crash of North Star Flight 810, TCA dedicated a granite memorial, inscribed with 62 names, which stands on a lonely and beautiful forest road leading to the lower slopes of Mount Slesse on the north side of the rushing Chilliwack River.

Above the names is the simple inscription: "In Memory Of The Passengers And Crew Who Lost Their Lives In A North Star Aircraft On Mount Slesse Dec. 9, 1956."

Four hundred people attended the dedication, conducted in all religious faiths, and TCA flight crews mounted a guard of honor.

And the final chapter in the sad saga of flight 810 was written on December 12 when the official government inquiry listed three causes for the disaster:

-The aircraft struck the third peak of Mount Slesse, B.C. at an altitude of 7,600 feet at a high rate of speed, causing total destruction.

-The cause for the aircraft being at an altitude low enough to strike Mount Slesse is undetermined, but there is a high probability that the aircraft, while flying on three engines, encountered either severe icing, turbulence, subsidence, or a combination of all three, or suffered some other difficulty of such a sudden or dire nature that the crew were unable to communicate with any agency or control the aircraft.

-For undetermined reasons the aircraft was not on Green Airway No.1 to which it had been cleared by Air Traffic Control.

*   *   *

Nine years after he read his innovative Burial On The Mountain service high on the snowy wastes of Mount Slesse, Judge Glen McDonald found himself involved in another airplane disaster.

A Canadian Pacific Airlines white, silver and red four-engine DC-6B had flown into the Vancouver International Airport on June 30, 1965. Empress Flight 90 carried the body of Grant McConachie, the president and founder of the airline, who had died suddenly of a heart attack in Long Beach, California, the day before.

At 6:30 a.m. on Thursday, July 8 the same DC-6B took off from Vancouver on a scheduled flight to Sandspit in the Queen Charlotte Islands and the northern port of Prince Rupert. The plane returned to Vancouver at 1:30 p.m. It was routinely serviced and refuelled and a new flight crew went on board. And at 3:30 that afternoon the aircraft— now officially designated as CPA Flight 21—lifted off on the long haul to Prince George, Fort St. John, Fort Nelson, Watson Lake, and Whitehorse in the Yukon Territory. There were six crew, including two stewardesses, and 46 passengers, among them four children, on board.

Shortly before 5 p.m. Captain John Alfred Steele, 41, of North Vancouver, radioed that he was changing course slightly in order to avoid turbulence ahead. There had been reports of thunderstorms over the flat and rolling Cariboo region that afternoon.

A few minutes later Air Traffic Controllers heard three loud, staccato cries of "Mayday!", the international distress call. Then— silence.

CPA Flight 21 had exploded at 16,000 feet, thirty miles west of the small ranching community of 100 Mile House. Horrified eyewitnesses were later to tell chilling stories of watching the big bird disintegrating, spewing out bodies and wreckage as it plunged to the trees below, the tail section and the shattered main fuselage landing half a mile apart. It was CPA's worst disaster.

* * *

The situation was first reported to the Coroner's Office by Canadian Pacific, and the early assessment was that the plane had been flying at 16,000 feet. The CPA public relations people called for help from us and the RCMP because they were getting calls from the press and panic calls from friends and relatives of passengers who were hearing sketchy radio news reports and rumors.

It seemed fairly definite from the start that there had been an explosion—cause unknown—either from within or without the aircraft. There was also a report of a severe thunderstorm in the area. But there was also a report that another aircraft had passed safely through, coming the other way, and there was nothing unusual or dangerous about the weather.

The prevailing attitude in those days was that thunder and lightning were of no real concern to aircraft safety, although there has since been some re-thinking on this subject. I once went aboard a P & O ship which had been struck by lightning at sea and was shown the burn mark on the funnel where the bolt had hit and then stopped. The old theory was that lightning would pass clean through a ship or an aircraft and then go into the earth or the sea, grounding itself. But that's beside the point. Back to the story of CPA Flight 21.

We knew by now that the tail assembly of the aircraft had come away from the main fuselage and bodies had spilled out as the plane plummeted to the ground. That was a hell of a grim thing to think about. The pilots would have had no control; all they could do for a minute or so was sit there and wait and watch. Jesus!

There had been that forward motion of the main section of the plane. It hadn't dropped directly down but had traveled on for a minute or so, spewing out its human cargo. This was a ghastly thought. We've all heard about how suction can drag people out of planes. I knew right then there would be bodies scattered and strewn along the ground for miles. Then I heard from the RCMP that this was indeed the case. The crash area was swampland, with tall grass and 18-inch deep water. Sure as hell, exploring and moving around in that stuff was going to be very, very difficult.

\* \* \*

The day after the tragedy *Vancouver Sun* reporter Jes Odam, in a dispatch from 100 Mile House, reported that logging mechanic Bill Wolfgramm, one of the first people to reach the disaster area, broke down and wept like a child at the horror of what he found.

He quoted Wolfgramm: "The tail of the plane was half a mile away from the fuselage and there was a constant trail of broken and bent bodies between them. There was no sign of life anywhere.

"I saw the body of a young child but I couldn't tell whether it was a boy or a girl. All we could do before it got dark was to pick up a few bodies. It was a terrible scene and one I'll never forget."

Wolfgramm's wife, Gerda, told *The Sun,* "He went in ahead of me and then came back and said there was nothing I could do. He was crying from the horror of it all. It was the first time I've ever known him to cry."

\* \* \*

My main concern was that the remains (nobody even considered the possibility of survivors) would have to come down to Vancouver for identification. After getting the okay from Attorney General Robert Bonner, I assumed jurisdiction and flew up by RCMP float plane. With me were some of my staff and Dr. Warren Lovell, an American pathologist and pilot who was an expert in probing airplane disasters. He had been recommended by Tom Harmon, my Chief Pathologist and a friend of Lovell's. A helicopter was waiting for us.

The Mounties had cleared a crude landing spot near a small sawmill about four miles from the main crash site. We landed okay. Immediately, the difficulties posed by the swampy ground were evident. The damn plane had to come down smack in the middle of a bloody swamp! But, with a jeep and a truck, we got to the main section of the aircraft. The wings, nose and most of the fuselage were intact; the tail was a half mile away.

The bodies, many of them still strapped in their seats, were strewn for two miles in all directions. We just made sightings and plodded and struggled along a line through the swamp until we found them. Some bodies were intact, although the suction had torn most of the clothing off. Other bodies were in pieces.

There had been 52 people on board that aircraft. We collected 146 parts of bodies. We put all these bits and pieces into plastic bags and loaded them into a refrigerated truck. It was a long and sad and arduous job. I walked the whole distance with the Mounties and did grisly swamper's work in the mud. The job took two days and a night. We had set up camp at the sawmill.

We marked every spot where a body or part of a body was found. This is routine procedure in investigating an airplane crash; you mark everything before you remove the bodies and pieces of wreckage. Every piece of luggage is tagged and the exact spot where it was found is marked. We preserved the site exactly as it was at the moment of impact. We put numbers on stakes, in different colors.

Then we made a grid. This was marked in detail, coded on a master chart on a blackboard and photographed. Now we had a large picture of the entire scene, with every detail recorded. It was really done just the way you plot the planting of vegetables in your garden so you know exactly where everything is.

There was now a very strong suspicion that the crash had been caused by an explosion—or implosion—within the aircraft. That was gone into later. Our immediate difficulty was identification. This was going to be extremely difficult. There was a lack of clothing and somehow every body would have to be put together as best we could do it for next-of-kin to view.

It was going to be a monumental job. Where to do it? I decided it would be best to take over the whole basement in the Vancouver morgue. It had space for about fifty refrigerated areas. We would turn it into a complete identification and pathology department.

So, a day or so later, at nine at night, the refrigerated truck drove up Cordova Street in Skidroad and backed carefully into the ramp in the alley leading down to the lower morgue. We had put up tables, including two autopsy tables, and had three pathologists on duty. The first thing facing us, of course, was the job of putting everything together to make up 52 people from 146 pieces. Assuming that we had, indeed, recovered everything from the swamp and the jackpine trees.

We had to match up everything—an arm here and a leg there—and fit in what clothing we had. All this was done meticulously. It's like doing a jigsaw puzzle. If the last piece doesn't go in, you must have one piece in the wrong place somewhere. It has to be perfect to be finished. We were finishing a giant human jigsaw puzzle and we finally got the job done.

The viewing by the next-of-kin was a very difficult and traumatic time. It took an entire weekend which I'll never forget. Men were crying and women fainted in the arms of the technicians. We did get positive identification from some relatives simply by showing them photos of the bodies and not putting them through the ordeal of actually viewing the remains.

Now we had to have a cause of death. Obviously, death was due to multiple and terminal injuries; fractured skulls, ruptured aorta, ruptured heart; all the usual causes of accidental death. But what had caused Flight 21 to fall out of the sky? I opened an inquest and adjourned it pending developments.

Meanwhile, a federal government inquiry was doing extensive work, including building a complete mockup of the DC-6B. This was assembled at the air force base on Sea Island near the airport and, at one stage, was inspected by the inquest jurors. The authorities had painstakingly put everything back together, the way we had done with the bodies. We all wanted to know why the aircraft's tail had come off.

\*　　\*　　\*

Four months after the crash, Judge McDonald reopened the inquest in his packed courtroom. The hushed court heard this dramatic eyewitness account of the last agonized moments of CPA Flight 21 from John Hyra, a forest fire guard.

"About four P.M. we heard a plane coming over. The truck was stopped and I watched it through the windshield. Suddenly I heard an explosion and I said someone must be parachuting from the plane, because a billow of smoke came from it that looked just like a parachute opening.

"The explosion was a very low-pitched bang and the smoke that came out was silky white in color. Then I realised what had happened. The front part of the plane seemed to continue to fly while the tail section seemed to hesitate, then fall down away from the front part of the plane. The front part of the plane continued to fly for about thirty seconds before it went into a spin. The plane's engines seemed to sound normal before the spin but then they developed a faster whine as the front part spiralled.

"Then it disappeared in the trees and there was a terrific blast as it hit the ground. Although I couldn't see the plane for the trees, I could see the fragments from the explosion rising hundreds of feet into the air."

The inquest also heard fascinating—but theoretical—evidence from explosive experts regarding the possibility that a dynamite bomb had been hidden in a rear washroom. The jurors, all experts in aviation, were also told of a potential explosive danger of aerosol spray cans and of a stewardess's pink nightie that was riddled with holes, possibly caused by acid.

And there were intriguing stories of a mystery man, with a round face and wearing a Tyrolean hat, seen near the after-end washrooms shortly before Flight 21 took off; of the fact that one passenger was an experienced powderman used to handling large quantities of dynamite; that two of the passengers had bought large sums of insurance at the Vancouver International Airport on the day of the flight.

The sensational inquest generated worldwide publicity and dragged on for days.

* * *

There were several theories being put forward now. One was that an accident happened near the aft port lavatory. There was a washroom on each side of the aisle. The area was next to where oxygen tanks were kept. Could these tanks have been the cause? It was also brought out that the stewardess's kit was stored in the area and contained aerosol cans of hair spray. This potential danger was amply domonstrated in court by a chemist who sprayed with a can, lit a match and shot out a flame four or five feet long. It was a spectacular sight. But there was a further question: how much explosive force would that create? Enough to cripple a big aircraft?

The investigators went over to James Island in Georgia Strait, where Canadian Industries Limited kept its explosives, and the experts there examined parts of the plane's tail section, as did analysts for the Department of Transport and the City analysts. They found nitrates in the assembly which were definitely consistent with dynamite—ordinary TNT. Could it have caused a huge explosive force? And how did it get there?

The investigators then got from CPA several toilets used in DC-6Bs. They put them in bunkers on James Island. First they put just two or three sticks of dynamite in and detonated them. Then they used five sticks and kept moving up until they had the same effect the explosion had had on the port toilet found in the wreckage. They concluded that the fatal explosion must have been caused by a bomb made of at least eleven sticks of dynamite, triggered by a burning fuse.

Working on this theory, we went back to the passenger manifest to find who might have had easy access to dynamite. We found out about the expert powderman on his way to a mining job in the Yukon. We also looked for someone who might have been jealous or, perhaps, carried a lot of insurance. There was no one on the fatal flight who was over-insured. There was, however, a large amount of insurance placed on one passenger. There were also reports that two passengers had bought huge sums of insurance at the airport but these proved erroneous.

The investigation was now being done at different levels but still the RCMP and other government investigators could say only that they had narrowed the case down to four or five vague possibilities concerning who might have had it in for somebody on the plane. There was never any conclusive evidence or proof.

How could a bomb have gotten aboard? In those days aircraft were not safe from breaking and entering. An airline would sometimes have a two-million-dollar aircraft parked on the ramp with no bloody key to lock the door with. Anyone could walk inside. And part of the airline routine requires the anonymity of an inspector. He must not be know to the employees. Sort of like an inspector who boards a bus and is unknown to the driver.

An inspector could board an aircraft undergoing an M4—routine maintenance, fourth class. This is when the ground crews put the pillows and blankets up, clean the ashtrays and sweep the floor. An inspector will sometimes go aboard to check if the job is being done properly. But he mustn't *appear* to be an inspector.

When Flight 21 was being thus serviced before taking off for Prince George, a cleaning lady aboard had been standing on a seat stowing pillows and blankets. She said later she spotted out of her right eye "a gentleman with a round, moon-shaped face" and a Tyrolean hat who walked past her to the aft port lavatory. She couldn't say if he actually went inside but she did recall seeing the door swinging as if he had gone in.

She said the man then walked back along the aisle and went down the ramp. The girl thought the stranger was probably an inspector and thought no more about it. She remembered the mystery man only when she had heard the plane had crashed. Nobody has ever found the man with the moon-shaped face and the Tyrolean hat. What was he?

It's just conjecture on my part but, at least, this girl's story put *somebody* in or near the toilet. It was, perhaps, a clue, a straw to be grasped. Was he an inspector? That's crazy. He surely would have come forward after the crash. Was he a confused passenger who had boarded the plane by mistake and then boarded another aircraft and flown away and perhaps never even heard about he crash? Or was he the planter of a bomb that would end the lives of 52 people?

Dynamite is not a commodity bought at the local hardware store. But it's in every construction and mining and logging camp in British Columbia. Every highway construction crew has it. It isn't that hard to come by.

But how was the timing figured out? A fuse had to have been burning for at least 90 minutes or so. This told me the deed must have been the work of an expert in explosives.

If there was a bomb in the washroom, why hadn't anyone seen it? Another mystery. Some experts said the dynamite could have been placed behind the toilet bowl, perhaps even behind the plywood wall itself. Who knows? We didn't.

Warren Lovell, the American pathologist, got involved with examining the pink nightie that belonged to a stewardess. It had been in her flight bag and had minute holes in it which were not explainable. They hadn't been caused by the crash. It looked as if they had come from acid of some kind, perhaps the result of corrosion in the area where the bag was, next to the oxygen bottles.

Dr. Lovell felt this was a major clue; whatever had caused the holes was from inside the overnight bag and was not an exterior force. But he also said later he was almost convinced that a bomb had caused the disaster. We also called in Dr. Tom Sterling, an explosives expert with the Canadian Armament Research and Development Establishment in Quebec. He testified that at least seven sticks of dynamite, weighing three-and-a-half pounds total, would have been needed to cause the damage done.

And we also had the testimony of Carl von Harten, a textile chemist who owned a dry-cleaning company in Vancouver. He was the guy who so dramatically demonstrated the effect a can of hair spray could have at an altitude of 16,000 feet.

The inquest jury found accidental death as a result of an explosion set off by person or persons unknown. It was definitely not mechanical failure or pilot error. Emphasis was put on that.

Now it was all over and we knew we had done our best. But it was like trying to guess how many angels can dance on the head of a pin. Everyone was by now convinced the crash was caused by an explosion involving nitrates.

But here was another problem: nitrates disappear quickly in the rain. Traces could have been washed away at the crash site. But the intricate chemical tests did show nitrates present from a low-level explosion, mechanically set off.

That was why we X-rayed all the bodies before they were released. In one we found two tiny bits of copper which could well have been from the casing of a dynamite cap. There was nothing more to be done. The one big question remained unanswerable.

*   *   *

The mystery of what happened aboard doomed CPA Flight 21 has never been solved and probably never will be.

Queen Elizabeth, through Governor-General Georges Vanier, sent this message of condolence to the relatives of the 52 killed:

"I am greatly distressed to hear of the tragic accident to an aircraft of Canadian Pacific Airlines in British Columbia. Please convey the sincere sympathy of my husband and myself to the relatives of the men, women and children who have lost their lives."

# A Jury of One's Peers

People often asked me over the years how inquest juries were made up. Where did we get the people? Was it done carefully and selectively? Was the process done on the basis of intelligence? Expertise? On the basis of familiarity with the circumstances of the death and the particular industry that was involved in that death? Or was it simply a matter of roping in whoever was available at the time?

Well, I guess it was a mix of all these, a sort of hit-and-miss business. And, somewhat surprisingly perhaps, it always worked. We always ended up with good and thoughtful and responsible juries. Well, almost always. There *was* the occasional lapse when things went wrong.

But I'm forever grateful to the hundreds and hundreds of jurors, good and true, who served in my Coroner's Court over 26 years. Especially to those who served so faithfully in the old days when they didn't even get paid for discharging their sworn duties, and who earnestly searched for the answer to that persistent question: "How come I'm dead?"

I always took the position that I knew nothing about the sources of my jurors but, of course, I did. In the old days, particularly, we often recruited many of them just by going into the beer parlors in the Skidroad area, such as the Stratford and the Empress. There was always a sort of captive audience of people there who didn't have much else to do with their time except spend their money on beer, and the pubs, of course, were very handy to the morgue. It was a rich market waiting to be tapped.

But we were a little more selective than that, even in those days. We didn't just go to the beer parlors. We always had a stalwart member, a corporal or sergeant, of the police force attached to the Coroner's Office, and he knew exactly where the old people were. Corporal Chuck Stuart, who was with me for many years, would simply go over to the old Carnegie Library at the corner of Main and Hastings, half a block from the police station, and he would have six subpoenas with him, blue papers—John Doe sort of thing—and he'd tap somebody's shoulder and say, "Wake up, Mac, you're on jury duty. It's just as warm over where you're going as it is here or anywhere else, so here's your subpoena and off you go now." The old folks liked the idea. They got free coffee and doughnuts.

We also got many jurors through the good offices of the two churches close to the morgue, St. James Anglican and First United. There was no pay in those days but we'd give the jurors coffee to keep them awake. The jury system back then was really a matter of "If you were lucky, you didn't get caught." But, what the hell? What's wrong with a free cup of coffee and a doughnut?

In those days there were always six jurors. For some reason, it's five now. An odd number. I always maintained that ignorance multiplied by six gives intelligence. Now I assume that ignorance multiplied by five also gives intelligence. The jurors would have a meeting and choose their foreman, usually the guy who talked the most and was able to write with a pencil. He was the one with the job of writing the verdict down. But it was always *their* verdict, as I always told them, not mine. That was the jurors' job and their's alone.

I made it a practice that after a couple of hours we'd take a break and I'd give the old folk a couple of bucks for coffee from the Ovaltine Cafe across the alley. Sometimes one of them would want a cake or a crumpet with it, but I only went for the two dollar trip. It was all nice and casual and friendly.

However, in due course we were able to benefit from the wisdom that sometimes—though rarely—is found in Victoria, seat of the provincial government, that inquest jurors should be paid, as jurors in other law courts were paid. As a result, we had an immediate upsurge in the number of people who wanted to go on Coroner's juries. So I had to say, "Well, this can't go on because we'll end up with professional jurors. We're going to have 'experts' who know all about what happened in some other case which isn't before them and has nothing to do with them."

So then we went to the Deputy Sheriff's office and, ultimately, to the list of people eligible to vote in the City of Vancouver and obtained our jurors from that. But that system developed its peculiar problems, too, because we'd have somebody from the ritzy Shaughnessy area down in the Skidroad morgue examining a sad and seedy case and wondering what the hell she was doing there, but there she was—dressed to the nines and with her chauffeur parked outside all day waiting for her.

Maybe that's democracy in action. Strangely, the system worked.

When you talk about a jury being made up of your peers, we did get a little bit of imbalance in that respect. But it did prove an interesting point—that death is the great equalizer in society. Certainly, when you had that shiny Rolls Royce outside of 240 East Cordova Street with that chauffeur sitting in it and the posh lady had probably had a special gown made for the occasion, and then sitting right next to her was Sweet Rosie O'Grady who just come across the lane from the Empress beer parlor and had just sobered up that morning from the night before—well, yes, it certainly did prove that death is an equalizer.

Then I would often find that perhaps a person couldn't see or couldn't hear or didn't give a damn, anyhow, yet he was an authority on everything on down. I always stressed that the foreman or any jury member could ask any damn questions he liked. Well, sometimes it turned out they wouldn't ask any questions when they should have. They just sat there, mute. And other times they wouldn't stop asking questions when they should have shut up.

But when you pick jurors at random you can sometimes get into deep trouble. And on one occasion I did.

\* \* \*

Ed Moyer was a man short in stature but long on the qualities that make a gracious and caring human being. He was also a gifted writer with a deep well of empathy for the poor, the underprivileged and the unlucky. He wrote for many years with warmth and wit and his police court column in *The Province* newspaper perceptively chronicled the daily misfortunes and misadventures of life's losers.

A Canadian of Irish ancestry, one of Moyer's proudest boasts was that he was the youngest Canadian to enlist in the forces in the Second World War. He joined the Royal Air Force in England when he was fifteen and ended the war flying as a tail-gunner over Burma. He once met Sir Winston Churchill and was mightily impressed by the great man's capacity for brandy and rude stories.

Eddie Moyer, with his easy laugh, puckish humor, sparkling blue eyes and penchant for the grape, was liked and respected by every fellow reporter and every policeman on the Vancouver force. In his many years on the police beat, first with *The Province* and then with *The Vancouver Sun,* he deservedly earned his reputation as the city's finest crime reporter.

But, friend to cops on the beat, detectives, superintendents, prosecutors, judges and strays nosing around the press room for a handout or a belt of cheap whisky, Eddie Moyer never forgot that he was, first and foremost, a newspaperman. That fact was amply demonstrated the day he was appointed foreman of a Coroner's jury. It came about this way.

* * *

This was during the British Empire Games in 1954, the games of the famous Miracle Mile race between Bannister and Landy. Vancouver had just built the China Creek Cycle Track on Broadway, one of the city's main crosstown thoroughfares. Cycling was the rage then and hundreds of guys were out on the streets, pedaling away like crazy to get into shape.

There was this one Italian who was in intensive training. He had been riding his bicycle along Broadway, following a truck. It's a cyclist's trick—get your bike behind a truck and you get a suction, a slipstream, that holds you. You don't have to work for a while. Even though you do breathe a bit of the exhaust fumes. Easy rider.

However, the truck in this case made a sudden right turn and the cyclist lost his balance and went under the wheels. He was killed. We had his bike and his body all wrapped together. We separated them down at the morgue and put the bits and pieces back together. The bits of the bike, that is. Well, there was no way I could have avoided an inquest into this death because there was such a tremendous interest in cycling at the time, much as there was later with the 10-speeds. So I decided I'd get some cycling guys on the jury and we'd try to figure out what was happening to bike riders in the City of Vancouver.

Everything was organized but when the inquest was to start we found we were short one cyclist, one juror. Usually, when we were one short, we'd just get somebody from Ted Fennell's analyst's office downstairs but, in this case, I didn't really like that idea because those guys worked for the city and someone might have suggested a conflict of interest.

So I'm sitting in court looking over at the press table and there was Eddie Moyer looking back at me, grinning like Peter Pan. He was covering the inquest for his newspaper. I guess he had nothing else to do that day. Well, we couldn't find anybody else in a hurry and we wanted to get on with the job so I strolled over to the press table and asked Eddie, "Would you go on the jury?"

"Fine," he said.

So I swore all the jurors in on the Bible (which actually turned out to be a copy of the Koran, as I discovered later, much to my amazement) and we heard the evidence of the death of Mr. Stromboli or whatever his name was. Then the jurors went away to their little room to consider their verdict.

Eddie Moyer, of course, had been made foreman of the jury right away. He seemed to know where the bathroom was or something. I guess because he worked for a newspaper, it made him the most qualified to write up the verdict. He had a pencil. He could spell.

After a while a knock came to my office door, signifying the jury was coming back. I went into court and waited.

But when the jurors returned, the foreman was nowhere to be seen. Now, the jury room had two doors, one leading to the courtroom and the other to the bathroom. So I just assumed that Eddie was responding to a call of nature. Hence the delay before announcing the verdict, I thought. So we all sat and waited some more. Eventually Eddie appeared, smiling as always.

He routinely read the jury's finding that this cyclist had been riding too close to the truck which turned and he skidded underneath it and died of multiple injuries to his head and chest, a rupture of the aorta and so forth. It was a clear case of accidental death.

Then Eddie drew himself up to his full five feet three-or-four inches and solemnly announced: "We, the jury, strongly recommend that bicycle-riding in the City of Vancouver be banned henceforth because of the accidents to cyclists and the concern of the travelling public." And he sat down.

I couldn't believe my ears. I looked across at Eddie and he was grinning from ear to ear, as if to say, "Well, you got me into this thing, now I'm giving it right back to you!"

"You son of a bitch!" I said to myself. "You got the headline you were hoping for! You sly bastard!"

I looked at the jury and asked, "So say you all?" They nodded and Eddie sat there with the smug air of a man with the satisfaction of a job well done.

I retreated to my office and said, "Jesus Christ, what do I do? All hell's going to break loose when this story hits the streets!"

Then my Court Officer came in. He was grinning, too. Smug.

"Do you know what happened?"

"I know what happened and I don't know what happened," I said. "What? What the hell happened? Tell me."

"Well, Mac, when they decided on the verdict, Eddie said he had to go to the bathroom. But he went to the telephone instead and phoned his newspaper and gave them the story so they could make the final edition and beat the other reporters in court. He says it'll be the page one banner for the street final and he was the one who dreamed up the recommendation."

"Son of a bitch!" I said again. "Where *is* the bastard?"

Eddie Moyer had vanished. He obviously wasn't phoning in his story. He had already done that before he even read the verdict. I guessed he made a beeline for the nearest bar.

I said a few choice four-letter words when I caught up with him but he just laughed like only Eddie Moyer could laugh and said, "Well, I was the foreman and that was the verdict and the rider. So I thought I really should give it to the paper before the other guys got it."

Eddie and I laughed about it for years after over our beer in the old West Coast Central Club next to the police station. But it did teach me a lesson: when in need, watch it!

\* \* \*

Twelve years later, when Eddie Moyer lay dying. Judge Glen McDonald visited him in hospital. They laughed gently about the celebrated bicycle inquest and Eddie's ingenious scoop.

\* \* \*

It's often a delicate area, the qualifications of the people on an inquest jury. In a situation where a death had resulted from an accident in a certain industry—the waterfront, construction, railroading, say—I would have my corporal go to the management area in that particular industry and find out who might be available for jury duty. Then he'd go to the union side and ask the head shop steward, or whoever was in charge, to give him some names. He would then put these names in his hat and draw three from management and three from the unions. From a policeman's hat!

There were some embarrassing occasions when we came up with a union shop steward from a plant involved in an accidental death and who wasn't too happy about management safety procedures at that plant. There were occasions when we came up with the manager of a plant who wasn't too happy about the union safety practices.

So we sharpened the method to the extent that we went to management, other than the management of the plant involved and to unions other than the unions which had anything to do with the particular plant. I never knew who was on a jury until the list was typed out, usually the day before the inquest. And if it was going to be a long inquest, we would have seven jurors instead of six, just in case somebody took sick or had to be excused for some other reason. We always tried to satisfy any complaints or questions.

We really did try to be selective in many cases. Our biggest argument in justifying what we were doing—this method of picking juries—was that at least the members of the jury should understand what was going on during testimony. In a maritime case, for example, we'd have people who understood what was the fo'c'sle of a ship and what was the stern and what was port and starboard. The same applied to building construction and railroading. These jurors would understand what a plywood two-ply was or what a two-by-four was, what a joint was, what a train was, things like that.

The worst difficulties, I think, arose out of my own ignorance, particularly in understanding railroad accidents. As a Master Mariner I had no difficulty at all with maritime accidents but railroads were of another world which I never could grasp. The jargon of the people who push trains into and out of Vancouver is a tongue the layman can never understand. So, unless you had some railroad men on the jury who knew what the witnesses and experts were talking about, you'd never know what the hell was going on. My God, these people would talk about a switchback and a throwover and a this-and-that-and-the-other and, if you stopped the evidence every time they used a name or term which to them was as commonplace as sneezing, you'd never get the inquest finished. And we always had a job to do.

I always tried in these situations to ask these experts simple questions so I could get simple answers and, if I had a jury of laymen, I tried to interpret the evidence into layman's terms. I was sometimes praised for that approach. But, certainly, if I had any success in that area it was mostly due to the simple fact that I always did my homework and tried to get the best jurors. I never had Crown Counsel in my court. Crown Counsel at inquests are a bloody waste of time. If a Coroner hasn't done his homework and doesn't know the facts of the case, the last thing he wants is somebody wandering in who knows even less about it and will then spend half-an-hour getting around to the point that, for example, a train ran over a man on the tracks and the man, being frailer than the train, died.

You've got to prepare yourself. I was never late for an inquest in 26 years but being punctual at 10 o'clock in the morning really isn't all that important, is it? The important part of my job was done the night before when I got all the reports in and learned the names of the deceased and the witnesses. And I was always prepared for the witness who absolutely believed what he or she saw but had only heard about it later, by hearsay and rumor. That was common.

But one must at least try to have people on the jury who are somewhat familiar with the particular industry which caused the death. I've been roundly criticized all over Canada and the United States for using this system. But I still think it's the best route to go. The only one, in fact.

Let's get into this deeper. There was a case a few years ago when a jetliner came in from Montreal to Toronto and made a heavy landing and crashed, killing 50-odd people. I was interested. I got permission from the British Columbia Attorney-General to go to Toronto to examine just how the authorities handled the deaths of so many people in one accident. Conveniently, there was a skating rink near the crash site. Beautiful if an airplane crashes right next door to an ice rink, where it's cold and equipped with all the facilities such as storage space and telephones and so forth. It's a damn convenient morgue.

Beatty Cotnam, who was then Chief Coroner for Ontario, was very well organized, just as any Coroner would wish to be in such an emergency. But one of the things I had an argument with him about came up when I asked, "Who are you going to put on the jury?" (The federal government, of course, subsequently held its own official inquiry into the crash but there also had to be an inquest.) Beatty said, "No, I'm not going to go your route, Mac. I'm going to get whoever we get by the luck of the draw."

Beatty Cotnam ended up with a baker, a housewife, a taxidriver, an expectant mother. If there was one thing they had in common, it could have been that they had flown on airplanes as passengers. My approach would have been very different.

I'd have said, "Look, this involves Air Canada so we don't take any of their pilots or engineers or ground crew and so on. Instead, we'll go to CP Air or Pacific Western or Nordair, or whatever, and put their people on the jury. Because somehow, these people will have to try and interpret the last words of the pilot when he thought he had only lost a wheel instead of an engine, or lost two engines or whatever it was that happened before he plowed in."

I will say this, to Beatty's credit. His reply to me was a simple one. He said, "Well, they've all been passengers on aircraft; haven't they got as much concern as the so-called experts who fly them?" I couldn't come up with an argument against that.

"As long as they can understand what it's all about, the technical stuff," I said. "But I think what you're doing is what the federal government should be doing. You're getting all the brass to testify regardless of what implication you get from that jury's mind."

I still believe that it's the juror who asks the most important question ever asked at an inquest. Not the Coroner, not a lawyer, but somebody who knows the job involved in the death and works with the same equipment and perhaps even knew the deceased. That person is bringing to that inquest the benefit of his own experience and knowledge. That, basically, is what the inquest is all about. Understanding and caring.

This happened so many times; one juror simply asking one vital question which suddenly causes some of the other jurors to say, "Yeah, maybe. Maybe that's right, I never thought of it that way." And they start asking more questions and all of a sudden they're questioning a witness and getting good answers. So maybe an expert on the jury takes a far more important role in the assessment of "How come I'm dead?" That question the deceased is not able to ask. That all-important question.

That, I think, was the strength of the way I did things. And it's interesting to note, in passing, that the Mining Act of the Province of British Columbia does require that at least three members of an inqest jury inquiring into a mining accident be miners. That's very interesting. When the Act was passed some years ago it stipulated that, if there were a cave-in or some other accident causing death, at least three people on that jury must be miners—people who went underground to work—and who would be able to ask the pertinent questions about safety and shoring up and all the rest of it.

Seems like an excellent idea. The way things work when you just take a list of names from the tax rolls is that you end up with all the experts on the witness stand speakng to the jury on evidence, but no experts on the jury itself. As a result, the Coroner finds he's spending most of his time trying to explain to the jury all the technical jargon and theories about this-and-that instead of letting the jurors get down to the nitty-gritty of how and why the person died. It makes the whole process more complicated and time-consuming.

\* \* \*

There was in 1969 one highly publicized inquest when, unwittingly, Judge McDonald had such an expert, not on the witness stand but as foreman of a jury. The court was probing the death, in hospital, of Nicholas Marino, a 50-year-old inmate of British Columbia's Oakalla Prison. Its findings, which severely criticized a prison physician, made headlines and raised questions in government.

\* \* \*

Under the British Columbia Coroners Act, any person who dies whilst incarcerated, that is, in jail in the custody of a peace officer, must be the subject of an inquest. It's mandatory. It's clearly spelled out in the Act. And quite properly so. The need for inquests in such cases has been amply demonstrated many times when there has been suspicion that the deceased had been ill-treated by guards or neglected when medical attention was needed.

Jail deaths are not pleasant deaths. Well, I don't think any death is pleasant but, to me, jail deaths sort of represent the real, sad end of the road. I think everyone will agree in principle. First of all, one simply shouldn't die. But if one *has* to die, don't die in jail. Or don't die in your best friend's wife's bed. Try to die so you can at least have some sort of final dignity.

At a jail death inquest, everything must be done with extreme care. And here, again, you run into one of those tricky little problems: who is investigating this death but the very people who arrested and incarcerated the deceased? So the Coroner must take every bit of evidence from every possible source, whether it be the real evidence or hearsay or whatever, in order to satisfy the jury and all the so-called Bleeding Hearts in our society of the true events and circumstances of the death. Nothing can be overlooked.

Now, there was this one case I'll never forget. God, how could I? It was an inquest into the death of an inmate in Oakalla Prison who had been transferred to the general hospital for treatment of a ruptured blood vessel in his skull. The cause of death was routinely proved by an autopsy and the jury found that this was obviously a natural death, caused by acute meningitis of the brain and a thrombosis at the base of the skull.

Of course, this seldom satisfies everybody in the next-of-kin field or the Bleeding Heart field. They'd like to say that the prisoner was beaten to death by his guards or was refused medical treatment or something like that. And this is what makes it so damned important to have the jury view the body with the pathologist present to note if there are any marks or signs of violence on the body which can be pointed out then and there.

I always made absolutely sure that my Coroner's Technician turned the body over from the back to the front on the stage right in front of the jurors. We always did this because it comes back again to that very important old principle: if you don't show the jurors everything, you may be sure somebody will eventually say, "Oh, they hid something from us."

So, in this case, it was all done. The whole story was taken from the jail doctor, the jail nurse, the hospital people and so on. Everything seemed fine. No problems.

Well, it struck me that the foreman of this jury was a damn good counsel who asked a lot of intelligent questions. He knew all about the procedures in jail: where you went when you had a sore tooth or a sore toe, and how you applied for treatment and so forth. I was most impressed. I thought to myself, "Well, at least I've got somebody intelligent on the jury who has taken away a lot of my problems because I wouldn't have thought of half the questions he's asking."

When the testimony was over, the jury came back into court and announced a unanimous verdict that the prisoner had died of natural causes. But the jurors were critical of the prison doctor, who they said had showed neglect, and they recommended that more due care and attention be given to inmates by all the jail staff. I said a silent amen to that; that's motherhood. So that was the end of it. Or so I thought.

But then Dick Schuler, a reporter with *The Sun* came up to me and said, "Glen, do you know who your foreman was?" I said I didn't because it was none of my business who the jurors had picked as their foreman.

"Well," Dick said, "he just finished doing two years in Oakalla."

"You're kidding!" I said.

So I called in Corporal Stuart and said, "Chuck, did you know who this guy was? Where did you get him?"

"Well, we got him from the Deputy Sheriffs—Premier Davie Barrett's Brownies. They went through the list and picked this guy out."

"Dick," I said, "you're right. Go ahead and make your story. I was caught out, but let me add something to the story. This guy asked more intelligent questions than I did or anybody else did."

It was legally arguable whether this guy had the right to sit on a jury or should have been disqualified but, somehow, it didn't seem quite right to have an ex-con as a jury foreman. You don't let the fox into the chicken coop. The lesson I learned from that case was that if I again had an expert of that guy's stature, I would bring him in as a witness but I wouldn't have him on the jury. And certainly not as foreman.

The jury came up with an excellent and positive verdict because, in fact, the prisoner had not received all the care and attention he should have been getting. By having an ex-con on the jury, yes, the system had in a sense been violated. But such a violation, I thought, helped the system out in the long run because, if it is necessary to examine every death in jail, then let's by all means do it as expertly as we can. And perhaps, in retrospect, the best and most qualified people who can help in such cases are the people who have been incarcerated themselves— the ex-cons.

\* \* \*

The *Vancouver Sun's* headline the day after the inquest said "EX-CON LED JURY" and the story described Judge McDonald's jury foreman as James Patrick Atkins, a parolee who had 46 convictions, mostly for forgery and impersonation, and who once was named a habitual criminal. Between his stretches in prison he had posed as Wing Commander Lord Atkins of the South African Air Force, Brigadier General Sir James Harris of the British Army, Air Commodore Lord Bluirro of the Royal Air Force, Bishop James Allan of the Roman Catholic church and David Simpson, MP.

*The Sun* also quoted Judge McDonald as saying: "I think it was an amazing coincidence. I'm sure it won't happen again."

And it never did.

Then there was the unfortunate occasion when a lady fell out of a window of the Empress Hotel next door to the Vancouver Police Station. As in the case of the fatally-injured cyclist, the inquest into this death led to one of the strangest jury recommendations Judge Glen McDonald had ever heard.

\* \* \*

This was in the late '50s. At that time Colonel Donald McGugan was a sort of one-man provincial Liquor Control Board and it was a standing joke that, when he was seen walking down the street, someone would observe that the liquor board was holding a meeting.

His regulation in those years was that all the beer parlors must close for one hour, between 6:30 and 7:30 in the evening. The idea was to make men go home to their families for dinner, but it seemed about half the male population of Vancouver just went to privately-owned clubs and carried on drinking until the beer parlors opened again, so it was a futile exercise. All of which didn't make the hotel owners happy, of course, and they were constantly lobbying the government to have the law changed. It was, in 1963.

When I was fairly new as Coroner, I decided one day, well, let's find out whose ox is being gored and, having been gored, perhaps these hotel people should supply the jurors for an inquest. The opportunity came with the death of Mary Joe, a native Indian lady who weighed in at somewhere around 260 pounds. The case also involved a logger, Johansen, a big, burly Norwegian who had come to town from a logging camp in the bush with two or three thousand dollars in the pocket of his jeans. It was a classic example of what so often happens on the Skidroad, when a man with lots of money is out for a good time and meets an unfortunate native person who shouldn't damn well be there in the first place.

Being rich and footloose and on holiday on Skidroad, big Johansen naturally drifted into a Hastings Street hotel near Woodward's Department Store and sat down in the beer parlor promptly when the doors opened at ten in the morning. And there he spotted his lady love, fat and friendly Mary Joe. Perhaps the light wasn't too good at that hour of the morning or Johansen wasn't seeing too well from the night before, but there was instant rapprochement. They spent the whole day together, delighting in their newfound friendship, until the witching hour of 6:30 arrived. Closing time. They were summarily ejected and couldn't go back for an hour.

So they left the pub and wandered along to the old government liquor store at the corner of Main and Hastings where Johansen stocked up with a bottle of rum, a bottle of rye, a bottle of scotch, and a bottle of gin. Then the lovebirds gravitated across the street and booked a room in the Empress Hotel (not to be confused in any way with the elegant Empress Hotel in Victoria) just behind the police station. Their room was on the top floor.

It was a hot and sultry summer's evening so they opened the windows and got down to the business of some serious drinking. Now, the windows in the Empress Hotel were, at that time, the largest of any hotel in Vancouver. Whoever the architect was, he had done a wonderful job. I suppose he had anticipated providing guests with a panoramic view of the harbor and the North Shore mountains. But, as it turned out, the view was a hardly inspiring one of the back of the police station and the morgue. But, of course, Johansen and Mary Joe weren't too fussy about the scenic vista after spending all day in the beer parlor. They were possessed of other, more immediate thoughts.

Well, I always seem to be in the wrong place at the wrong time or something. I'm sitting in my office this evening, working late and minding my own business, when the telephone rings and somebody says someone just fell out of the Empress Hotel. Oh! Great! At least it wasn't far away. There was no difficulty walking down the lane and, sure enough, there was certainly someone lying there who had no pulse, no heartbeat, no anything. There were multiple fractures of the skull, ruptured aorta and so on. It was a drunken and now obviously dead Indian lady named Mary Joe. That was all we knew.

It was no problem to move her the few feet from the alley to the morgue, so that was done. The body was undressed and examined and autopsied and, of course, the cause of death was multiple internal and external injuries. She also had a very high degree of alcohol in her blood, .30 or .28, something of that order. In the meantime, we had to tell the cops. The hardest place to find a policeman in Vancouver is within 500 feet of the bloody station. They all see to be so busy doing paper work or something that you have to call a man in from Shaughnessy or West Point Grey or the Fraser Valley, almost, to investigate a case right outside their own back door.

However, the cops eventually showed up. I told them I thought poor Mary Joe had come out of a room in the hotel because I could see a window open up on the top floor. Well, about half an hour later somebody went into the room and there was dear old Johansen fast asleep on the bed.

After some effort, the cops managed to wake him up. They asked him where his friend was. Now, there's a real Sherlock Holmes question, "Where's your friend?" First of all, did he *have* a friend? I don't think the guy even knew who he was or where he was, let alone if there had been somebody with him. But he looked foggily around and, sure enough, there were a few personal possessions of Mary Joe's— cigarettes, a handkerchief, a lipstick. Johansen tried to pull himself together and tried valiantly to reconstruct the events of the day, but all he could say was that he didn't know what had happened to Mary. "She was right here. I've been with her all day. She's my friend." And that was that.

The difficulty Mary Joe had encountered was simple. She had answered a call of nature. All the beer of the day had had its effect on her kidneys and she had gone into the bathroom to urinate while Johansen was snoring on the bed. Now, this is where the old Empress Hotel comes into the twentieth century, so to speak. The owners, in a fit of ambition, had decided to modernize the rooms by putting toilets in. However, because of the way the building was designed back in the early 1900's, this meant they had to raise the floor to put the piping in. And, in order to put the toilet bowl and seat in, they had to raise the floor another foot.

So the pressing problem thus presented to the would-be lady urinator was that she had to climb up six inches and then another foot in order to rest her buttocks, finally, on the toilet seat. Which isn't exactly Sir Edmund Hillary or Sherpa Tenzing Norgay climbing Mount Everest, but I suppose it's pretty close to that kind of challenge when you've been drinking since ten in the morning on Skidroad.

What happened was that Mary Joe had completed her natural duties and, in stepping down the eighteen inches from the toilet to the bathroom floor, had tripped and lost her balance and toppled through the open window falling five storeys to her demise. And, of course, while she was performing her acrobatics in the bathroom—somewhat in defiance of the laws of gravity or, perhaps, with them—good old Johansen was busily sawing logs on the bed, blissfully unaware of what was going on. Certainly, his contribution to the proposition, or hypothesis, of what had happened was decidedly negative, as indeed, everying else he could say was negative.

So, a few minutes after Mary Joe made her sudden descent from the bathroom to the pavement, here I am standing in a very highly-populated area of the city with lots of people milling around trying to figure out what had happened. I knew right away I had to hold an inquest because here was a very serious accident occurring near a very popular hotel.

Then I got the bright idea that I should have some owners or managers of hotels on the jury because this accident occurred following a day of heavy drinking in beer parlors which, in turn, was followed by more drinking when those beer parlors were closed. I decided this was a hotel problem which should be examined and discussed by people in the hotel trade. As it turned out, I couldn't have been more naive.

The owners and managers reported for jury duty eagerly and with great gusto. I thought they were really going to get somewhere. My simple premise was that these enormously large hotel room windows should have steel bars put across them so guests couldn't fall out. And I also put to the jury the question of excessive drinking in beer parlors, anticipating some censure, in the verdict, of people who drank too much. So we went happily along and heard all the evidence, which the jury accepted a hundred percent.

When the jurors returned with their verdict it was obvious I had missed the point entirely. They found that Mary Joe, whilst intoxicated, had fallen out of the hotel window and had suffered these massive injuries—fractured skull, ruptured aorta, fractured almost everything else—and that her death was to be classified as accidental. But I was absolutely staggered when they added: "We, the jury, strongly recommend that the Attorney General of the Province of British Columbia be advised that the practice of closing beer parlors between 6:30 and 7:30 p.m. should be abolished because people are being forced to go to the liquor stores to buy hard liquor and taking it up to hotel rooms and becoming so intoxicated they are falling out of windows."

It seemed all they were concerned about was having the pubs stay open for that extra hour so they could sell more beer and make more money. Well, one always tries to maintain the decorum of the court, so I heard the verdict and the recommendations read and then I read it all back to the jurors and asked, "And so say you all?" and they nodded their heads in all seriousness. So I just said, "Thank you, Mister Foreman and jurors. I shall undertake to have this recommendation transmitted to the Attorney General forthwith, and I thank you for discharging your services here on behalf of the deceased." That was it.

Then Johansen, who had been snoozing in the back row of the court, came to and came up to me and asked, "What do I do now?"

"I think you'd better pay for your room," I said.

*    *    *

The simple fact that death is the great equalizer in everyone's life was never emphasized more dramatically than on the day Judge Glen McDonald held an inquest into the death of a young native Indian woman on the seedy strip of violence, frustration, humiliation and despair that is Vancouver's Skidroad.

On the jury were two women from directly opposite poles of the social strata: one from upper-class Shaughnessy, the other from Skidroad itself; one who arrived at 240 East Cordova Street wearing furs and riding in a long and shiny car driven by a uniformed chauffeur, the other who trotted over from her dingy hotel room just two blocks from the morgue.

This odd couple were brought together by the death of a third woman, a total stranger to both. And they each learned that day that death is a common bond shared by all, regardless of race, rank or creed. Death protects no favorites and shows no class distinctions.

*    *    *

I was the first Coroner in Vancouver—perhaps the first in Canada—to have women on my juries. It was just that I had read the Coroners Act many times and, when it referred to juries, it just said "men." But "men" was the only terminology used in those days so I said to myself, "Well, that doesn't exclude women." The very first time I had women on a jury it made quite an impression on the local women's groups and made headlines.

It was a positive step I was very proud of. I found that a woman's mind was often more conducive to dealing with certain situations we were faced with than a man's was. In those days, of course, we had inquests into abortion deaths and I felt women on a jury could understand such things a little better, perhaps, than a man could.

Then there came a memorable inquest I'll never forget and which, for some of us, underscored a very valid point about the Coroner's job in society. One morning a Rolls Royce, or maybe it was a Bentley or a Daimler, rolled up to the front of the Coroner's Court. There was a chauffeur at the wheel and a most elegant lady got out and came up the stairs. Naturally, we were all curious at this unusual spectacle and were peeking out of the windows. What was a Rolls Royce doing in Skidroad at quarter to ten in the morning?

Every morning my Chief Technician had a list of the deceased who had been admitted to the morgue the night before, with their addresses and next-of-kin and so on, and on this morning I couldn't see anyone on his list who came from a district which might be representative of a

Bentley or a Rolls Royce, complete with chauffeur. So I was even more curious by now, and I went to see Corporal Stuart. I discovered that this posh lady was a juror who would be inquiring into the squalid death of a young girl on the Skidroad.

The inquest started at ten and was going well when I noticed, looking down from the bench, that one of the jurors was a gal I recognized from the Empress and the Savoy and the Stratford beer parlors. Well, she was reasonably presentable for that hour of the morning but she had obviously been out on the town and wasn't too much with what was going on. Whereas the other, rich lady, who was sitting next to her, was very much with it and had even put her little pince-nez on and was carefully studying all the exhibits and making notes and comments. I just thought to myself, "Well, east has finally met west and the twain have met at an inquest forum. How fitting."

The case involved the death of an Indian woman from a drug overdose. Out of curiosity, I went to meet the jury when the verdict was in. I found these two ladies having a long and earnest discussion and I introduced myself as Coroner McDonald. They nodded and said how interesting the morning had been and then they left, together, discussing with great seriousness the problems facing Indian women on the Skidroad.

I thought: Well, maybe the pattern is wrong but, at the same time, there is that same concern about life and death whether you come from Shaughnessy with your chauffeur driving, or whether you walk over from your Skidroad hotel after a night on the town. Death is the great equalizer. The death registration still reads "The Province of British Columbia" and, more important, it has a date on the bottom as to when the person died and the cause of death. Homicide. Suicide. Accident. Misadventure. The juries always found out.

So they left, this rather odd couple, and the chauffeur was waiting in the car and when they pulled away from the Coroner's Court, he was driving two ladies instead of one. I don't know where they went. I don't know whether they went up to Shaughnessy for a glass of sherry or to the Stratford for a beer. But I know they had met and made friends because of someone else's misfortune, and they had each learned something that day.

# *Floating Coffins*

A spokesman for the Canadian Merchant Service Guild said Monday night the union will seek a full investigation into the presumed sinking of a tug with five men aboard.

The 61-foot steel-hulled tug *Haro Straits* was reported missing Sunday off Point Roberts. Search and Rescue officials and the ship's owners said Monday they were fairly certain the tug sank in the gale that lashed the British Columbia coast Sunday.

The tug's crew were identified as: Captain John Carstens, of Ruskin; mate George Ramsdin, of Haney; engineer Tom Greer, of North Vancouver; deckhands Ole Rysstad, of Prince Rupert, and Fred Pullen, of Nanaimo.

News Item, February 29, 1972

On that stormy Sunday, Judge Glen McDonald was with his wife, Mardie, at their country home in Crescent Beach, a small community on the Pacific Ocean, 35 kilometres south of Vancouver.

They were snug in the living room in front of a blazing fire of fir and alder logs. They listened to the trembling and shuddering of the house in the gale and the rain lashing the windows fronting the beach. It was not a night to be outdoors.

They became aware of unusual and erratic lights flashing far out across the black water and, through Judge McDonald's old navy telescope they watched the eerie spectacle of searchlights stabbing and sweeping the angry sea and bright orange flares falling slowly, as if they were slow-motion shooting stars, from the rain-shrouded sky.

They knew someone out there in the storm was in distress. So the McDonalds put on their boots and heavy jackets and they called their dog and they went out to the beach, heads bowed to the unforgiving gale.

Judge McDonald didn't know it then but the sinking of the *Haro Straits* was to become yet another case that would eventually find its way into his courtroom in Vancouver's Skidroad.

\* \* \*

We walked along the beach. We could see a lot of ships off the tip of Point Roberts (a peninsula that juts across the 49th Parallel and is part of Washington state) with searchlights on. There were aircraft from Search and Rescue dropping flares. The wind was from the southeast, 50 or 60 knots and gusting higher, and it was raining heavily.

We had heard on the radio that a towboat had apparently foundered about three-and-a-half miles off the point, towing two empty wood chip barges up from Washington. She had routinely reported in that afternoon to another ship of the company, saying she was northbound and experiencing heavy winds and seas, but hoped to be in the Fraser River on schedule.

The tide was well out and we thought if the crew had taken to liferafts, the gale might have blown them in along the beachfront. A lot of the neighbors were out, too. We wanted to do anything we could to help.

We couldn't do anything, as it turned out, and in the morning we read that the tug had just vanished. The chip barges were found but as no sign of survivors. Five men had disappeared without trace.

The sinking added one more sad chapter to the long history of tugboats foundering in British Columbia waters, one of the wickedest coasts in the world. It set me to thinking about all these needless deaths.

I'd held a lot of inquests into tugboat and fishboat sinkings. The ships always seemed to capsize in a matter of just a minute or two. That was the terrible part. The quickness precluded any hope that the crew could get off or, if men were asleep, could be wakened in time to get to a liferaft. The steady loss of life was of great concern to the Merchant Service Guild, the Seamen's Union, the shipowners, the underwriters and the federal Ministry of Transport.

I felt that here was another catastrophe. I had a gut feeling. And it wasn't long before my fears were proven. I wasn't directly involved at that stage, but I knew I was going to be before too long. In the Coroner's job, if you don't have a body, you don't have jurisdiction. So it was just a matter of waiting and saving the clippings from the newspapers, keeping informed so I would at least be aware of some of the facts.

The fact that loss of life on tugboats was so high on the west coast of Canada and not nearly as high on the east coast was of great concern to everyone in the shipping industry and to me, because of my background as a former member of the Canadian Merchant Service Guild and Master Mariner. Safety at sea was, naturally, something I was very interested in. I spent four years' apprenticeship at sea and 18 months to get a mate's ticket and another 18 getting a master's ticket. I knew the bloody cruel sea. There were questions of ship safety and metacentric height relating to buoyancy; the danger of capsizing, loading principles and the principles of the Plimsoll line—how far you can load a ship down—and the difference between a ship that is towing or is, itself, on the end of a towline as opposed to a ship that's not towing or being towed. These are all very important matters that any seaman should understand.

I'd also taken a year's sabbatical with the Dillingham Corporation, sailing as master of a tugboat towing a barge from Vancouver to Honolulu and back. So I had some expertise in the towing business and when I studied the reports of the Haro Straits' sinking, it was like going back to the classroom. She was a 60-foot vessel, equipped with modern gear. And yet her sinking seemed to fit a pattern which had been demonstrated regularly over the years.

To my mind these vessels were no more than tin cans with tremendous horse-power. The sound of the engine alone would be continuously in the ears of the crew. That didn't suggest they weren't safe but it did suggest they could pull more than one tow at a time, which they frequently did. And, as naval architects had said at previous inquests, these tugs were designed to a registered tonnage of 1.89 or 1.92, or something below a registered tonnage of two because, as such, they would move into a different and more demanding classification. Registered tonnage simply means 100 cubic feet per ton of the tug's space, less engine room space, less navigational space, less crew's quarters space.

The only thing really measured was the walking space between the engines or in the afterdeck locker, or lazarette, and it was the pride of not a few naval architects—often on orders from the owners—that they built under the two-ton registration so they wouldn't have to go through steamship inspection and other costly inspections.

It has always seemed odd to me that Canadian government marine regulations for the west and east coasts of Canada are the same, bearing in mind the very different conditions encountered. The west coast tugboat industry is physically protected by the presence of the mass of Vancouver Island to the west of the mainland. You can, for example, paddle safely from Vancouver to Nanaimo in a canoe. But no one would ever suggest paddling a canoe from Halifax, Nova Scotia to St. John's, Newfoundland. Usually, you're not in the open ocean on the Pacific coast. But sometimes conditions in this area can be actually worse than conditions in the North Atlantic because they change more suddenly and mariners are frequently faced with short, choppy seas in the Strait of Georgia instead of the big, rolling swell they'd find in the Atlantic.

These small but high-powered tugs would be working 24 hours a day, coming off a regular run or contract jobs only once every two weeks to change crews. The engines were seldom turned off. They're tremendously efficient vessels, no doubt about that. But they're also hugely high-powered for their length and draft. This had been grapically shown at several inquests, particularly in cases when a towline was not leading directly astern but was on a quarter, either 45 or 60 degrees on either the port or starboard side, but still pulling with all the stress needed for the tug to control the movement of the barge in tricky tidal waters in a gale or a strong swell.

This was where metacentric height comes in. If a towline is attached to a winch and from the winch to a bollard and then to a barge, and you have an adjusting lever on the quarter of the tug, that ship will list 10 degrees, 15 degrees, even twenty degrees but will still have sufficient center of gravity within the vessel to right itself should the towline part. However, if the towline doesn't part, an added strain from external sources—wind, tide, current—is put on the towline and a further pulling-over of the vessel occurs. The metacentric height between the center of buoyancy and the tug and the center of gravity of the tug will meet. At that point she either capsizes or rights herself. If there's any added tension, she will almost certainly capsize. And it happens viciously quickly, throwing people over the side or trapping poor sods below decks in the inrushing water.

That's not oversimplication or being overly dramatic. The few survivors there are can readily attest to what I'm saying. At one inquest, I asked a survivor to put his forearm upright on the witness box and then put it down, like in arm-wrestling, to demonstrate how fast the tug keeled over. We timed him at under thirty seconds and, again, at under twenty. That was damn scary.

The danger arises from the utilitarian and spartan design of these tugs. A sailing ship, for example, has a deep and heavy keel which compensates for wind blowing against the square footage of the sails. The tugboat is not so equipped. It's dealing only with the tow itself and the weather. Why not cut the power of the engine; why not cut back? But the job of a towboat is to control the tow and deliver it safely. That's what towboats are for. If she loses control of her tow, other damage can be suffered as a result. And there's no alarm signal to warn the skipper or the mate that he's facing a dangerous and possibly fatal situation.

It's that damn swiftness and finality that's so awful. I handled many of these cases over the years by way of inquiry rather than by inquest, simply because there were no bloody witnesses left alive to tell us what had happened, what went wrong. In most cases, all the families and friends could do was arrange a memorial service and hold a wake. They had no answer to the question "How come I'm dead?" because there was no one left to give it. It was a very sad situation.

All this was running through my mind when the *Haro Straits* sank. Ironically, the gale on that fateful Sunday was just a front passing through the area and next morning the sea was as calm as it could be. That's one of the fickle and terrible things about the Strait of Georgia; the weather can come up fiercely and quickly and without warning and then calm down just as quickly. The chop is short and high and nasty and completely different to the swell of the open ocean. I'd far rather be caught in a storm halfway between Cape Flattery and Hawaii than in Georgia Strait.

The chip barges were found the day after the *Haro Straits* went down. They were still attached to the towline and were pointing down, as if they were anchored. The tug itself was found a week later 400 feet down on the bottom. The cost of raising the ship was prohibitive as far as the owners were concerned and, in fact, raising her for inspection was not even required by the insurance underwriters. But there were a hell of a lot of unanswered questions and pressure was put on the Ministry of Transport in Ottawa, really because of this long and relentless toll of tugs capsizing on the west coast. So it was decided she would be raised and we would search for clues that might help in preventing future disasters.

*     *     *

Judge McDonald opened the inquest into the deaths of the five crewmen aboard the *Haro Straits* on March 21, 1972, three weeks after the tug had gone down.

No bodies had been recovered at this stage; the ship still lay on the bottom of Georgia Strait and the proceedings—before a five-man jury of experienced seamen—were brief, the only testimony covering weather reports and radio exchanges between ship and shore.

The jury returned a verdict of death by drowning and Judge McDonald adjourned the inquest indefinitely, noting that a federal government inquiry was being set up to try and determine the cause of the accident.

His next involvement with the ill-fated *Haro Straits* came the following November when the tug was at last being raised by a 150-ton crane mounted on a barge.

Once again, Judge McDonald and Mardie were at their Crescent Beach home when they saw activity far out on the water.

*     *     *

We could see the workers trying to attach the crane's cable to the tug, using a two-man submersible. Mardie and I went out in our 26-foot former Air Force crashboat, the *Flicker,* to see what was what. We were interested. It was foggy that morning but we got off the Point Roberts bell buoy and watched. It was obviously a tricky job in the treacherous conditions of tide and current. We hove to alongside and I introduced myself. The crew on the barge said they were faced with strong currents 400 feet down. But they managed to get the bridle around the tug and raised her, pumped out the water and towed her to the Coast Guard dock at the mouth of Vancouver's False Creek, by the Burrard Street Bridge.

I went down there, too, to look. The ship was filled with tons of silt. I took two of my technicians to help me go over her and, hopefully, find if there were any bodies. We shovelled a lot of sand and debris out and found one, the corpse of a deckhand, in the lazarette at the stern. There was no trace of the other four men. Now, this was very interesting. Let me explain.

The Canadian Merchant Service Guild had said its members wanted the tug raised one way or another and the guild's business agent, Harry Chapman, was quoted in a newspaper as saying, "We want a full investigation to find out exactly why she went down." The story added that the union had in the past charged that steel-hulled tugs are unsafe if they are not equipped with flotation compartments. Chapman was quoted: "If a steel tug is built properly, with three compartments, there is no safer vessel afloat. She must have two watertight bulkheads so that if one compartment is flooded the others keep her afloat. Some steel tugs have no bulkheads, some have one and some of the owners have put in a second one." And the article also quoted C.S. Cosulich, the president of Rivtow Straits Ltd., the tug's owners, as saying the *Haro* Straits had been inspected by the government's transport ministry and found safe for service.

It was interesting that the Guild had mentioned watertight compartments. The body we found was that of a crew member who would not normally be in the ship's engine room. Nor would he be in the after lazarette area unless a sudden rush of water had forced him in there—had physically forced him through an open hatchway. The torrent of water would then follow the body in. We also found a lot of sand in that part of the ship. All of which underlined the point the Guild was making: if you put in more than one watertight compartment, this creates a honeycomb effect so some areas will have air in them and the ship won't founder.

The tug was hoisted out of the water and examination showed some evidence of what had probably happened. The government inquiry was being set up and I had adjourned my inquest. I had done all I could—established that all on board were dead, presumed drowned, and death was accidental. This was important because it now transpired that the Workers' Compensation Board of British Columbia had no jurisdiction on tugboats regarding marine accidents. These were for the federal government to investigate. But, as far as insurance was concerned, a death certificate had to be forthcoming so next-of-kin could claim insurance monies.

Unfortunately, no changes were made in the regulations regarding the design and building of tugs following the *Haro Straits* tragedy. I think, though, that more caution is now being exercised by the industry—both by owners and crews, by masters and mates. But, to my knowledge, no official changes were ordered and the same regulations still apply to Canada's east and west coasts. There was no requirement made for extra watertight compartments even though the concern—and this must apply to the naval architects as well—was that all tugs should have at least one watertight bulkhead. But, of course, if that bulkhead is not closed, the insult to the vessel still occurs and it's a wasted exercise, anyway.

But there haven't been as many capsizings in recent years and I can only attribute this to greater caution. The owners and crews are more careful and have gained more experience in using these high-powered tugs. The Haro Straits was only 64-feet long but she had horsepower that normally would be in a 200 or 300-foot vessel.

Difficulties came with progress. Construction methods had improved tremendously during the war. Steel hulls, aluminum hulls, the welding—all were now a way of life. No longer were tugs made of great timbers laid down as a keel and built from the bottom up, with ribs. With modern techniques a tug or a fishboat could be built upside down and, in the course of construction, the plates would be welded together. Then she'd be turned over, put in the water and fitted out with engines and navigational equipment.

But when you build a ship upside down and weld the plates, you put extra strain on the molecular structure of those plates. I've seen a lot of Liberty and Park merchant ships which cracked at Number Two or Number Three hatch, just forward of the bridge. The cracked plating was always parallel to the weld. The weld itself held but the area two or three inches away was fractured.

In the west coast towboat sinkings, no survivors could ever describe the shearing or tearing of a plate near a weld. So that begged another question: recovery of the vessel for examination. It was determined, in the *Haro Straits* case, that no shearing of a plate had occurred. The ship had suffered damage to her propeller, according to evidence at the inquiry. This is understandable. Tugboats hit logs all the time. Anyone familiar with the Strait of Georgia knows the amount of debris and deadheads that propellers run into. In my view, the *Haro Straits* sank because her barges were on the quarter and pulled her over and under to her doom.

*     *     *

The official inquiry into the sinking of the *Haro Straits* released its report in October, 1973, more than a year and a half after the tragedy. It said the tug had probably been pulled under in high winds by the weight of the two barges after her engines stalled. Mr. Justice Frank U. Collier of the Federal Court of Canada, the head of the inquiry, said he concluded from expert evidence that the tug sank quickly. He said the vessel's propeller had struck a heavy object which stalled the engines. Then, somehow, the ship took on water. Mr. Justice Collier added that no attempt had been made to release the tows, probably because the crew members were busy with the engine problems and events happened too quickly.

The judge attached no blame and made no recommendations. But he did comment on the proposals of the Canadian Merchant Service Guild, saying, "Without meaning to sound flamboyant, trite or ponderous, I say that one must recognize that the hazards of the sea and the elements still overtake vessels, no matter what safety precautions and equipment are taken or are available."

He added that a quick-release system on the ship's towlines would probably not have averted the sinking. The Guild recommended that such a system be installed aboard all tugs. The federal government made the system mandatory in 1976.

* * *

Let's move on to the fishing boats on the west coast. Commercial fishing in British Columbia is a huge industry and there has been an appalling fatality rate over the years among the fishermen. A fishboat—gillnetter, troller or seiner—is not required to have a Plimsoll line on the hull. This line was introduced by Samuel Plimsoll, a Member of Parliament in the British House of Commons and the leader of English shipping reform, away back in 1876. He brought forward the simple theory that ships were sinking because they were overloaded.

He was ridiculed in the House. He wasn't a seafaring man but he obviously was sensible and had compassion for sailors who went down to the sea in ships and didn't come back. He was, in fact, ridiculed to the extent that one English shipowner actually put Samuel Plimsoll's design—a circle intersected by a horizontal line to denote both winter and summer loadings—on the funnels of his ships to show the world how foolish he thought the idea was. Throughout history, safety regulations have never come in overnight or been easily accepted. But, eventually, the British Parliament accepted the Plimsoll line and embodied it in the Merchant Shipping Act, on which Canada's Act is based.

We had a hell of a lot of inquests during the annual herring season in British Columbia as well as the seine boat seasons for salmon and halibut. The juries always recommended that some form of Plimsoll line be marked on the boats so the crew knew, and the owners knew, how far a vessel was loaded. You'd think that's a sound, commonsense regulation. But the trouble is that fishboats don't load alongside a dock. They do their loading out in the ocean where there are no inspectors or anyone else to police them. Fishermen are no less greedy than anyone else. The more fish, the more money. As simple as that.

There are further complications. There are no centerboards on fishboats, no longitudinal board to stop the boat from keeling over. Herring are slippery bastards and can slip suddenly over to one side, compounding an already serious listing problem.

So you have the Godawful situation where fishboats are loaded so deep the sea is awash on the afterdecks. They have too many bloody fish in them. That's one reason why the fishermen like to sell their catch to the packer out on the fishing banks. Then they can get swiftly on with the job of catching more fish. It makes economic sense but not safety sense.

Before a ship can sail from, say, Vancouver to New Westminster, she must report to the shipping master and the port warden. The density of the water is taken alongside the vessel and the Plimsoll line is examined. A ship loading in the Fraser River at, say, 10/19 specific gravity is allowed to go down on her Plimsoll line a bit if she's heading into the ocean because she'll come up out of the water slightly when she gets into the salt water.

But everyone says you can't enforce this rule as far as fishing boats are concerned. Why bother with a Plimsoll line when you're dealing with fishboats of 60, 80 or 100 feet? But these boats are getting bigger and bigger all the time. It's too damn dangerous.

There's a lot of heavy equipment aboard, too. There are the gullies—the big wheels you see suspended from the top of the masts. They're very heavy. There are radar sets and other navigational equipment, the engines and the rest of the gear. All this is weight above the center of gravity so we must return to that matter of metacentric height. When a fishboat gets into trouble and leans over, and if the fish in the hold slide over as well, plus you've got the added weight of the equipment up top, the boats can and do capsize.

There's the matter of training or, rather, the lack of training when we talk about safety at sea. Here's a case in point. This was back in the fall of 1965. The *Aleutian Queen* was a big and powerful fishboat sailing out of Vancouver, 68-feet long and worth about $140,000. She had been fishing off the north coast of Vancouver Island, a notoriously rough and stormy area. Somehow, she was in collision with a Russian trawler and she sank. There were three men aboard the fishboat, the owner and skipper, his 21-year-old son and a cook, aged 49. The skipper and his son were saved but the cook drowned.

At the inquest, the evidence was that the *Aleutian Queen* had 20,000 pounds of fish in her hold and was heading for a port on the island because of stormy weather. But the son testified that his father told him he had fallen asleep in the wheelhouse shortly before the collision and that the wheel wasn't lashed at the time. The skipper had apparently been up all night and dozed off at the wheel while the other two were also asleep. A fine example of a combination of greed and lack of training.

The son told us he had heard the Russian trawler blowing her whistle and the next thing he knew the ships had hit. After doing everything they could to keep the fishboat afloat, they abandoned ship. They threw the inflatable life raft over the side. But, unfortunately, the cook had no training in using it and it landed in the water upside down. The cook vanished while the other two struggled to get the raft right side up. Largely because of this, the jury found the skipper negligent because he had failed to insure the safety of his ship and crew.

The jurors decided the crew was not adequately instructed in the use of life jackets and the damaged area of the vessel had not been thoroughly examined by the crew immediately after the collision. The jury strongly recommended that the Ministry of Transport require all vessels to carry proper lifesaving equipment and that the department should supervise crew training in safety matters.

There has never been a school for people who go down to the sea to fish. By tradition, it's a matter of learning the job by working at it. You start young when a relative or friend takes you on board, and after a few years you know your way around. That's probably the most practical and the best training there is. But for cooks, for example, who are not planning to move up and buy their own boat or make a living out of the actual fishing, this lack of training can—and does—prove fatal. Most skippers don't have the time to train people in safety and they sure as hell don't have the inclination.

I was involved in at least four cases when fishermen had fallen overboard soon after their vessels had sailed, heading out to sea. The circumstances were simple and followed a pattern. The men had left a party, said goodbye to their friends and relatives and had got stupid drunk. Then they'd go up on deck to urinate, trip and fall over the side. Finis. Of course, that sort of thing can never be controlled or patrolled. It's just a question of plain common sense. Some should have the good sense to stay sober and the rest should go to their bunks, sleep it off and go to work the next day.

\* \* \*

The years 1975 and 1976 were grim for British Columbia's fishermen. A dozen fishboats had sunk by the spring of 1975, the most disastrous season in the history of the multi-million-dollar herring fishery.

Thirteen fishermen had lost their lives in just two weeks in the pursuit of a delicacy attractive to foreign palates. The spawning herring were being stripped of their eggs and the cured roe sold to Japan at breathtaking prices.

The lost fishboats had been built as long ago as 1913 and as recently as 1974; they varied in length from 30 to 80 feet; some were metal-hulled and some were wooden; some were loaded and some were empty.

The one thing they had in common was that in March of 1975 they were all out in the vastness of the Pacific Ocean chasing the Almighty Dollar with fishnets. The stormy weather, over which no government has control, seemed to be the only common denominator in their sinkings.

But people wanted to know why the boats were sinking so often and they were asking angry questions: of the packing companies, of the federal Ministry of Transport, of the Workers' Compensation Board of British Columbia, of the Canadian Armed Forces rescue coordination center.

When the carnage continued in the 1976 herring season, Judge Glen McDonald decided it was time to ask some questions of his own. As Coroner—and as a master mariner himself—he wanted to find out just what was going on out on the fishing grounds.

So, in April of 1976, he convened an inquest into the deaths of four fishermen who had died in three separate accidents at sea the previous February and March. He empaneled a jury of six experienced mariners and fishermen and the inquest received extensive media coverage.

* * *

I was bloody furious about this appalling loss of life in these short herring seasons in the years when prices were so high the Japanese brokers were even buying catches right out on the fishing grounds. I decided to have an inquest into these four deaths at the same time. There was nothing in the Coroners Act saying I couldn't do this. And it didn't turn out to be difficult.

The common denominator, apart from the bad weather, was simply that all these boats had been overloaded by greedy people who wanted to make as much money as possible to pay their bills, to get loot to carry them through to the next fishing season. There was no control by the provincial Workers' Compensation Board because they had no jurisdiction; there was no control by the federal Ministry of Transport because they also had no jurisdiction except for the issuing of a registration number and a radio transmitting licence.

But there was absolutely no checking-out to decide if a vessel was fit to put to sea. A fishboat master is just like a guy who owns a million-dollar pleasure yacht; he owns the boat; he's got a key for the engine and presto! He can go. And he goes. Too often, there's a tragedy. We have never recognized the need to be responsible at sea.

Fishing boats are also becoming faster and faster and more and more powerful and expensive. There's an enormous capital outlay involved. Simply, there are too many damn fishboats for too few fish and there are too many greedy fishermen. Many of those deaths in the mid-seventies were absolutely unnecessary.

There were bigger and bigger herring bonanzas and the prices were forever going up. It was crazy. Greed was rampant. That's human nature, I guess. And it wasn't the herring themselves the fishermen wanted, although they were sold for fertilizer and pet food. It was the herring roe, which had to be taken right at the time it was prime for the palate of the Japanese market. That was where the loot was.

Competition was fierce. It was like watching seagulls spotting scraps of food thrown over the side of a ship. They converge on it and fight for it. That was the way it was with the fishermen and the fish. The men could hear by radio how other boats were doing 20 or 30 miles away and they'd head for the same area, steaming all night at full speed ahead. They even had their own codes, by God, so they could try to fool rival skippers when the fishing was good.

In one case, a herring boat was barreling up the coast near Porlier Pass. There was a well-known rock in the area that wasn't marked with a buoy or a light. Well, the crew were in such a hurry to get to the fishing grounds by first light they ran hard aground on the rock. They were cruelly exposed to the elements. The radio was knocked out and by the time they were spotted, one guy had died from hypothermia. Here was another tragic example of the need for education and training.

Before inquests involving fishing deaths, I always got in touch with Homer Stevens, who for years was boss of the fishermen's union, and with representatives of management. They would supply us with good, senior, qualified fishermen for the juries and, actually, we had a seminar on safety at sea every time we held an inquest. The damn trouble was that it was always too late for the guy who had lost his life. He couldn't ask, "How come I'm dead?"

\* \* \*

At that much-publicized inquest in 1976, the jury of experts, two Pacific coast masters and four fishermen, found that all four fishermen had died accidentally and unnaturally. But the jurors added that they deplored the inaction of both the federal and provincial governments on safety recommendations that had been put forward after the disastrous 1975 herring season.

They called search and rescue facilities on Canada's west coast totally inadequate and urged the establishment of a marine college to provide commercial fishermen with special training. They also said all commercial fishermen should be licensed.

The jury noted that, following the tragedy-marred 1975 herring season, the federal government had set up a West Coast Fishing Vessel Casualties Inquiry. And it added: "We. . .deplore the lack of action by federal and provincial authorities in implementing recommendations endorsed by this inquiry. We urge speedy action before yet another winter herring roe fishing operation comes around."

The jurors had deliberated for five hours before bringing in their verdict and recommendations for safety on the fishing grounds. Judge McDonald thanked them for their efforts and added, somewhat wistfully, "I only hope somebody will have heard your message."

His might have been a voice crying in the wilderness. But he at least had the satisfaction of knowing he had brought the tragic matter of the "floating coffins" into the glare of the public spotlight.

\* \* \*

There were many good recommendations like that. Had they been followed up perhaps we wouldn't have needed more inquests. It came out time and again that the fishermen all admitted it was that consuming greed to get the fish that caused the accidents. Avarice was the culprit. The sad part of the whole scenario was that the inquests were the result of tragedies that simply should never have happened. I wrote an article for *The Vancouver Sun* in which I pointed out that concern for those lost at sea comes only after the fact, at the memorial service and the wake.

In that piece, published in 1967, I wrote: "How many more must literally go down with their ships before the authorities do something about it? By more, I mean more than the 28 lives lost in British Columbia fishing and tugboats last year.

"By authority, I mean the Department of Transport, which functions under the Canada Shipping Act—an act which, when proclaimed by Queen Victoria, was then as archaic as the non-existent rules of safety of the Phoenicians. There has been no change since.

"But there have been fantastic changes in our fishing and tugboat industries which would have stunned the minds of those who drafted the English Merchant Shipping Act—which Canadians plagiarized without blush some 100 years ago and without blush perpetuate today."

And that, remember, was written in 1967.

Hell, it'll always happen to the other guy—never to me! That's the prevailing attitude. Without discipline, training and education and at least some seagoing qualifications, nobody is going to obey international rules of safety at sea or maintain proper safety and navigational equipment. We make people pass a test to get a driver's licence. And, when you consider the elements and the risks on land as opposed to the weather and the other risks at sea, it just doesn't make sense. It should be the other way around.

I've asked many insurance underwriters, "Why don't you give people a better deal on a premium if he submits himself to some schooling, like a night course in navigation and safety at sea?" But the underwriter, as well, takes the position that hopefully, nothing will happen. To him it's just a matter of paying out money. To those aboard the ships it means their lives. We haven't changed the rules since Queen Victoria passed the Shipping Act and the Plimsoll line was introduced in 1876. Well, we've come a hell of a long way since then.

*　*　*

At the inquest into the death of the cook aboard the fishboat *Aleutian Queen,* the Coroner's jury recommended that the (then) Department of Transport require all (fishing) vessels to carry proper lifesaving equipment. It also strongly urged the department to supervise crew training in safety. The B.C. Vessel Owners' Association and United Fishermen and Allied Workers' Union were urged to submit their views to the department on the subjects of training and the use of life jackets.

That was in 1965. In the years since, many more British Columbia fishermen have died as they confronted the cruel gales of the north Pacific, tracking the herring, the salmon and the halibut. The toll of lives in the west coast's towboat industry was to prove as inexcusably high. In October of 1984 six fishing boats sank off the west coast of Vancouver Island when a sudden storm raged in on a fleet of 370 salmon boats. Three men and a woman died from either drowning or hypothermia. A Coroner's inquest heard testimony suggesting inaccurate weather reports and a poorly equipped Coast Guard cutter.

In January of 1982, a provisional agreement was reached between towboatmen and the Council for Marine Carriers, representing towboat operators, regarding the supply of survival suits aboard vessels venturing into unprotected waters. Survival suits would be placed on all tugs sailing open seas.

Too little, too late?

And in March of 1983 a Canadian Coast Guard report said more than 90 percent of west coast fishboats checked so far that year had failed voluntary inspections. There were 23 reported incidents of fishing vessels in distress in 1982, down from 36 in 1981. The report said many of these cases could have been prevented with proper safety equipment and measures.

The report criticized the continuing practice of overloading with herring catches and cited a general lack of life rings, improper navigation lights, no horns, absence of life jackets, lack of flares and failure to inspect fire extinguishers.

The authors described the poorly lit and under-equipped fishboats as potential "floating coffins."

# *Now You Don't Even Want To Know My Name. . .*

You call me Chief and you do well for so I am. The blood of Chieftans flows in my veins. I am a Chief, but you may ask where are my warriors, their feathered heads, their painted faces? I am a Chief but my quiver has no arrows and my bow is slack. My warriors have been lost among the white man's cities, they have melted away into the crowds as once they did into the forests, but this time they will not return. Yes, my quiver is empty and my bow is slack. . .

> Chief Dan George
> Burrard Indian Band
> North Vancouver, B.C.

*       *       *

Frances Chow, 32, of no fixed address, died of pneumonia after her 32nd arrest for being in a state of intoxication in a public place. . .

> News Item
> *The Vancouver Sun*
> 1963

*       *       *

It is estimated that the cost of allowing native Indian women to die on the Vancouver Skidroad totalled $1.2 million over the last six years. . .five hundred and seven Indian women came to court on drunk charges in the last year. . .

News Item
*The Vancouver Sun*
1963

\* \* \*

Let us bring this life of Frances Chow down to cold dollars and cents. Let's take the figures involved—the cost to the taxpayer—with no emotion, no Christian endeavour, no sociological implication. The cost to the taxpayers for the last six years of Frances Chow's life computed at $2,543.40—arrests, bookings, jail facilities, court facilities, time spent in Oakalla Jail. . .

*Judge Glen McDonald*
Vancouver Coroner
1963

\* \* \*

A sight that never failed to upset Judge Glen McDonald was the squalid scene that reached out to clutch him every morning when he arrived at his office next to the police station in Vancouver's Skidroad.

It was in *McDonald Alley* behind the Coroner's Court at 240 East Cordova Street where, at nine in the morning—in the stifling heat of summer and in the bitterness of winter—he came upon Old Mary and her friends, Annie and Michael, and sometimes perhaps, Joseph and Johnny.

Empty beer and wine and whisky bottles lay beside the huddled forms, discarded brown paper bags rustling softly in the breeze. The Indians were asleep in the morning, dreaming gentle dreams of yesterday and of a tomorrow that might never come. Never dreaming of today. They were smiled on by the summer sun, kissed by springtime rains, blanketed by winter's white robe. Where were the warriors gone to?

Judge McDonald parked in the slot marked *City Coroner* and walked to his office. He knew it would be sooner, rather than later, when Old Mary or Annie or Michael or Joseph or Johnny would be lying, stiff and cold, on a white slab in his morgue. He had seen it happen many times.

\* \* \*

I was passionately interested in and profoundly saddened by what I saw every day on the Skidroad. Every seaport has its Skidroad and Vancouver's is one of the worst insofar as being an insult to human dignity. Skidroad is the graveyard of native Indians. It entraps them and sentences them to death. I found this hard fact out as soon as I went down there as Deputy Coroner in late 1953.

Over the years we had an average of one dead Indian a week at the morgue. In 1958, for example, there were 45 such deaths. I could count on one traffic fatality and one Indian fatality every week. That was routine. And that was just in the City of Vancouver, not the province of British Columbia.

The most common causes of Indian deaths were alcoholism and malnutrition. They didn't bother to eat. They drank instead. There was seldom a big hue and cry in those years for the betterment of their condition. They were labeled drunks. That was it. Many Skidroad Indians were from up-country. They were lured by the bright lights and stayed in the big city. It was that simple and that tragic. And it goes on today.

After they'd done their time in jail, they would take the bus ticket which the munificent government gave them to get home to the reserve, sell it, get a few dollars and head for Skidroad where they mistakenly thought the bright lights were magic and the streets were paved with white man's gold. Five years later, almost to the day, you could safely say they'd be dead and lying on a slab in the morgue. That was the grim cycle. When Skidroad trapped them, they never left.

There *were* many efforts made by many concerned groups, like the churches and the Vancouver Indian Center Society. They tried to corner these sad people and get them back home where they belonged. The vital need for education was stressed but the politicians never listened. Indians were forced to stay at the minimal level of education. The cause of Indian drunkenness is, of course, the seamy side of the tapestry of the way Queen Victoria's government handled our Indian affairs and the way our own federal government has handled them over the years and continues to handle them. Booze couldn't be taken onto the reservation so the natives went to the beer parlors. As Charles Dickens wrote, "the law is a ass."

This leads into an interesting question, one which occurred to me at the very beginning of my career as Coroner. I asked myself, "Are Indians physically and anatomically not equipped to handle alcohol?" Or does the problem stem from social causes?" What was the answer?

To find out, Tom Harmon, my Chief Pathologist, and I did some autopsies together. We did a white drunk, dead of an overdose of booze. Then we did an Indian drunk, dead of an overdose of booze. We went the same route again and again. Then we compared the liver with liver, heart with heart, kidneys with kidneys, spleen with spleen, brains with brains. We made microscopic and histological examinations and comparisons of people of different races who had the same lifestyle. And we consistently found there was absolutely no anatomical or physiological differences in organ structure. None whatever. Was it, then, a sociological problem?

This is still an ongoing argument among anthropologists and sociologists and politicians and maybe some day someone will come up with an answer better than the one Doc Harmon and I came up with. To my mind, it's a sociological thing. Some social scientist should get his butt out into the field and find out exactly why the white man isn't suffering from this self-abuse, or social abuse, to the devastating degree the Indian is.

A past cause of these problems—inherited, remember, from Queen Victoria's day—was that the Indian felt browbeaten. As a consequence, he just gave up. He was told by the government, "You just stay here on your nice reservation and we'll make sure you don't starve to death. And, by the way, don't drink! You can't handle it!" For God's sake! The Indian saw the white man working five or six days a week, having his Saturday night out and his Sunday day of rest, and then back to work on Monday for another week. Why couldn't *he* have those things?

The Indian felt left out, denied of opportunity. He was prepared to work and he would have worked as well and as damn hard as the white man. But the Indian's hopes and dreams faded away when it finally dawned on him he was being treated as a second-class citizen. In fact, until he got the right to vote he wasn't a citizen at all. The Indian's lassitude and despair grew with his frustrations.

My father was Marine Superintendent of the Empire Stevedoring Company in Vancouver and sometimes he would bring captains of Japanese ships home for dinner. As a kid, what surprised and delighted me was to hear both father and the skippers say the best bloody stevedoring gangs they ever saw working were the Indian boys from the Squamish band in North Vancouver. They said they worked harder and more efficiently than any of the white men. The Indians were okay, I knew.

Many years later, I found out the cold truth about Skidroad. The handsome. dark-eyed young Indian girls were attractive to a white man with a roving eye. The girls did a trick for money. They were looked after. But the white man never stayed around long enough to even buy breakfast or chat and make friends. Ergo, the bitter Indian saying:

"You made my ass happy five times last night and now you don't even want to know my name."

The girl took the white man's money and bought more beer and wine. She forgot to eat. The white man went his way and forgot the Indian. She was still on Skidroad.

Sadly, in my years working in the area I never saw a native Indian girl working for wages—as a waitress in a restaurant or even washing dishes in the kitchen. For some reason they just seemed unable to change to a way of life that would get them out of the beer parlors.

The male Indians gravitated to Skidroad, too. They also took a fancy to the phony Goddamn bright lights. They thought they meant a better life. But they probably knew in their hearts that the end of their road wasn't far away and an early death probable. It was fatalism.

Many well-meaning lectures were given over the years at the Vancouver Indian Center and by dear May Gutteridge at Skidroad's St. James Church. But they were really exercises in futility. Sad but true. The Indians seemed not afraid of death. They had that gentle philosophy that death is inevitable and must not be resisted.

They're generally happy people, despite the lingering and overriding aura of sadness they bear with them. If there's a fight among them in a beer parlor, it's usually over nothing more serious than who is going to be a certain girl's boyfriend that night or whose turn it is to buy a round of beer or a bottle of wine. They always seem to have money but, sadly, it's seldom used for going home where they belong. The money goes to the white man's liquor store or pub. They see no future back where they came from. Instead, they see the neon lights of the city where there's no future either.

They spend their days in the pubs and when night falls they find somewhere to sleep—a cheap room, a park bench, a back alley. Life is simple. They do a bit of shoplifting. They seldom fight. They don't constitute a big chunk of the criminal element in society. They have strong bonds of loyalty. They're lotus-eaters. They get something for nothing. Why work?

It was, after all, the white man who told them, "You keep your land. You will call it a reservation. You stay there. Don't bother us and we won't bother you. If you need help we will give you money."

Canada became the land of the immigrant hordes flowing in from the Ukraine, Hungary, Italy, Great Britain, Ireland, Spain, Portugal, Germany, China. It was now their land; it no longer belonged to the Indians.

The *quid pro quo* is that the Indians stay on their reservations. And there's so much bloody hypocrisy. I've yet to see a Royal Visit to Canada during which the organizers didn't march out the Indians in their "traditional" regalia—usually made in Taiwan or Hong Kong—to chant and beat their drums and dance around to the delight and cheers of everyone but themselves. The visiting Royals may think we see this spectacle every day. It's a bloody insulting charade and nothing more.

The Skidroad Indian problem became a very personal thing. I saw the desapir every day. When I parked in the alley behind the morgue the drunks would be coming out of the Police Station where they'd spent the night in the tank. Half, perhaps three-quarters, were Indians who had been locked up for their own safety. Others were waking up in the alley itself. They slept there if it was raining or snowing or sleeting. Some would catch pneumonia and die. That was that.

For me, it was like going every morning from one world into another. This transformation became just a part of the skyline of the city. Unfortunately, it was also the gutterline of the city. I'd say to myself, "Sooner or later one of these Indians is going to be in my morgue." And it happened, all too often. It became a common occurrence over the years.

I remember four Indian gals, about 22 or 23 but already getting fat on beer and at the same time suffering from malnutrition. I saw them many mornings in *McDonald Alley*. Later I saw all of them in my morgue.

"Well, old Sally's in the morgue now," one of the staff would say. I'd say, "That's too bad." I meant it.

I began to think that having an inquest into a Skidroad Indian death was much the same as having an inquiry into why the sun comes up in the morning. Where was the point in it? I sat down and did some homework to find the cost of the problem to the taxpayer.

The cops apprehend the drunks and jail them, for their own protection, in less than sanitary or pleasant surroundings. They stay overnight and appear before a Provincial Court Judge, all the necessary official papers having been typed out. There is a Crown Counsel and the Salvation Army representative is there, plus an Indian social worker, plus, perhaps, the jail doctor or nurse. There's sometimes a short prison sentence handed out for some mild misdemeanor. And everybody knows full well the Indian will likely be back in a week or two after release. That was the routine.

I multiplied out all the salaries of the arresting officers, the booking officers, the jailers, the officers of the court, the nurse, the doctor, the court reporters and the judge. Then I multiplied this by the number of arrests in one particular month. All this showed it was costing the City of Vancouver about $60 million a year to perform this continuing charade.

(The figures would be different today, of course. They would probably show a Skidroad Indian death once every two or three weeks instead of every week as it was in the '50s and '60s. There are various explanations: the development in and around the Skidroad; freedom now for the Indian to drink wherever he chooses, even in the poshest cocktail lounge; a decrease in the drifting-away from reservations.)

Understandably, this costing-out report got a lot of attention at City Hall. People immediately cried, "Let's strike a Committee!" Committees were duly struck and did whatever committees are supposed to do. Aldermen and alderwomen came down to my office. There was a hell of a lot of talk-talk. But nothing was ever damn well done!

When Indians came to the morgue to claim their dead, I saw how refreshingly free their thinking was from the white man's red tape. They didn't understand bureaucracy and they didn't want to learn. All they wished was to take their dead back home to their own cemetery on the reserve. They'd usually drive up Cordova Street in an old and battered pickup truck and park in the back alley.

I'd say, "Well now, you've got to have a casket or something to put the body in. Here's the death certificate but you must go to the Vital Statistics people. They'll give you a permit to bury, remove, cremate or whatever."

They would do all these things meticulously. They were strong family people, calm and stoic in their grief. I often thought they should be angry with us whites and blame us for their family tragedies. But they were never like that. They were impassive but also grateful for our help.

After the formalities were complete, the Indians would go away and come back with a plywood box they'd had somebody make. As a matter of fact, we knew a retired carpenter just down the street and he'd nail something together for a couple of bucks. And off they would go, back up to the Cariboo or the Okanagan, wherever they belonged, where they could hold their own sad service in peace, far from the bright lights of the big city.

These visits to claim their dead also provided the Indians with a few adventures. One time a group of relatives and friends started their wake a bit too early. In the pickup truck, in fact. There was a highway collision in the Fraser Valley near the village of Hope. The Mounties who investigated were astonished to find a body in a plywood box in the back of the truck. They called us and asked if we knew anything about it because they just couldn't understand why these drunken people were transporting a body in a wooden box on a public highway.

"They're just doing their traditional duty," I said. "They're absolutely allowed to do that as far as we're concerned. They can do it unless you people in Hope have a bylaw stating they can't take a body through town to a cemetery."

The Horseman was dubious about all this, but finally agreed, adding, "Anyway, we'll keep them in the slammer overnight for their own good because not one of them is in a fit condition to navigate. We'll let them go in the morning, with their body."

This gets me back to where I started; this Indian inability to cope with the city. It impressed me deeply that the next-of-kin would drive hundreds of miles to claim the body, go through the white man's legal bureaucracy of getting forms signed, have a crude plywood box built, put the corpse in it and quietly disappear to the country from whence they had come. It was a touching ritual. Hell, the white man would just go to a funeral director and say, "Okay, you look after it and send me your bill." The Indians looked after their own in their own way.

Mary and Sally. Those names live in my memory. Mary was a

denizen of the Skidroad who tried really hard to help her fellow Indians. She was also very well-known to the Police Department, having floated in and out of the drunk tank for years. We saw her around every day. She was easy to spot because she always wore a pair of sparkling white gloves as she wandered up and down the back lanes, looking for her friends, people in need of her help. There were many.

Mary was aging. By this I mean she was about thirty, which is old for a woman indulging in a vast daily consumption of beer, cheap wine and rotgut whisky. But she cared. She organized groups of Indian girls in the basement of the St. James Church where they were fed. Then Mary tried to start them on the way back to their reservations.

The tragedy was always that the gals didn't want to go back. They felt there was nothing to go back for or to. Unless they were dead. Then they would go back in that plywood box in the back of a pickup truck. That was okay. Mary, I'm sure, was very frustrated. And one sad day she was found in a Skidroad room, having suffered from the usual high levels of alcohol and pneumonia. Mary was dead, still wearing her little white gloves.

The word spread quickly and the next morning thirty sad Indians presented themselves in my office. They had come to see Mary. It wasn't a matter of identification. They had come to pay their last respects, in the only way they knew how, to one who had been their friend. But, ironically, nobody knew from what reservation poor Mary had come or where she should go home to. She was buried in the hated city of the bright lights.

\* \* \*

There was someone on duty at the morgue 24 hours a day. Sometimes, at two or three in the morning, a knock would come to the front door. Indians stood shyly on the steps of 240 East Cordova Street.

"Is Joe in this place?"

"Yes. Joe is in this place."

"We want to see Joe."

The Indians would file quietly into the morgue and they saw their friend Joe. They chanted and they danced. They said goodbye. Then they went away into the night.

\* \* \*

I was then a director of the Vancouver Indian Center Society. We met once a month and tried, with what limited funds we had, to help people like Mary help the others. We realized that guidance and leadership were important within the Skidroad community itself. But it was always an uphill battle. There were insufficient funds and a damnably insufficient desire or even interest on the part of the politicians and the public. And the Indians knew that we knew it was an impossible job. They knew—and seemed resigned to the knowledge— that life in the big city could lead only to tragedy. Perhaps they felt they were already in their Valhalla.

The lady who was called Old Sally. Who could ever forget? Sally was very well-known on Skidroad, at the seedy hotels and flophouses and, of course, in all the beer parlors. People looked on Sally as a toothless, lazy and amiable buffoon. She was a hell of a lot smarter than we thought.

In those days the beer salesmen would start their rounds in the morning at ten o'clock opening. They'd go from one beer parlor to another and there was a welcome flow of free beers turning up on the tables, courtesy of the brewery reps.

When a salesman had given away his allocation in one beer parlor he'd go down the street to another. Well, the Indians—and a lot of white folk, too—would immediately follow. It was like the Pied Piper of Hamelin. There was this constant, amusing procession up and down the streets of Skidroad going where the free beer went.

Old Sally was usually at the head of the parade. She had been the first to realize that this bonanza of free beer was taking place. She didn't give a damn what brand of beer was being handed out as long as it was free and cold and tasted like the Nectar of the Gods. Which it did at ten in the morning. She'd tell her friends to meet her at such and such a pub. Free suds were flowing. Just how she got her underground information nobody knew but the CIA or the Mounties might have done well to study her methods. Dear old Sally was never wrong.

This sort of thing was a part of the Indian way of life. They accepted it and were happy with it. By contrast, at that time of the day the white man would usually have a grim, worried look on his face. How could he pay the rent or the mortgage or keep his wife happy or meet his payroll or pay for his fancy new car?

The Indians, meanwhile, were enjoying themselves. Maybe they had the right idea.

*   *   *

*I am a Chief but my power to make war is gone and the only weapon left me is my speech. It is only with tongue and speech that I can fight my people's war. . .*

Chief Dan George
Burrard Indian Band
North Vancouver, B.C.

*   *   *

The village of Vanderhoof is a small farming, ranching and logging community nestled dustily amid the rolling hills and arid plateaus of north central British Columbia, far removed from the metropolis of Vancouver.

Life in Vanderhoof in the early 1970s was generally quiet. Ranchers, farmers, loggers and tradesmen worked and lived side by side. Cowboys and Indians shared the amenities of the village's few pubs and cafes. There was little animosity. But the gentle ambience changed abruptly in the early morning of July 3, 1976.

On the previous evening, the village's 2,400 residents had something special to celebrate. It was Vanderhoof's 50th anniversary. It was a night to be remembered. So it turned out to be; but in a way nobody wanted.

In the early hours of Saturday morning on a hill just south of town, Coreen Gay Thomas, a 21-year-old pregnant Indian girl from the Stoney Creek reserve, was struck down and killed by a car driven by 22-year-old Richard Redekop. Redekop was a white man.

And in the agonized weeks that followed, it became clear that this was not simply another unfortunate accidental death on the road. That single motor vehicle accident turned into a nightmare of accusation, counter-attack, bureaucratic bungling, rumor, counter-rumor, suspicion and—sometimes—violence.

When Judge Glen McDonald of the Vancouver Coroner's Court arrived, he found the village of Vanderhoof a community divided, seething with bitterness, ugliness and racial tension. It was, he said, like a charged powder keg waiting for the fuse to be lit.

\* \* \*

I'd been called in as Supervisory Coroner for B.C. I knew right away this was going to be a bloody sticky affair. I had read the news reports. The celebration had started in the afternoon and carried on with games and fireworks and finished with a big street dance in the evening. The Redekop lad was driving his girlfriend home and on a hill just outside of town came upon a group of about forty Indians walking home to the Stoney Creek reserve, several miles away. No trans-portation had been laid on for them. Some people said the Indians were playing "chicken"—staying on the road as long as they dared in the path of oncoming cars, defying the drivers in a crazy contest of nerves. Who would get out of the way first? In this case Coreen Thomas had lost. Redekop's car struck her and she died. The RCMP investigated at about three in the morning. It was a nasty situation.

The whole background was disturbing. It came to light that a couple of years before, Redekop's younger brother, Stanley, had also been involved in a fatal accident on the same road. That had resulted in the death of Coreen Thomas's cousin, Larry. No charges were laid and there had been charges of an RCMP whitewash.

In Coreen's case, the local Coroner, a Vanderhoof realtor named Eric Turner, at first said no inquest would be held, then changed his mind after pressure was put on by the Thomas family and other Stoney Creek Indians. He agreed, reluctantly. As if all that weren't enough, Turner then abruptly withdrew from the upcoming inquest after it was confirmed that he had been convicted of a criminal offence involving a hit-and-run driving accident ten years before. It was a confused and ugly state of affairs and the Attorney General had asked me to take over.

Here was another classic and tragic case of white man versus Indian. There seemed, on the surface, absolutely no reason why an Indian girl—or anyone, for that matter—should be walking on a road and deliberately challenging a young man driving a car. Then it came out that, in their hearts, the Indians had felt the celebration had been put on solely for the benefit of the white people. Why, they asked, did the white people not even lay on transportation back to the Stoney Creek reserve?

Tension was running high as hell and now the atmosphere became even more charged because at this time we were all reading about the infamous Wounded Knee incident south of the border. One of the American Indian leaders was in British Columbia, fighting extradition, when Vanderhoof was having its troubles and we learned later, had actually been in the area helping the Stoney Creek Indians mount their protests.

We also learned later that the Mounties at one stage had the village of Vanderhoof secretly ringed with sharpshooters armed with high-powered rifles with telescopic sights. Vanderhoof had enough damn troubles of its own without someone from outside stirring things up more.

The inquest opened in late September, two-and-a-half months after the accident. We started in the gymnasium of the Nechako Secondary School, moved to the local Royal Canadian Legion branch and ended up in the basement of the library. We were wandering all over town because we kept running out of space. There were 200 people present some days. That was a measure of the public interest and concern. I wanted absolutely nobody denied entry. This was vitally important. The situation clearly demanded a thorough investigation in public. If this was not done, rumor would beget rumor, facts would be distorted and people could easily lay an accusation of conspiracy—conspiracy by the white man to allow one of their own to kill an Indian and get away with it. I wanted none of that. So that inquest was made as public and as accessible as was humanly possible.

As usual, the mutual process of voluntary segregation took place; Indians sat on one side of the court, whites on the other. I opened by instructing the jury—three natives and three whites—and emphasizing as strongly as I could that their duty was not to conduct an inquiry into a sociological problem but was simply to inquire into how, when, where and by what means Coreen Gay Thomas had come to her death.

The jurors deliberated a long time before bringing in their verdict but when they did, it was one of unnatural and accidental death. The jury said the driver was negligent in that his car was moving too fast into a crowd of people on a main road in darkness. I told the court that the village of Vanderhood had had all its lights turned on that gala evening to celebrate a festival that ended in tragedy. Since then, there had been a lot of tension and ill-feeling. I sincerely hoped the lights would now go on again in a spirit of renewed friendship and understanding between the Indians and the whites. I like to think that's what happened.

\* \* \*

VANDERHOOF—Richard Brian Redekop, 23, of Vancouver, was found not guilty Wednesday of criminal negligence and dangerous driving in the July 3 death of Coreen Gay Thomas, 21, a resident of the Stoney Creek Indian Reserve, nine miles southeast of here. . .the case attracted national attention when local Indians used an inquest into the Thomas death last September as the focal point for native rights issues. . .

News Item
*The Province*
Vancouver, B.C.
June 23, 1977

\* \* \*

When I think about that Vanderhoof case, my thoughts also turn to the much-publicized Fred Quilt case of November, 1971. There were many similarities: Indian versus white man; mutual distrust and fear; suspicion of a cover-up; a deep-seated resentment between the native people and the Royal Canadian Mounted Police; an absolutely vital need for all the facts to be brought fairly and squarely into the open.

The Fred Quilt tragedy took place in the interior of British Columbia, in the Williams Lake area of the Cariboo, hundreds of miles from Vancouver. Quilt was a 55-year-old Indian from Alexis Creek who was arrested by the Mounties following a traffic accident. He died two days later of a ruptured intestine. There was evidence that he had fallen from a truck during the arrest but the Indians claimed the Mounties had jumped him and beaten him, causing the fatal injuries. Another classic confrontation.

The inquest, held at Williams Lake in January of 1972 by Coroner S.S. Leith, returned a verdict of accidental death but attached no blame. The Indians promptly labeled it a whitewash, partly because there were no natives on the jury. And they later formed a Fred Quilt Committee which petitioned the Attorney General to have one of the arresting RCMP officers charged with manslaughter. Attorney General Leslie Peterson called me in to review the evidence and receive any new and relevant evidence that might be forthcoming from the public.

I ploughed through the three books which formed the transcript of the inquest. But this inquest had been an obvious failure. Neither Indian nor white was satisfied. I told the AG another inquest should be held to hear new witnesses and examine any new pathological evidence produced. I said, "Let's get to the truth of this thing because the allegation is being made that Fred Quilt was badly treated by the RCMP. Murdered, in fact. That's bloody serious."

A County Court Judge was then appointed and he held a second inquest, in August of 1972, which produced the same result as the first. The jury could not decide if Quilt's fatal injuries were caused by the RCMP or if he had sustained them from a fall when getting out of the truck. Back to square one. And five years later, on her deathbed, Fred Quilt's widow, Christine, confessed to a friend that she had backed the pickup truck into her husband as he stood behind it, urinating, that night on the Chilcotin road back in 1971. She added that Quilt was helped back into the cab and was sitting there when the Mounties arrived. Not a word of this had come out at either inquest. The new Attorney General, Garde Gardom, decided at this time that the books should be closed forever on the controversial Fred Quilt case.

\* \* \*

*How easily one says, oh, hell, what's*
*the use and then he dies within himself.*
*How easily drink, drug and vice come*
*when pride and personal worth are*
*gone. . .*

Chief Dan George
Burrard Indian Band
North Vancouver, B.C.

\* \* \*

CHILLIWACK— The Indian who held Elliott Henry in his arms as Henry died from the effects of an initiation into spirit dancing delivered a tear-choked plea Wednesday to retain what may be the last hope for native people to defeat the ravages of drug and alcohol abuse.

Stephen Point, 26, told an inquest here that he helped guide Henry through a rigorous four-day initiation into spirit dancing, only to lose a pickup truck race with death to Chilliwack Hospital.

Point, an experienced spirit dancer, said Henry became gravely ill on the fourth and last day of his initiation and was rushed to hospital in a truck driven by another member of the Skulkayn Band. . .

News Item
*The Province*
Vancouver, B.C.
May, 1978

\* \* \*

Breakfasters in the busy, cosmopolitan and sophisticated city of Vancouver were fascinated and not a little puzzled to read such a bizarre item of news over their morning toast and coffee. The city of Chilliwack was, after all, only 75 miles east along the Trans-Canada Highway and it, too, was a busy and modern community, the hub of the lush farming belt of British Columbia's Fraser Valley.

What strange and mystical rites of ancient Indian lore were being carried out there in virtual secrecy? Was it conceivable that in today's society the local natives had taken the law into their own hands and reverted to savage rituals and customs the white man had assumed were long ago buried and forgotten?

Did a primitive form of worship involving sacrifice, violence, purging of the soul, ridding of the devil and invocation of the spirit really exist today, so close to Canada's third largest city? Judge Glen McDonald was to find out.

* * *

The inquest into the spirit dancing death of Elliott Henry was a weird yet utterly fascinating experience for me. The Chilliwack Coroner had told us some of the local Indians had held some sort of ancient native ritual in the tribal longhouse just outside of town and Henry had been brought to hospital suffering from dehydration and possible internal injuries. The Coroner suspected his condition was the result of what the Indians call a last chance rebirth, a four-day tribal ritual conducted in and around the longhouse.

Elliott Henry, who was 28, was an alcoholic. He had been taken, against his will, to undergo the longhouse initiation, during which he was supposed to find his guiding spirit which would rid him of the demon alcoholism. The ritual included fasting and taking little water during the four days, a gruelling run through the snowy countryside, a nude dunking in the icy waters of the Vedder River and being rubbed with rattles made of deer hooves.

This age-old ritual of the spirit dancer, held only in winter, had once been—along with the traditional Indian potlatch—officially banned by the government. The white man presumed it had been forgotten. But it had been enjoying a secret comeback since the 1950s and was now being used to cure Indians suffering from alcohol and drug abuse. This was the case with Elliott Henry.

Witnesses told us that the deceased had violently resisted submitting to the ritual and had been dragged, kicking and screaming, from his house one morning and carried to the longhouse by fifteen natives. We heard medical witnesses testify that Henry's alcohol-abused physical condition was such that it couldn't withstand the rigors of the ritual. The jury found that he died an unnatural death due to misadventure caused by a pulmonary embolism (blood or fat clots in the lungs) and cardiac arrest during his initiation as a spirit dancer. And the jury recommended that such initiations be halted at the Skulkayn longhouse until the rites could be made safe for those being initiated and that the Indians should publicize the fact that the ritual dance is a spiritual belief and not necessarily a cure for social problems.

Here was a case—not of Indian versus white man as in the Vanderhoof and Fred Quilt cases—but a case of misunderstanding or non-comprehending. It certainly pointed out the need for more understanding on both sides. We had, for example, testimony from Dr. Norman Todd, Henry's physician and an expert on Indian spirit dancing. He said 80 percent of native people who had undergone the ceremony had, at least temporarily, solved their alcohol and drug problems.

But we also heard evidence that Elliott Henry had wanted no part of the thing and had been virtually kidnapped, abducted from his home to undergo the initiation. Could his death then be legally viewed as manslaughter  or even homicide? It was extremely thought-provoking—a man dead and two disparate cultures colliding as a result and earnestly trying to figure out what to do for the benefit of all concerned.

The evidence was voluminous and complex and often mystifying. Part of it demonstrated clearly that the native Indian cannot, in some cases at least, get along with the white man's whisky. Just as a lot of white people can't get along with it, either. Henry's mother had been very concerned about her son's drinking problem which often made him abusive and violent. But, rather than turning to the white man for help, she went to the tribal initiates. She asked them to arrange the ceremony that would cleanse her son's spirit and rid him of his Devil.

This kidnapping thing concerned me as much as anything. The initiate's consent was not needed and in Henry's case a group of men simply dragged him to the longhouse, rattling their deer hooves and chanting as they went. We learned later that this element of surprise was most important to the whole ritual.

Henry was blindfolded, put in a small enclosure and kept there without food or water until evening. Then he was carried in a horizontal position around the longhouse—a large building—to the hypnotic beating of drums, rattling of deer hooves and chanting of ancient Indian songs. This was the start of the process of forcing the Devil out of his system.

I asked some of the participants if they had themselves taken such an initiation. They said, yes, they had. Had it helped them with their alcohol problems? They were very candid: yes, it had. "I used to drink a quart of whisky or a gallon of cheap wine every day," one told me. "Now I only have a beer now and again." His Devil had been purged and his soul purified.

The ritual has been documented by anthropologists and sociologists and psychiatrists over the years so I was able to read a lot about its origins and purposes. Physically, as well as carrying the initiate around the longhouse to drumbeats and chanting, the participants wielded deer or reindeer hooves tied to sticks with which they "rubbed" or beat the initiate's body. They weren't supposed to use much force but in Elliott Henry's case examination showed massive bruises on his abdomen. Pathologist Dr. John Sturdy testified also that the beating with the rattles may have dislodged fat from Henry's stomach area which eventually clogged his lungs, contributing to death.

The sound of the rattles is said to drive the Devil away. Then the initiate gets what is called his "own song." His spirit is now pure. During the four days of the elaborate ritual Henry was given only some water and a little reindeer broth to drink. Obviously, such treatment would lead to dehydration and this condition was readily diagnosed at the autopsy. There were other rigors to endure. He was put in a tent in the snow and ordered to sing a song. The initiates would then decide if he had finally got his "own song." And the final act was when he was marched, naked, to the Vedder River and forced to plunge in. There was ice in the river that winter.

All sorts of theories can be put forward as to what causes this "song" to be born in a man's spirit. It could well be that the initiate is by now hallucinating as a result of the harsh treatment. Perhaps he truly believes the Great Spirit has come down through his forefathers and is ordering him to change his ways. Perhaps he's just plain bloody scared. And the ceremony doesn't come cheap. The cost is borne by the family or friends of the initiate and can run as high as two or three thousand dollars, depending on how elaborate it is.

In Elliott Henry's case, death rather than the cleansing of the spirit was the result. His body was too debilitated by booze to withstand the harsh rites. Then we learned there had been some similar deaths in previous years in the Fraser Valley. Should these tribal initiations be discontinued? Outlawed, perhaps? Some people suggested the folks who had conducted the initiation weren't experienced enough or were too enthusiastic in their zeal to exorcise the Devil from Henry's body. Perhaps the repeated blows by the deer hooves had caused irreversible damage.

Again, we had three Indians and three whites on the jury. Sometimes I think this jury ritual is perhaps a form of racism in reverse—going through the back door. But the procedure satisfies people who would be severely critical if we didn't do it, if we had an all-white or all-Indian jury. The main thing, once again, was to get all the evidence out in public.

Somewhat to my surprise, everyone was completely candid and open in giving testimony. The Indians said, "You, the white man, brought alcohol into our lives as well as TB and VD. But you haven't got a cure for alcoholism in our people any more than you have a cure for it in your own people—unless they go cold turkey. This is our system of cold turkey. We have a long history of this treatment and it has had success."

This raised the question: if the white man did bring you alcohol, why did you perform this ritual in pre-white man times? There was no answer to that because there's no record that the sole reason for the ritual was for treating alcoholism. This re-birthing and getting your "own song" was possibly used over the years for other reasons—for ridding a person of a congenital or genetic defect, such as epilepsy. This was their treatment. We can't say if it's right or wrong.

One jury recommendation was that any prospective initiate should have a medical checkup first to ensure he could stand up to the rigors of the ritual. I suggested at one stage that perhaps a consent form should be obtained. But those well-intentioned ideas were knocked on the head by the required element of surprise. The nature of the initiation is that the person must be taken unawares and so is shocked. It would defeat the whole purpose of the thing if he were to see a doctor first or sign a paper.

I can understand this shock effect business. The initiate would certainly remember being carried around the longhouse, blindfolded, being beaten with reindeer hooves, dunked in an icy river and going without food for four days while his spirit is being cleansed and his own song found. Obviously, he wouldn't want to drink booze anymore if he thought he'd have to go through that ordeal again. I sure as hell wouldn't. Would you?

The jurors, in trying to reach a verdict, were chiefly concerned with two words—accident and misadventure. But they also had to look at the possibility of manslaughter and, even, homicide. The initiate in these rituals does not, after all, willingly consent to that which is about to happen. He's kidnapped, in fact. In Elliott Henry's case, the RCMP and Crown counsel did at one stage consider laying charges of murder or manslaughter against all the participants in the ceremony. And even if death doesn't transpire, there's still the kidnapping and the matter of an assault on a person without his consent. Eventually, the jury made it a sawoff. The verdict was unnatural death due to misadventure. A satisfactory compromise.

For me, the Henry inquest was a curious and revealing experience. I was all of a sudden thrust into an alien world, speaking to people of a culture I didn't properly understand. They, in turn, couldn't properly understand why I was there asking all these questions. The proceedings were filled with subtleties and nuances that sometimes baffled both sides equally. There was even some conflict and confusion among the Indians themselves. One theory put forward was that the participants at the ritual weren't really serious but were young men out to have a party, paid for by the Henry family. But we established there was definitely no alcohol involved. Such a thing would *really* have been hypocritical. This was a crucial point. Neither Crown counsel, the Mounties nor myself came up with a shred of evidence that there had been drinking.

Another important and tricky point arose. The Skulkayn longhouse was on reservation land, which could be considered private property. Had the Mounties gone underground in advance of an initiation and raided that private property to stop a traditional native ceremony, would they not be at fault, at least morally? It would be like marching into a church and interfering with people's religious beliefs. The Mounties, as a result, really hadn't known quite how to handle the case or what to do regarding the prevention of similar deaths in the future. future.

The inquest was important in that perhaps we did manage to steer the people on the right course so deaths wouldn't occur at initiations in years to come. Maybe we accomplished something constructive. It was a grey-shaded and puzzling anomaly. Here was the white man, come to the Skulkayn people because of a death. He had not only brought whisky into the lives of the Indians, now he was bringing his Coroner's Act, his ritualistic courtroom procedure and his equally formal investigation. But I felt that holding that inquest was a good thing for everyone involved. Maybe we all learned something about one another. The rites are still being conducted. There have been no more deaths.

\* \* \*

> But after the winter cold and icy winds,
> life again flows up from the bosom of
> Mother Earth and Mother Earth throws
> off dead stalks and the withered ends for
> they are useless and in their place new and
> strong saplings arise. . .
>
> Chief Dan George
> Burrard Indian Band
> North Vancouver, B.C.

\* \* \*

Cormorant Island, a bleak huddle of forest and rocks lying off the northeast coast of Vancouver Island, is aptly named.

The isolated island's inhabitants are 1,000 native Indians, 800 whites and countless numbers of seals, sea lions, seagulls and cormorants.

It is a lonely place and the community of Alert Bay is frequently cut off from Vancouver Island by storms.

The Indians of Cormorant Island, mostly fishermen, are of the proud Nimpkish band renowned for their exquisite wood carvings.

One day—January 22, 1979—something very bad happened to the

Nimpkish. One of their members, eleven-year-old Renee Smith, died in St. George's Hospital in the village of Alert Bay. Renee's family said the little girl had not been properly treated by the white man.

Now she was dead. They wanted to know how come she was dead. The Nimpkish were very angry. Many signed their names to a petition and they took it to the British Columbia capital of Victoria and in that place they gave the paper to Garde Gardom, the province's Attorney General. He promised the Nimpkish people he would see what he could do.

Three months later Judge Glen McDonald packed his suitcase and boarded a bobbing floatplane in Vancouver's Coal Harbour and flew up to Cormorant Island. His job, once again, was to clear the air and bring out every fact, no matter how unpleasant, for everyone to see. His job, once again, was to sort out a tangled skein of accusations, resentment, bitterness and misunderstanding between Indian and white man. He, too, wanted to know how come Renee Smith was dead.

* * *

Renee Smith had died, we learned at the inquest, of severe generalized peritonitis, a ruptured appendix and acute gangrenous appendicitis. But we still wanted to know *why* she was dead. She had gone with her uncle, Leonard, who was looking after her because her parents were away, to the office of Dr. Jack Pickup, the community's only physician. She had stomach pain. It was suggested she should go to the hospital. Renee said no and was taken home. So she didn't get the complete examination she should have had that day.

Next day the pain was worse. She went to St. George's Hospital where she was again examined by Dr. Pickup. But a diagnosis was not made because the girl was suffering from a very bad cold and cough which could even have been pneumonia. This condition prompted concern about performing an appendectomy because of complications resulting from anesthesia and a possible pneumonitis or bilateral pneumonia coming on. Renee stayed at St. George's and her condition grew worse. Then she died.

The Indians were dissatisfied and angry. They had visited the girl regularly and seen her steadily worsening condition. They had wondered why more wasn't being done for her. They refused to accept the fact that death was due to natural causes—a ruptured appendix—as had been decided. They felt Renee Smith had not been clinically treated properly; that her treatment had somehow been bungled. They wanted to know how this could happen. The local Coroner, William Deadman, had held an inquiry into Renee's death. But, since he was also officially connected with the hospital, the Indians felt this was a whitewash. They demanded a full and proper inquest. That's how I got involved.

There was not much love lost over the years between Dr. Pickup and the Indians; there was an increasing feeling that he should not be the only practising physician in the Alert Bay area and that a second doctor should be made available. The Indians had made representations to that effect to the Department of Indian Affairs, in Ottawa, saying they wanted their own medical board and their own doctor. They had also asked to have Dr. Pickup's licence suspended. As a result of all this, the ambience was none too pleasant when I arrived with my court reporter, Walter Gottschau, and Coroner's Investigator, Bart Bastien. I asked the RCMP to give me all they had on the case and then we went to work coordinating things, obtaining necessary witnesses and so forth.

When we flew into the island community we were unaware that this was a matter which had split the town of Alert Bay right down the middle. The gravity of the situation didn't occur to us until the morning we went to inspect the courtroom. This was large enough for the usual routine business of Alert Bay but wouldn't be big enough for this inquest. It was obvious that the courtroom would be so crowded there would be standing-room only, with many people left outside. I decided on the spot that if we were going to do this thing properly we should do it somewhere where everyone could sit down and everyone could clearly hear all that was being said.

We opened proceedings in the cramped and crowded courtroom, anyway. I swore in the jury and we adjourned. Again, we had a mix of Indians and whites plus a spare juror. Then we hustled around and got hold of the caretaker of the Royal Canadian Legion branch. We started again. But *that* hall wasn't big enough. There were too many people, not enough room, not enough chairs. Finally, the school board lent us the high school gymnasium and supplied all the needed chairs. The inquest was held on the basketball court—except for one day when it was booked for the finals of a curious game involving a soccer ball and hockey sticks. The finals, it seemed, were extremely important. We adjourned for that day.

One gets used to this sort of thing in small communities. You use any amenity you can lay your hands on. I was also concerned about proper acoustics and the gymnasium worked out well. Acoustics were very important in Alert Bay because so many of the Indian witnesses would whisper shyly, as opposed to speaking up loudly and clearly like the white man. This is the way many Coast Indians speak so you must have amplification if everyone is to hear what's being said in court.

We put up at the Bay Hotel and I found myself billeted directly above the tavern. It wasn't the quietest room I've stayed in. Everyone in the pub, whites and Indians, seemed always to be discussing the Renee Smith inquest so it was obviously out of bounds to us. I took breakfast, lunch and dinner in my room and became a virtual prisoner for almost a month. It was the only route to go if I were to remain impartial.

People sometimes came up to me on the street to offer information. But, because it was always hearsay piled on hearsay, I had to tell them,

"Thanks but no thanks, unless you have something that's really important or new. But if you want to tell Harry Rankin, the lawyer who's acting for the Smith family, and if he wishes to tell me what he intends to produce, I'll be pleased to hear that request. You must understand that when we talk at an inquest everything is fully open to the public and is taken down and transcribed." I didn't want to be accused of being influenced by one side or the other.

Everyone eventually got the ground rules straight as we went along. But there was still that strong feeling of antagonism between the whites and the Indians. The whites, who generally supported Dr. Pickup, felt he had been a good and conscientious physician who had served the community well for many years. But there was absolutely no doubt that the community was now split into opposing camps because of the death of young Renee Smith. This was glaringly evident at the inquest. The chairs on the left were for the Indians and the chairs on the right were for the whites. This wasn't done by design. The people just came in and drifted naturally to one side or the other. That forum graphically illustrated the mood of the town. Yet there were close friends on both sides. When a day's hearing was over they would sit and talk at the same table in a coffee shop or in the pub. Curiously, Renee Smith had brought them all together as well as dividing them.

From the very start, the evidence was complicated, sometimes confusing and often contradictory. The girl's uncle told us that Renee was crying with pain and could barely walk when she first went to the hospital but was merely given painkillers by a nurse and sent home. He said he couldn't identify the nurse. Two nurses testified that medical procedures at the hospital were not all they might have been. There was confusing and conflicting testimony about some of the medical reports and records in Renee's case; allegations that some were not kept during her five-day stay or had gone missing. And my pathologist, Dr. Tom Harmon, testified that the girl could have been operated on right up to the time of her death. Nurses who had attended Renee testified that every day produced a worsening of her condition. Yet, still no diagnosis had been made and, medico-legally, a doctor must have a diagnosis before his patient can go into surgery.

What usually happens in a case of appendicitis is that the doctor diagnoses the condition and then removes the appendix. That is the accepted procedure subject, of course, to complicating factors such as a possible infection of the lungs which could affect the anesthesia procedures. In Renee Smith's case, we soon got into the question of whether a patient with a possible ruptured appendix, who had heavy sweating and a high temperature and who was obviously going into a state resulting in peritonitis, should be operated on. There are two medical opinions on this.

The lawyers for both the Smith family and Dr. Pickup called in internists to give their opinions, Dr. Leslie Patterson and Dr. June Mills. They disagreed as to the procedure which should or should not have been followed in the Renee Smith case. Dr. Patterson's approach was that appendicitis could be treated without surgery. To prove his point he told of how Karen Magnussen, the well-known Canadian figure skater, had suffered an appendicitis attack while performing and had had it treated with antibiotics. She recovered fully, without an operation. This testimony, of course, was somewhat in defence of Dr. Pickup's position of why he had not operated on Renee Smith.

And when Dr. Pickup took the stand he said his concern was that the girl was not in a sufficiently stable condition—because of her cold and chest condition—to withstand an anesthetic and undergo surgery. This was his medical judgment, or opinion. The other side took the position that if an appendix is about to rupture or *has* ruptured, a doctor has only one course to follow—to go in and remove the source of the infection that is affecting the whole of the abdomen. Death usually results if such infection isn't halted. It was interesting—to me, at least—that throughout these long technical discussions of methods and procedures in treatment neither Dr. Mills nor Dr. Patterson ever once referred to any difference between an Indian's appendix and a white person's appendix. We were dealing with the same anatomy, the same physiology. Often, the jurors interrupted the medical experts to have them explain some baffling medical jargon in layman's terms. This they willingly did and at one stage the inquest became almost a medical school class on the treatment of appendicitis and accompanying complications. It was like sitting in pre-med school, which I had done years before.

The question was asked of Dr. Pickup, "Would it not have been better, if you were in doubt, to have flown the sick girl to a hospital in a larger community such as Port Hardy or Nanaimo on Vancouver Island for consultation and further examination?" This, of course, raised the subject of the weather. Could the girl have survived a rough airplane flight in her condition? The question was so important it was pursued to the point where we brought in the meteorological reports in the area for the days Renee was in hospital. They showed that perhaps a plane could have taken off but the flight would have been risky. A bumpy flight, of course, would probably have caused a rupture to occur or an existing rupture to become worse, causing the poison to spread throughout the bowel.

Then the case took a totally unexpected and unusual turn that caught everybody off guard. Leo O'Connell, an undertaker from the Vancouver Island town of Campbell River who had examined Renee Smith's body, took the witness stand and said he thought the girl might have been raped.

Rape! Now, this was something that had to be completely explored. And it was. The matter was put to rest only after my pathologist, Tom

Harmon, explained that Renee had had the beginning of her monthly period at the time of her illness and this would have caused a certain irritation which could be misinterpreted by a layman. Renee Smith had definitely not been raped. All the same, rumors and misinterpretations continued to pass around the community. Even the faintest suggestion of rape was another complaint for the Indians to lodge against the white people.

As an aside, I should mention that the Alert Bay inquest was commenced under British Columbia's old Coroners Act and a new Act was proclaimed while we were proceeding. I took the position that we would abide by the old Act and if the jurors wished to find and state in their verdict that there was negligence, it was entirely within their field of jurisdiction to do so. I stressed this point because the new Act contained a specific section saying an inquest jury is not competent to find negligence. And, as it turned out, this very area was extremely important in the outcome of the Renee Smith case.

Actually, I never believed that a Coroner's jury's finding of negligence was the same as a finding of negligence by a judge or by a judge and jury in other courts. They're coming to a conclusion after having followed the strict rules of evidence and therefore are more capable of being wholly definitive than an inquest jury is. We do allow hearsay evidence at a Coroner's inquest, identifying it for what it is and, therefore, allowing the jury to perhaps find something to be negligent. But I never used the word negligent in any address to any jury. I always said, "If you find a person, or persons, to blame you may indicate that." But I always warned them not to be flighty and come to any hasty conclusion or be persuaded by elements which were not really there. I always advised them not to think that somebody has to be blamed because somebody else is dead.

What, after all, are the definitions, the parameters, of negligence? I suppose reasonable cause would constitute what a reasonable person would do under reasonable circumstances and that if everything were reasonable, then that would be what a reasonable person would do. But we were not always considering just a reasonable person and reasonable circumstances. In the Alert Bay case, for instance, we were considering a professional man who was entitled to exercise his professional judgment in the practice of his profession.

The jury was extremely thorough in the matter of the death of Renee Smith. Every facet of the case was investigated meticulously and completely. The jurors had sat through days and days of complex and often contradictory testimony. They had taken copious notes and they had asked many positive and intelligent questions. They had delved into the tricky question of the parents and guardian issue. They had examined the question of stricter enforcement of hospital bylaws and regulations. They had wanted to know all about the charts and records that were kept—or, perhaps, not kept—on Renee Smith.

They had also wanted to know all about the X-rays that had been taken and had been delayed in returning to Alert Bay because they had been sent to Vancouver Island for processing by regular parcel post. At last it came time for the jury to retire.

* * *

The jurors filed slowly back into the school gymnasium five-and-a-half hours later. They had reached a verdict.

-Renee Smith's death was natural and was to be classified as accidental due to negligence.

-Dr. Jack Pickup was negligent in the death of Renee Smith.

-Renee Smith died of severe general peritonitis, ruptured appendix and acute gangrenous appendicitis due to failure on the doctor's part to apply adequate medical care and procedures.

The jurors recommended:

-An investigation by the provincial health minstry and the College of Physicians and Surgeons into medical practices of the doctor and general standards of medical care in Alert Bay.

-The Registered Nurses' Association of British Columbia inquire into the nursing care at St. George's Hospital.

-The college and the local hospital board make every effort to obtain another doctor for the community immediately.

-Oral communications between patient-nurse-doctor and the hospital administration be improved.

-Parents or guardians be fully informed of all circumstances in cases involving children.

-Stricter enforcement of the hospital bylaws and regulations.

-Medical charts of Renee Smith be sent to all investigating bodies for their consideration.

-Residents of Alert Bay become more involved in the administration of St. George's Hospital.

-Treatment and hospital consent forms be re-designed for clarification, and greater onus be placed on persons signing these forms.

-More reliable and faster means be found of getting X-rays and test results to and from hospital—by private carrier rather than relying on the postal service.

Judge McDonald thanked the jurors for discharging their sworn duty and assured them their recommendations would be forwarded immediately to the Health Minister, the Attorney General, the medical groups mentioned, hospital administration boards and all provincial Coroners. Then he packed his suitcase and flew home to Vancouver. The long and gruelling inquest into the sad death of young Renee Smith was over.

* * *

How can a death be natural and also be classified as accidental? That sounds like a contradiction. Well, we do not have in the English language the appropriate words to fully express what the jury concluded. A ruptured appendix is, of course, a natural occurrence. It's a fairly common illness and sometimes results in death.

Perhaps, then, when the jurors used the word *accidental* they meant that all cases of ruptured appendix should be successfully diagnosed and operated on which, in the Renee Smith case, of course, was not done. I think this was why the jury used the word *accidental* in the verdict. But it was the jury's verdict and it certainly stood.

The jury also recommended that everyone in Alert Bay, Indians and whites alike, should become more involved in the administration of St. George's Hospital. I thought this most appropriate and wise because it really squared up to the old sociological problem; the whites were running the hospital and the Indians were receiving treatment in it. Why not share the responsibilities equally? Also, there was a feeling that there should be Indian nurses at the hospital.

I had a good reason for telling the jurors I would forward their recommendations to the appropriate authorities and they would have a definite progress report within six months. It was always my practice that, when an important inquest was held which produced significant findings, I would advise the jurors—who had given of their time and trouble—of any results that could be attributed to their findings. I liked to be able to tell them that something positive was going to be done as a result of the good job they had done. Something that would, perhaps, prevent a similar death in the future. And, looking back over jury verdicts of 26 years, I'd say some 33 percent were acted on in some way, shape or form. Usually in a positive and rewarding way.

Before we left Alert Bay, I made a point of talking to the RCMP and the nurses and Dr. Pickup and Richard Smith, Renee's father. I asked, "Did we bring out all the information you feel should have been brought out? I don't want to hear any suggestion of a whitewash. We spent a lot of time up here in this lovely spot and now we're leaving. But I don't want to read in the newspaper about something we've overlooked."

They all said, no, we hadn't overlooked anything. Renee's father said the tragic events had been very hard on all of us. What he was really saying was, "Let's not have it happen again. Let's make damn sure such a thing never ever happens again. Everybody—Indians and whites— said amen to that."

\* \* \*

On June 10, 1979, Judge McDonald received a letter from the government of the Province of British Columbia in Victoria. It read:
Dear Mr. McDonald:
I want to thank you on behalf of the people of British Columbia, as

well as myself and the Attorney General's Ministry, for your thoroughness in conducting the inquest into the tragic death of Renee Smith at Alert Bay.

The Coroner's function is to bring out before the public all the facts in a fair and impartial manner. This you have done in the highest tradition of the Coroner's office.

Yours sincerely,
Garde B. Gardom
Attorney General

\*　\*　\*

*The signs of this rebirth are all around us. There are more and more of our young men and women graduating from high school and their numbers will grow and grow until the Red Man of Canada will once again stand firm and secure on his own two feet.*

Chief Dan George
Burrard Indian Band
North Vancouver, B.C.

\*　\*　\*

# The Day
# The Bridge Fell Down

Tuesday, June 17, 1958 was a glorious day in Vancouver. The sun blazed from a cloudless sky to dance on the dappled waters of the blue Pacific; the soaring North Shore mountains stood out purple and clear; small birds sang in the tops of the tall trees in the gentle forests of Stanley Park at the water's edge; swimmers and sunbathers swarmed to Spanish Banks and Kitsilano Beach.

The temperature at the International Airport climbed to 81 degrees Fahrenheit by mid-afternoon and inched even higher on the baking, sun-scorched downtown streets. There was little wind to bring relief to shirt-sleeved workers aching to get home to swimming pools, gin and tonics tinkling in tall, frosty glasses and mugs of cold beer.

At the eastern end of the harbor the rust-red skeleton of Vancouver's new second crossing of Burrard Inlet thrust a thin finger of steel probing across the water from the city to the North Vancouver shoreline. The huge bridge, made necessary by the pressure of traffic on the handsome Lions Gate Bridge to the west and the rickety old Second Narrows span, had been building since February, 1956. It was to be officially opened early in 1959.

Scores of workmen—steelworkers, ironworkers, painters, engineers—toiled high on the bridge's girders on that Tuesday. From the ground they looked no bigger than ants darting to and fro at their work. The unthinkable happened at 3:40 on that gorgeous sunny afternoon. It was the day the bridge fell down.

Judge Glen McDonald of the Vancouver Coroner's Court had just consumed a lunch of Dover sole and Stilton cheese in the exclusive Terminal City Club on Hastings Street a block from the downtown waterfront. He was lingering in the company of good friends when someone came in and said the bridge had fallen down.

\* \* \*

I had been looking out of the window at the harbor and when I came back to my table somebody said, "My God, the bridge has fallen down!" It was so unreal, so unthinkable, because there was only one bridge that conceivably could have fallen down and that, of course, was the new second crossing of the inlet in the harbor.

I went back to the window. In those days, before a new highrise office tower was built, you could see from the club all the way to the east end of the harbor where the bridge was going up. I remember seeing vividly that it now looked like a set of fallen domino tiles or a collapsed meccano set. It was an unbelievable sight. But there it was.

We all went up to the roof of the club and we just stood there and looked and looked. No one said much. I suppose we were all too stunned to take it in. It was incomprehensible that such a thing could have happened. We just kept staring. Ironically, we had been talking at lunch about the new bridge and wondering when it would be finished.

My first concern, as Coroner, was if there had been a loss of life and, if so, whose jurisdiction was it, North Vancouver's or Vancouver's? It further occurred to me that most of the men working on the span would be from the Vancouver city area itself. But, in any event, if there had been a loss of life, how were we going to get the bodies all together and identify the victims? Later, we would consider the cause of the bridge collapse. But the immediate thing was that the bridge had collapsed. This was the hardest thing to grasp and comprehend but it was the harsh reality of the situation and could not be denied.

My next thought was to get back to the office as quickly as possible. A quiet lunch had led into an afternoon of horror. However, I did phone the Coroner in North Vancouver from the club. He hadn't heard about the collapse and I said, "How can you handle it at your end? Maybe they're closer to you because it was your side that fell down. Do you want to waive jurisdiction and, if there is loss of life, I'll look after the bodies and ultimately decide whether you hold the inquest or I hold the inquest?" He said, "We can't handle a case like this. We're not equipped for it. If it is a bridge collapse, it's an absolute bloody disaster! There'll be so many bodies we couldn't possibly do the work here."

At the office I immediately got hold of the Attorney General in Victoria and told him we had this crisis, this catastrophe. I told him the way I would proceed unless he ordered otherwise. He said okay, I should handle things and keep him advised as we found out more of what had happened. The RCMP were on the scene by this time on the North Vancouver side and our city police were busy as hell on our side. We were told there were at least 12 people dead, squashed and mangled by the bridge itself or drowned.

* * *

What happened on that terrible day was a horrifying scenario of groaning, twisted, shattered tons of steel as two spans of the Second Narrows Bridge collapsed without warning and plunged into the Burrard Inlet. Seventy-nine workers were either hurled, screaming, 210 feet to the water below or rode down on the buckling girders. Many were trapped or crushed in the tangled wreckage. Others, dead or injured, were swept down the harbor by the swift-flowing current.

Pleasure craft, search and rescue boats, a Royal Canadian Mounted Police boat and the Vancouver City Police boat were on the scene of the carnage within minutes, later to be guided in the desperate search for survivors by the crews of hovering helicopters. Eighteen workers died, twenty were injured and a skindiver drowned two days later searching for bodies.

It was the worst single disaster in Vancouver's history and the massive rescue effort was modelled on a coordinated plan that had been mapped out to cope with a possible major plane crash at the International Airport. * * *

The Coroner's Court was only a couple of miles from the disaster scene. By this time a lot of phone calls were coming in because the media had heard the news and wanted to find out how many workers were dead. Did we know? We didn't know. We didn't know anything definite at that time, none of the details. Then some of the employers started calling. A friend of mine named Joe Boshard, who used to run Boshard's Painting, called me. He had some men who were up there painting the girders that day using rust-proof paint. He said maybe there were more he didn't know about and he wanted to know where they were, if they were alive or dead.

* * *

It turned out that 27 workers from Boshard's painting firm went down with the bridge. Two of the lucky ones were inspector Byron Maine and painter Tommy Moore, who both survived with minor injuries.

Maine told reporters, "I was standing with a foreman on the second section. We heard a terrific rumbling, just like a shunting train. We ran like hell and leapt to the third section. When the bridge was going, the noise was unbearable. Nobody had any chance to think of others. We just had seconds to look after ourselves. When the crash was over, in the quiet that followed, we could hear the cries of the injured down below.

We couldn't get down to them."

Moore said, "I was right in the middle of the second section when I heard this terrific roaring. I looked around and saw the front end of the bridge disappearing. The section I was on began to shake like an earthquake so I grabbed one of the steel cross-sections and hung on. When the section hit bottom I scrambled up again on the bridge approach."

*   *   *

I asked Joe for his workers' names and he gave some to me—four or five. He said it might be difficult to identify them because his workers and the others would have arrived at the site in their street clothing, their civvies, with their identification in these and then would have changed and put on their boilersuits. They would have no identification in their pockets other than cigarette packs or lighters or small stuff like that. Indeed, that was the way we ultimately did identify some of the workers to start with, before the next-of-kin were allowed to come in—by whether they smoked a particular brand of cigarette or carried a certain lighter.

But Joe added, "You can perhaps identify my men if they're there because they're sure to have a lot of paint on their overalls. They usually do put more paint on their clothes than on the building or the bridge or whatever it is they're painting." I thought to myself, "Well, you always find a little bit of humor in these things as you go along. Yet, tragically, it's going to be pretty damn conclusive if I find a man with a lot of rust-colored paint on his clothing. I'll know he must be a painter. That's obvious. Certainly, what experience I've had with painting—I can always tell what color I've been putting on just by looking at the color of my clothes."

Eventually, the Harbor Patrol people talked to me—the National Harbors Board. I told the Attorney General that we were proceeding, this was the way we would handle it. We would do the identification in our facilities at 240 East Cordova Street, next to the police station. I saw right away there would be a logistical problem and I knew the hospital morgue facilities in North Vancouver weren't big enough. Our facilities were really the only ones available. We could take 10 or 12 dead people at once in an emergency. We had the view room for the identification and the waiting bodies would be kept in the basement.

Anyway, a hospital is not supposed to be for the admitting of bodies. A hospital exists, basically, to admit the sick for treatment. People who are alive and will, hopefully, get well. So you can't possibly overload a hospital morgue with the victims of a disaster. There would be a lot of problems such as hysterical next-of-kin coming in to identify or hoping to find that their loved ones were alive and being treated. That's why the city morgue was made the site. Then the bodies started coming in.

The crew of the city police boat brought several over. What had happened was that the scaffold areas of the bridge went down and the steel girders had collapsed into the water, pinning the men and holding them under the water until they drowned or died of severe and multiple injuries.

The police boat guys brought these poor, shattered men over to the dock at the foot of Main Street, just a couple of blocks from the morgue. It was the quickest way of coming from the disaster scene. There was now heavy traffic on the Lions Gate Bridge because of rush hour and cars being rerouted from the old Second Narrows Bridge. Using the boat was the best way to deal with the situation.

We laid the bodies out on their stretchers on tables. Positive identification was not immediately possible. So we knew we would need the help of the next-of-kin—wives, sons and daughter, fathers, friends. We knew it would be tough.

The phones were still going crazy and there was the usual concern by our staff when dealing with tragedy. But nothing much could be done on the telephone. You can only do so much that way. Ultimately, it was a case of the families coming down to the morgue and doing the identification in person. This is never an easy or a pleasant task and the morgue staff always has to have a great deal of sympathy and empathy with the public. We all knew this was going to be a rough one. A long and bad night lay ahead.

The technique of identification on such a large scale is to find out the name of the person the caller is asking (often hysterically) about, and then telling them we'll get back to them as soon as possible. But it's not that simple. Understandably, everyone wanted to come down at once. So, aware of what we were in for, I phoned over to the St. James Anglican Church across the street, as I always did in a crisis and asked the people if they could stoke up their coffee urns and get their sandwich wagon rolling. I also called the Salvation Army and the United Church. Everyone said they'd come right over. I also called the Catholic people and the priests and the sisters came with no hesitation. People are like that in emergencies. They help. They want to.

The whole Coroner's Courtroom was soon full of people and more wanted to come in. Now we tried out a routine which we had sometimes practiced before. We hoped it would work. The plan was to get the bosses at the Dominion Bridge Company and Swan Wooster Engineering to send their superintendents and foremen down to the morgue to make at least some preliminary identifications.

*　*　*

At the scene of the tragedy the frantic rescue operation was still underway as the first bodies were arriving at Judge McDonald's morgue in Skidroad. Police boats. Fireboats. Search and Rescue boats.

Tugboats. Fishing boats. Pleasure cruisers. Ambulances. Police cars. Fire engines. Helicopters. Skindivers.

Journalist and author Doug Collins, who was then a reporter with *The Province* newspaper, described the scene this way:

"From the helicopter, it looked like a toy bridge that a boy had kicked in anger. Except that even from up there the atmosphere was charged with tragedy. The pilot brought his machine close in at photographer Ville Svarre's direction, and we could see covered forms being loaded into the ambulances on stretchers. A couple of police boats darted out from beneath the wrecked superstructure.

"Svarre leaned out of the little door to take his pictures. I took a few notes, felt sick and the helicopter headed for home.

"And the morbid thought crossed my mind that some wouldn't be going home."

Ed Cosgrove, a reporter-photographer with New Westminster's *Columbian* newspaper, was driving across the old Second Narrows span when the bridge fell down beside him. He remembers:

"I couldn't believe my eyes. I stopped the car, grabbed the camera and ran down to the water and started shooting. I was the only cameraman there. The guys were struggling to get out of the water but most of them couldn't move, they were pinned or injured too badly. They were yelling, screaming. It was gory as hell. People were pulling them out. One young woman stripped off her blouse and wrapped it around a workman who was in shock, shivering and bleeding. I couldn't believe how calm she was.

"I kept shooting until I ran out of film. I've always felt guilty for not trying to help the guys. I shoved the used roll in my left pants pocket and reloaded. I was running down the pier when I felt the roll slip down my leg. I watched it fall into the water and sink. Christ, what a feeling! I'd forgotten there was a hole in the pocket I'd been after my wife for weeks to mend. I've thought since that maybe it was God's way of punishing me for shooting instead of helping."

Cosgrove shot three more rolls of film and was awarded a special citation that year in Canada's National Newspaper Awards for his dramatic coverage.

The first news of the enormity of the disaster was being flashed across Canada and around the world by the Canadian Press news agency. Ed Leitch, a CP teletype operator, had seen the bridge collapse from his mother's home overlooking the harbor.

"At first I thought it was a heat waver," he recalled, "and then it went down. I phoned our Vancouver news bureau right away. But the desk editor wouldn't believe me. I guess he thought I'd gone a little crackers. Finally, he filed it."

In Skidroad the city morgue was filling up, with both the dead and the agonized relatives and friends. The long, horrible hours of waiting and praying were just beginning. The pathologists and morgue attendants would soon be bloodied.

* * *

The appearance of a body crushed by a girder or a steel beam is not pleasant for anyone to look at, not even for medical people used to such sights. We had them all that night. There were multiple fractures; there were compound fractures; there were limbs missing. It was far worse than what we got from automobile accidents. We were dealing here with an average weight of 165 pounds for a body and the crushing force of girders pinning these poor men. It was like the jaws of a huge steel machine with a force that couldn't possibly be resisted. It's awful to think about but some of the men were almost truncated—cut in half, crushed in half. Some were no longer human. They looked like abstract Picasso paintings. Twisted, garish, unreal. That's why the identification had to wait. We wanted to do at least something to tidy the bodies up. Disasters in 1956 and 1965 involved more deaths but in 1958 this was our worst experience. The memories of that night still haunt me.

My morgue attendants—or coroners' technicians, as they're called now—were busy cleaning the bodies up as much as they could without concealing or destroying the actual cause of death. This would be determined by the pathologists who had now arrived—Tom Harmon and Eric Robertson. What we were trying for at this stage was just a temporary identification pending the arrival of the next-of-kin who would make the final and ultimate determination of whether or not a victim was, indeed, a loved one or a known one.

I philosophized but I was also practical. This terrible bridge collapse had brought the most bodies to the morgue we had ever had at one time. We had a plan for such an emergency, although we had hoped we would never have to use it. The plan to cope with this disaster went back to a strategy we had mapped out for a similar disaster like a plane crashing in Vancouver. It was detailed. We had a place for the priests to give the last rites and we had a place for the identification of the remains. Tags were made. We removed the bodies as quickly as possible. We tried our damnedest to help the grieving.

So the long and difficult process of identification began. The cigarette packs helped. A couple of Joe Boshard's painters smoked MacDonald's Export cigarettes, which come in a green pack. And, indeed, we did find two bodies with Export packs in their pockets so we thought we perhaps had these two men identified. But, again, nothing was definite at that time. Who knows if a few moments before the bridge collapsed somebody may have given a pack of cigarettes to somebody else, or something like that? In some cases we had to go to examination of the teeth, extrusion and articulating of all the teeth. This was done in cases where there was definite doubt because we wanted to be absolutely

114

positive. But we got within reach of the ball park and when we had reasonable assurance from a superintendent or a foreman, or other men who had been on the job, we allowed the next-of-kin to come in.

* * *

The morgue and adjoining rooms were filled to overflowing by this time. The Coroner's Courtroom itself was pressed into service. The calamity had occurred during daylight and most of the immediate rescue efforts were completed by nightfall. The injured were in hospital; the dead were in the morgue. But work went on at the scene in the eerie glare of floodlights, and skindivers would resume the search for the missing at daybreak.

The hysterical calls to the Coroner ended at last. While many next-of-kin waited for news in hospitals in Vancouver and North Vancouver, others came fearfully to the old morgue building. They shared a common denominator in their grief. They hoped and they prayed that it wasn't true; that there had been a mistake; that the still form on the stretcher in the view room wasn't the body they dreaded to see.

* * *

This was a very delicate problem requiring utmost sensitivity on our part. We handled the job with compassion. Each body was on a stretcher, with clean sheets and pillowslips, made as cosmetically acceptable in appearance as the tragedy allowed. We had nurses over from the city jail, next door, and we had our own men with ammonia capsules in the palms of their hands in case somebody fainted during identification. This quite often happens. The attendants would hold the relatives so they wouldn't fall down and apply the ammonia to the nostrils and help them all they could. It was all we could do. And we also had the padres and the priests and the strong coffee. It's really not the answer to what people need at a terrible time but at least it was something to help them through the ordeal.

By this time, of course, people were sensing and fearing the worst and, when a person finds that worst fear confirmed it's an inexpressible shock. We were now going on to 10 or 11 o'clock. It was a slow process. Everyone had to be patient because there was no way we could expedite the matter of identification and we wanted no mistakes.

In fact, expedition would have made things worse because often an identifier will lie to himself or herself, hoping that that which is so obviously a fact cannot be. It's a desperate and positive attitude to a negative knowledge that people know they will have to ultimately face. Identification is only as good as the identifier. But when people are identifying loved ones, they'll sometimes say things like, "It looks like my husband but I could be wrong." They're hoping, of course, that the facts turn out to be wrong. They want them to be wrong.

We had everyone more or less accounted for by eleven that night. One by one, friends would take the grieving relatives home. By one in the morning, we could proceed with the autopsies.

Grief comes in many forms and we ran into pretty well all of them that night. We had all sorts of problems—problems of crowding, language, religion, emotion. Identification was made even more difficult because of whole families coming in together and we had a lot of small children running around, parents having had no time to get babysitters. It was a very tough trial for a family caught up in a sudden emergency over which it had no control. A lot of the relatives of the iron workers and painters were new Canadians of Italian descent and the English language was difficult for them even at the best of times. Anguish and grief made things almost impossible.

We tried our best to find out whether a dead man was Catholic or Protestant but there were some foul-ups about this that night. I remember there was one Italian lady, who was unfortunately now a widow, there with her family. I had phoned over to Holy Rosary Cathedral and a monsignor sent a priest down. So this priest was busy giving the last rites and, just when I was congratulating myself for being most religious and most understanding, there was a hell of a lot of weeping and wailing from the view room near my office. The priest shot out of the view room and came in and said, "They're not Catholic."

"What do you mean?" I said. "They're Italian."

"Yes, but they're from northern Italy and they're Anglican."

Well, I just got hold of one of the priests from St. James Anglican . He gave the last rites of the high Anglican church and quiet was restored.

This seemingly unimportant incident pointed out to me that you can't come to any conclusion in the Coroner's business based on your own opinion unless you know all the facts. I didn't know, in this case. That taught me that when we took down the names of the next-of-kin we must in future ask the family's religion. I had hesitated to do that until then for the simple reason that all next-of-kin, hopefully, are not coming down to the morgue to make an identification. But if you ask them about religion, well, you've virtually told them that a husband or a son or whoever is dead. That's not a pleasant thing to do.

There were other problems with the identification that night. One thing we had to do was bring the workers' clothes over from wherever they had changed into their work clothes that morning. To bring these street clothes over so we could figure out—from the height of a body, the build of a body—who they belonged to. And, of course, in the clothes was usually identification such as a driver's licence or credit card. The system didn't always work, however, because of the crushing of skulls and the fracturing of legs and so on, often wouldn't allow us to get a proper height or build of a body.

116

But that method plus the usual routine methods such as dental records and fingerprints, when possible, and the help of foremen, workmates and employers, all advanced the process. Then the final and positive identifications were made by the families. Tattoo marks also helped. Again, the hardest part was that simple fact that the identifier was hoping against hope that it wasn't the loved one lying there in the morgue. But, of course, those who had survived the disaster had already phoned home to say they were okay. The word got around quickly, I guess. Most of the workers and their families knew each other because these high steel men are a rare breed of cat and take enormous pride in their work, and rightfully so. They're a close-knit family in themselves.

The autopsies went on into the early morning. These were very necessary in view of the insurance claims that would obviously be forthcoming, perhaps lawsuits against the construction company and the engineers and the involvement of the Workers' Compensation Board of British Columbia. There were toxicological questions about the possible use of pep pills or sleeping pills or alcohol by some workers which could have possibly caused them to fall. Exposure to carbon monoxide fumes was another question that had to be answered. Of course, in this accident the causes of death seemed quite obvious. But the point was that the cause of each worker's death had to be demonstrated so the question was clearly answered and there could be no doubt raised in the future. We did all the tests and took no chances.

All this work was performed and concluded. There was no point in stopping, as long as the pathologists and the morgue technicians were able to carry on. We had refrigerated vaults on the main floor for twenty bodies and another forty cadaver seats in the basement. So we moved everything down to the basement and were well-organized at last. And when all the bodies had been positively identified to our satisfaction, we just waited for instructions for their removal to funeral homes. It was a long and hard and heart-wrenching night.

* * *

The grim identification process over and the autopsies performed, Judge McDonald now faced the task of setting an inquest date and empaneling a competent jury to look into Vancouver's single worst disaster.

The inquest opened on June 24, exactly one week after the tragedy. It was held to probe the deaths of 15 men who died in the bridge collapse. Three other men were still missing.

The jury, composed of two engineers and six ironworkers, heard, from the autopsy reports, that eleven of the men had died of multiple injuries and four had died of asphyxiation from drowning.

* * *

I had been concerned about how we were going to get a jury that would be able to understand all the technical jargon we were obviously going to be hearing. One always hears the expression *a jury of your peers*. Now, if the jurors in this case were to be peers of the experts in bridge construction, it wouldn't make sense to use the route of merely going to the tax roll and picking people who just happened to come out on the draw from, say, 100 people. You might end up with a butcher's wife or a candlestick-maker's mistress, or you might get someone who had never even driven across a bridge or knew anything about bridges or perhaps his only connection with a bridge was when, as a kid, he built one with a meccano set.

So I decided to go to the unions and ask them to supply a list of men who might be eligible for jury duty and then go to the management people and ask them if they would supply another group who might be acceptable. Not going, of course, to the principals in this case, the Dominion Bridge Company and Swan Wooster Engineering. I wanted to have people on the jury who had absolutely no axe to grind. We drew from the hat from the lists supplied by the unions and management. I explained to counsel at the opening just how the jury had been chosen. If they had any challenges, would they say so now? Nobody challenged and we went ahead.

There were twelve lawyers representing the survivors or their next-of-kin, the unions, the companies and the provincial government which had commissioned Dominion Bridge to build the span. I said I would try to stay as close as I could to the rules of evidence, omitting hearsay, explaining that the only hearsay would be the evidence of the various experts who were known to vary in their opinions as to why the bridge collapsed. We were really doing an exploratory job here, the better that these experts could find out answers to certain questions and so the jury could at least decide whether this was accident, suicide or homicide, and to say how it happened. And, if they were able to so conclude, to possibly suggest what might be done in the future to avoid a bridge collapsing while under construction.

It was a case of the old Latin expression used in law, *ipso loquitor,* which, when translated, means the thing speaks for itself. After all, bridges aren't supposed to fall down when they're being built. It seemed there must have been negligence somewhere so I knew there would be many arguments and disagreements.

The testimony concerned itself with such questions as the tidal effect in Burrard Inlet, a possible major earthquake, a sliding change of the surface on which the temporary bridge footings were placed, poor design and lack of accurate follow-through in the construction. It was rather ironic that a company engineer was on the bridge when it went down and maybe he knew there was a danger. He was taking sightings because there had been some concern that there had been a shift or a drop or something and that things were not entirely correct. He died.

Much of the testimony was extremely complicated and technical and the jury members knew enough to realise that this was an area of expertise that didn't come into their sphere of knowledge and should be left where it belonged. We were sitting only to determine, without fear, favor or affection, who the people were who had died and the causes of death. But if the jurors found any fault or blame, they could add that. Any jury recommendations would be forwarded to the proper authorities such as the Attorney General, the provincial Minister of Highways and the companies and unions.

The verdict was what one would have expected. The jury found that the deaths of the workers were unnatural and accidental and that another man died of accidental drowning while looking for some of the missing bodies underwater. The jurors also said they were unable to come to any firm conclusion as to what had caused the bridge to collapse and they therefore had no recommendations.

That was their verdict and, when you think back on it, that's really all they could say. Well, anyone could have stood up and said, "We the jury recommend that no more bridges fall down in the future" which is sort of another way of saying we believe in motherhood. My job was done and I stepped out of the picture.

\* \* \*

The subsequent Royal Commission into the disaster, which had been set up by the provincial government within hours of the collapse, fingered two crucial engineering errors built into a temporary bridge support as the cause of the accident and nailed the Dominion Bridge Company with the primary responsibility.

Chief Justice Sherwood Lett of the British Columbia Supreme Court wrote: "It must be recognized that human errors may and do occur and where the safety of the public and erection crews is concerned, reasonable safeguards in the form of adequate and effective checking must be provided."

The grim chapter in the history of Canada's third largest city was officially over, six months after the disaster. But it will never be forgotten. A tarnished bronze plaque mounted on a pillar at the south end of the bridge, seldom seen by the thousands of motorists who cross the span every day, notes the date of the accident, lists the names of those who died, plus those of four men killed earlier in the construction of the tragedy-marred project and the drowned skindiver, and bears the words:

"In memory of those who lost their lives in the process of construction of this, the Second Narrows Bridge."

And every year on June 17 a brightly-colored floral wreath flutters gently down into the waters of Burrard Inlet from the bridge's center span to mark the Iron Workers' Union's memory of the day the bridge fell down.

# The Coffin
# That Refused To Sink

The embarrassing case of the P & O Line coffin that refused to sink happened in the 1970s and was one of the most bizarre that Judge Glen McDonald had encountered during his 26 years as Vancouver Coroner. He still chuckles about it.

But, like the equally unusual incident of the collapsed accordion player from Seattle, it taught him a lesson. Both cases were perfect illustrations of the pitfalls that can waylay a Coroner and the yards of bureaucratic red tape he can find himself tangled in.

Sometimes Judge McDonald bent the rules, sometimes he broke them, and sometimes he ignored them completely and made up his own. He constantly tried to brush the cobwebs off what he saw to be clumsy, restrictive and outdated bureaucratic requirements and let fresh air in to permit the dead to be treated with dignity and the living to be educated and, as a result, protected.

He had, over the years, become increasingly concerned about the complex matter of jurisdiction when death occurs at sea or in the air. He had also become intimately, personally involved with "kitchen" or "cafe" deaths in public places and the need for their full investigation.

He developed his own philosophy as to when the ordering of an autopsy is absolutely essential for the benefit of the deceased's next-of-kin and the public. He pondered the considerations of inquests as opposed to inquiries. He weighed the merits of the Coroner's system versus the largely American Medical Examiner's system—a la televi-

120

sion's crusading Quincy—when it came time to answer that persistent question "How come I'm dead?"

* * *

In the last decade the cruise ship business has burgeoned greatly in the Pacific, mainly with luxury voyages to Alaska, with many liners of various flags sailing in and out of the Port of Vancouver, Canada's busiest seaport.

The one common denominator among the passengers is that most of them are geriatric. They're in their 70s and sometimes 80s. Some are wheelchair cases; some are heart condition cases; some appear to have every terminal disease known to medical science.

I was always concerned by the fact that our provincial Department of Vital Statistics has a very archaic statute which, in fact, goes right back to the days of the first sailing ships coming into Vancouver, to tie up at the old Hastings sawmill. The statute states that a Master at sea has the right to bury a body at sea, making a sufficient entry in the rough logbook, which is later transposed to the fair logbook, which is ultimately sent back to the port of registry of that vessel. In these days of the flag of convenience, that would probably be somewhere in Liberia or Panama or Greece.

Unfortunately, some of the more decrepit tourists sailing in and out of Vancouver aboard these luxury cruise liners drop dead at sea. But our Department of Vital Statistics says, in effect, that they have not died in the province of British Columbia. They are, therefore, not eligible for a certificate of death to be issued in Vancouver when the ship docks.

The ship's agent would routinely inform my office that he had been informed that a passenger somewhere between Alaska and British Columbia had become a late passenger. The ship was bringing the body back. That was no problem. The crew would simply put the body in a plastic bag and stick it in the deep freeze along with the turkeys and hams and booze and whatever else was in there. Another corpse in the freezer.

(Incidentally, to digress, I should mention that the embalming process used by funeral parlors is really not that great. No funeral director will say it's intended to preserve a body for long. Bacteriological changes take place, maggots and so forth. I conducted two disinterments in my career and the bodies we dug up certainly didn't indicate any sign of perpetuity in remaining the same forever after. Embalming is merely a cosmetic procedure in effect for a very short period of time.)

There's always a doctor aboard these cruise liners so we know that what is called a certification of death has been made. The doctor gives this to the captain and he enters in the log the ship's position when the death occurred and the approximate time of death.

This, of course, would all be outside the province of British Columbia so there was no way a proper death certificate could be issued unless the Master—let's assume we're talking about a British ship— went through an elaborate international protocol that directs he must send a copy of his fair log to Somerset House in London where a death certificate would eventually be issued and sent to the ship, probably in six months' time. That's a cumbersome and time-consuming procedure which any ship's captain would prefer to avoid.

So our procedure in these cases was simple. A couple of my staff would go down to the dock, wait until the passengers were ashore and then quietly go aboard and take the body away. The deceased would usually have a spouse or relative or good friend with her, or him, who, naturally, would want to know what arrangements could be made.

Now, there were several concerns I had about this procedure, both as Coroner and as a Master Mariner myself. As far as the shipping company was concerned, they wanted that body off because the ship would soon be sailing again. They wanted a release for the body. I gave them a release. And, further, they wanted to know the cause of death. I gave them that, too. All against the rules.

I had made it a rule—and it was purely my own rule and without any jurisdiction because if the Vital Statistics people had had their say I shouldn't even have been involved—that we did autopsies, plus the standard toxicological tests, on anyone who died at sea and was brought into the Port of Vancouver.

My reasoning was simple. There was always the chance of accusations being hurled later. Had a person died of food poisoning? Or a lack of proper medical attention? Or even been murdered? Although that probably only happens on television. But if you haven't done the autopsy, you don't know the answers. But I was told by the bureaucrats at Vital Statistics that I couldn't sign a certificate unless the death had occurred within the province of British Columbia. Nonsense!

So I just conveniently ignored the fact that the ship's surgeon had certified death somewhere out at sea and I certified that the death was on arrival at the Vancouver City Morgue at 240 East Cordova Street, which just happens to be in the province of British Columbia. It was an artifice. It was, in fact, a bloody lie, but it was the only way we could allow the next-of-kin to transport the remains and to be issued a permit to bury, cremate or remove. Without that certificate, that can't be done. And also, without the certificate, insurance monies can't be collected.

The whole farcical situation cries out for some sort of amendment to the Vital Statistic Act. And the same rules apply when you're dealing with death aboard an aircraft. If someone is certified dead by a physician on a plane 40,000 feet over the middle of the Pacific Ocean, that's certainly not in the province of British Columbia. Then the body is landed in Vancouver. What to do?

So, when I was appointed Supervisory Coroner for all of British Columbia in 1969, I simply instructed my Coroners in the Municipality of Richmond, where the International Airport is, to go ahead and assume that the body was alive when it landed in British Columbia so we could circumvent these outmoded bureaucratic requirements and properly observe the humanity of the situation. The body was then certified dead here and that was all there was to it.

I'll never forget the case of the floating coffin because it was so damn weird and hilarious. It all started when an elderly dodderer aboard a P & O passenger ship was careless enough to expire at sea. The ship berthed in Vancouver. But the widow insisted that her late husband remain on board so he could be buried at sea with a flag on the coffin. A nice thought. Maybe he was an old navy man like me.

Well, it was very simple because I had no legal jurisdiction to demand that the body be landed in Vancouver, anyway. The Master was the man in charge and the ship was sailing under the British flag. So, after discussions with the captain and the agents and the company solicitors and the widow's attorneys in Los Angeles, I just supplied a death certificate.

My conscience wasn't in too much turmoil because, after all, the body was in Vancouver on board a ship and in a deep freeze. I went down and looked. Yes, there certainly was a dead body there. The widow was able to identify her late, lamented husband. The ship duly sailed. All seemed to be shipshape and I forgot all about it.

About a year later I got a call from the Coroner at Pacific City, a community on the coast of Oregon state. He said a funny thing had happened, that a local fisherman had come in with a coffin snared in his net and there was a document in it which said: "Vancouver Coroner— Glen McDonald."

The Coroner asked me, "What do you want me to do?"

"You don't do anything," I said. "Give me your phone number and any other number you're going to be at for the next two or three hours and I'll get back in touch with you."

I immediately phoned the P & O agents in Vancouver and said, "Look, what the hell happened with that case we had a year ago when everyone agreed they would bury the body at sea?"

In the old days, by the way, the ship's sailmaker would make a sack out of canvas and the last stitch went through the nose, just to make sure the guy was good and dead, and they put some old firebox weights in the tail of the sack and it went over the side. That was that.

But in this case the coffin box had been made out of plywood and the carpenter hadn't put enough holes in it. It didn't sink. Or if it did sink, it floated back up. It got caught in the fisherman's net something like 150 miles east of where the ship's course had been on her way down to Los Angeles.

The agents, of course, knew bugger all about it. But they contacted the ship by telex—she was in the Caribbean at this time—and were told that, yes, the body had been buried at sea at such and such a latitude and longitude and all the rest of it. It appeared this ceremony had not gone like a burial at sea should. The coffin had risen from its watery grave to haunt us.

Here was a situation fraught with danger. If the news got out the consequences would be highly embarrassing for all concerned, including me. The stuff ulcers are made of. So I took one more ulcer on myself and phoned back to the Coroner in Pacific City. I said, "Do me a favor. Bury that damn body and send me a bill. The whole affair is unknown as far as we are concerned. I know it's going to cost you some dough but you'll be getting a cheque from the company's agents. Meanwhile, don't hit the bloody headlines or say anything to any of the media."

"No," he said, "we're not doing that."

"What about the fisherman?"

"Well, there's a slight problem there."

"What's that?"

"He wants to be paid for salvage."

"Christ!" I said. "The greedy bastard! Find out what a reasonable salvage fee is for a coffin off a luxury cruise ship and I'll make sure he's paid, too. And, by the way, get this guy sworn to secrecy, tell him if he doesn't keep his mouth shut we'll sue him for desecration of a dead body or something. We'll think of something you have down there in your statutes."

So the guys who dug the grave were paid and there was a salvage fee paid to the fisherman of about $250. I don't know what the price of fish was that year but I don't think he did any fishing for a couple of days. And that was the last I heard of it. Thank God.

That was an example of the stupidity of our relationship with death in international waters or air space. We have not, as yet, faced up to the problem. There's no question that something must be done about it by someone—the United Nations' International Court of Justice at the Hague or some other body. We need international rules at sea and we need an easily available international death certificate.

Take a situation where you have, say, a Greek-owned ship with a Norwegian Master and a Pakistani or Chinese or Filipino crew. One of the crew dies. What do you do? Well, if you went through the proper procedure—because that ship, sailing under a Panamanian flag, owned by Greeks and commanded by a Norwegian, is sort of a mini-world unto itself—you'd have to make an international application for a certificate of death.

You'd put all the necessary documents through the International Court. Then they'd go to the port of the ship's registry and from there to where the company is registered, or incorporated. The language used in the logbook would have to be translated into English. And, finally, the death certificate would be issued in the Hague two or three years later.

This would be a real, honest-to-God international death certificate. But meanwhile, the ship's Master would still have the body on board and the ship would be sailing merrily around the world. Also, the crew would want to go to the funeral of their dead shipmate. Seamen can be very loyal and sentimental. But how can they go to a funeral when there's no death certificate and no permit to bury, cremate or remove? Without these you can't even have a bloody funeral. It's a ludicrous situation.

So that's why I went through this charade of signing death certificates for people who didn't—according to Vital Statistics—die in the province of British Columbia. Technically, they didn't. I said they did.

But for my breaking a silly law, a ship would have to have sailed with a body still on board. And that's the last thing a seaman wants—that's the end of the world. That's like sailing on Friday the Thirteenth.

\* \* \*

Jack Wasserman, who for many years was *The Vancouver Sun's* urbane, witty and well-informed items columnist, radio open-line host, television interviewer and man-about-town, collapsed and died on the night of April 6, 1977. He was 50.

Wasserman, Vancouver's counterpart of San Francisco's Herb Caen (who was a good friend) or Toronto's Dick Beddoes (also a good friend), was making a light-hearted speech in the ballroom of the Hotel Vancouver at a roast honoring the redoubtable British Columbia timber baron, Gordon Gibson, Sr. He dropped dead in front of 650 of the city's tuxedoed elite.

Naturally, because he was well-known and liked and highly respected as a superb investigative reporter, people wanted to know what had happened. Had Wasserman been a victim of food poisoning in a public place?

Judge Glen McDonald, also a close friend, made sure the public learned the facts, just as Wasserman the reporter would have wished. Had he been able to do so, Wasserman most certainly would have asked "How come I'm dead?"

\* \* \*

The thought of suing a restaurant, a hotel, a nightclub, a cruise line or an airline because of death from food poisoning might well occur to a next-of-kin. This was one reason I put emphasis on the need for autopsies in these cases of "cafe" or "kitchen" deaths.

When I heard about Jack's death, I went right down to the morgue and said, "Bring that body down. He died in a public place at a public function and he was a friend of many people. There'll be a hell of a lot of questions asked if we don't do an autopsy."

So I got hold of Jack's widow and told her this was now a Coroner's case. We did the autopsy two hours after his certified death at St. Paul's Hospital and it told us what we had suspected—that Jack had had a previous heart attack, and this was a sudden onset of myocardial infarction, coronary thrombosis and coronary atherosclerosis.

Food samples from the banquet were brought down to the lab and examined. There was no evidence of any toxicity, so we knew we had an honest-to-God, unfortunate, sudden but natural death. It wasn't a good experience for me. I've never liked attending or assisting at autopsies of people I know. But, in the back of my mind, I knew that if the job wasn't done questions would be asked and speculation and rumors would spread.

So, my standing orders to my staff and all Coroners in the province were that, whenever in doubt, don't hesitate to order an autopsy, regardless of whether the deceased is plain old John Doe or a public figure like Jack Wasserman. Somebody wants to know what the cause of that death was. I played no favorites. It was a rule for all. Death comes to kings and queens and the man in the street.

\* \* \*

Ministry of the Solicitor General of Ontario. Memorandum to: Ontario Coroners. Re: The Cafe Coronary—Heimlich Manoeuver. May 6, 1980.

Several recent Coroners' investigations have indicated asphyxiation death due to food impacted in the throat—the so-called Cafe Coronary.

The cause of death has been ascertained at autopsy. In most instances the deceased has been given the usual cardiopulmonary resuscitation; obviously useless in these cases.

No attempt to clear the airway, use of the Heimlich Manoeuver or similar action, has been undertaken. Most cases occur in mental retardation or chronic care facilities, homes for the aged, and, of course, in cafeterias or dining areas. The incident occurs at or immediately following mealtime, and it would appear that doctors, nurses, and other attendants do not exhibit a high index of suspicion re the Cafe Coronary syndrome when circumstances should suggest this possibility.

Coroners should consider dissemination of this information to the appropriate persons as indicated above and possibly also to industrial nurses and health care centres.

\* \* \*

The autopsy rule must be applied in these "cafe" deaths: choking on a piece of steak, getting a fishbone lodged in the throat. There's always the possibility of civil action being taken against the purveyor of the food or beverage and if you haven't done the autopsy and the toxicology you're not able to answer vital questions after the body has been removed. You've lost the evidence.

Here's a classic example of how important an autopsy can be. Several years ago Bill Ellis, a well-known Vancouver advertising executive, was flying to Montreal on business. He had a few drinks, and the stewardess served steaks. Bill Ellis started eating. Then he started choking.

There were three doctors on the plane. They thumped his chest and tried mouth-to-mouth resuscitation. No good. They then assumed Ellis had died of heart failure at 30 or 40,000 feet somewhere between Calgary and Toronto. In Toronto, his body was taken to the Coroner's office. Death had occurred over Saskatchewan or perhaps Manitoba. But Ellis was now under the jurisdiction of the Ontario Coroners Act.

Bill was a personal friend and I got the news from his widow. I knew the Chief Coroner in Ontario and got the results of the autopsy which showed that a piece of steak had lodged in the throat. It was clear this was an accidental death caused by choking, a classic case of the Cafe Coronary.

All those doctors and the stewardesses had to do was look at the dinner tray to see there was a piece of steak missing from the plate. God, the steaks on airlines aren't that big—you could easily see a bit was missing. But no way did they realize it was this that was pressing down on the glottis and the epiglottis. If they had gone that route they could have done a tracheotomy, cutting into the trachea so Bill could breathe.

Bill Ellis's death might well have been written off as being caused by a heart attack had the autopsy not been done. But I became more deeply involved when the body came home to Vancouver. His widow, June, and I and Dr. Charlie Gould, another family friend, planned to scatter the ashes in the waters of Howe Sound, a favorite fishing spot of Bill's. But, before the cremation, June called me and said the insurance people were quibbling about paying double indemnity for an accidental death caused by a bit of steak in the throat. They were dubious about the evidence. The body was then lying in the Hollyburn Funeral Home in West Vancouver. So I decided to play detective. I got my pathologist, Tom Harmon, and we phoned the funeral parlor. We said we had the widow's consent to open up the body of Mr. Ellis and examine his throat. We went over with a Polaroid camera and opened up the throat and, indeed, there was still some steak left in the glottis and epiglottis. So we took pictures of it and showed them to the insurance people.

They had said they would pay double indemnity in a case of accidental death only if the cause were from outside and they took the position that this was a cause of death from inside. Well, to me it seemed like arguing about how many angels can dance on the head of a pin. The steak came from outside. It sure as hell didn't suddenly grow inside the throat. But for Dr. Harmon and I taking an interest in the death of a friend, I doubt the insurance people would have paid up. But they did—on the steps of the courthouse.

* * *

Judge Glen McDonald also learned on one occasion that the exact time of death can also be a most important matter in the subsequent paying of insurance monies. This case involved the collapsed accordion player from Seattle.

The Vancouver Coroner, himself, had been a rousing barrelhouse piano player and enthusiastic squeezebox squeezer for many years. One of his proudest moments was when he played the concert Steinway in the grand ballroom of the Cunard liner *Queen Elizabeth* in the middle of the North Atlantic. It was during the war when she was a troopship and his less than discriminating audience was composed of rowdy sailors, soldiers and airmen who were at the time playing poker and singing dirty songs.

But, being an aficionado of the accordion, Judge McDonald was immediately and sympathetically interested in the unfortunate demise of the player from Seattle.

* * *

The police report on a sudden death—one not associated with an accident or a homicide—has the exact time of the certification of death typed on it. The officer would attend at the hospital, take down the name of the deceased and the next-of-kin, and would then try to notify those next-of-kin. Part of his information was, of course, who certified death and at what time. This was standard procedure and it was followed when this accordion player died.

He had come up from Seattle to do a gig. He had some friends in town and after the show they went to the Niagara Hotel and had a party. I had heard of him and spotted the name on the police report.

He had had a heart attack and snuffed it, playing his squeezebox for his friends. He was certified dead at the Vancouver General Hospital at 12:10 a.m. on a Saturday.

I read the police report on Monday morning and just thought it was sad to see a good accordion player go that way. Yet he was playing when he died and that, at least, was a comforting thought. Well, a few days later—after his widow in Seattle had gone to the Musicians' Union and claimed the life insurance policy which the union had for all its members—I got a call from the union local's shop steward. He asked if I could tell him what time the accordion player had died. I said, "Well, in British Columbia I think we are the same as you in Washington State. The same time."

(By the way, the only people who can certify death are qualified physicians and surgeons licensed to practice. Not paramedics, not ambulance drivers and not Coroners or anyone else. It has to be a

Hollywood movie idol ̶ ̶ ̶ Flynn was all smiles when he arrived at the Vancouver International Airport in October, 1959. Three days later the swashbuckling Sultan of Suave lay dead on a slab in the City Morgue on skidroad. Flynn's sudden death caused the coroner's office to have its most publicized night in history.

Part of a once-powerful Merlin engine is welded to a crag 7,600 feet high on the snowy slopes of Mount Slesse, stark evidence of the force of impact as the TCA aircraft slammed into the mountain during turbulent weather.

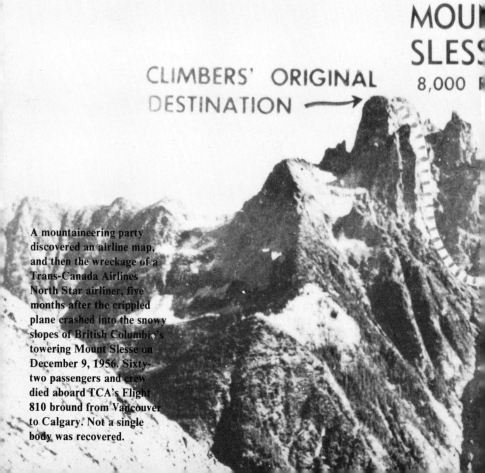

CLIMBERS' ORIGINAL DESTINATION →

MOU
SLESS
8,000 F

A mountaineering party discovered an airline map, and then the wreckage of a Trans-Canada Airlines North Star airliner, five months after the crippled plane crashed into the snowy slopes of British Columbia's towering Mount Slesse on December 9, 1956. Sixty-two passengers and crew died aboard TCA's Flight 810 bround from Vancouver to Calgary. Not a single body was recovered.

This granite memorial at the foot of Mount Slesse was dedicated by Trans-Canada Airlines to the memory of those who died in the crash.

WRECKAGE FOUND HERE

LANDING INSTRUCTION SHEET FOUND HERE

The shattered wreckage of Canadian Pacific
Airlines' Flight 21 lies strewn over swampy
woodlands in British Columbia's Cariboo region.
The DC-6B was en route from Vancouver to
Whitehorse, Yukon on Thursday, July 8, 1965
when it crashed. This followed an explosion,
believed to have been caused by a bomb planted in
an aft washroom. Fifty-two people perished.
*VANCOUVER SUN*—Ken Oakes

The tug *Haro Straits* was raised from the depths of Georgia Strait in November, 1972, nine months after the ship sank and five crewmen died in a treacherous gale. Judge Glen McDonald held an inquest into this and other tragedies involving B.C.'s towboat and fishing industries.

A dazed workman awaits rescue amid the twisted wreckage of Vancouver's new Second Narrows Bridge which collapsed while under construction on June 17, 1958. Eighteen workers died and twenty were injured in Vancouver' s worst single disaster.
ED COSGROVE

An ironworker awaits rescue amongst the destruction. The old Second Narrows Bridge can be seen in the background.
ED COSGROVE

The body of one workman lies pinned as another is helped by a rescuer in a workboat.
ED COSGROVE

**Helping hands gingerly hoist a stretcher bearing a workman injured in the collapse of the birdge, a disaster caused by engineering errors.**
ED COSGROVE

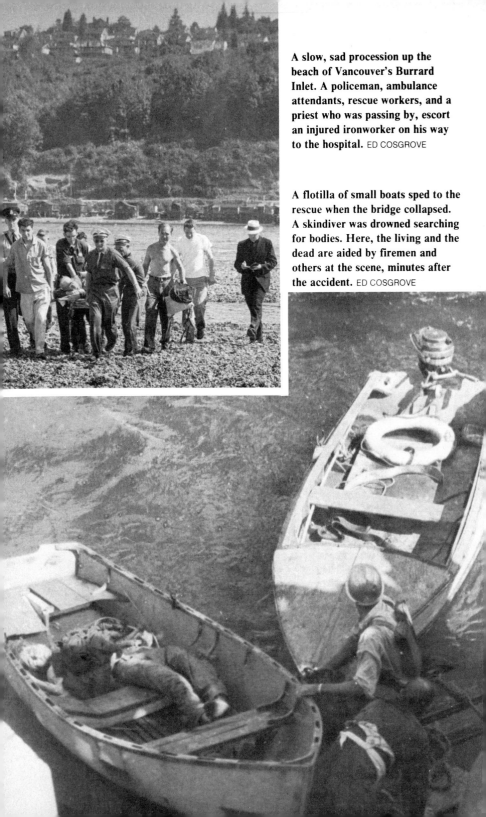

A slow, sad procession up the beach of Vancouver's Burrard Inlet. A policeman, ambulance attendants, rescue workers, and a priest who was passing by, escort an injured ironworker on his way to the hospital. ED COSGROVE

A flotilla of small boats sped to the rescue when the bridge collapsed. A skindiver was drowned searching for bodies. Here, the living and the dead are aided by firemen and others at the scene, minutes after the accident. ED COSGROVE

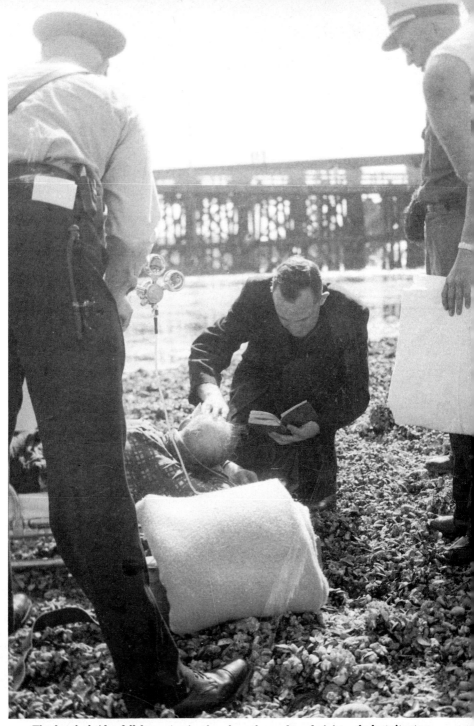

**The day the bridge fell down. A priest kneels on the sand to administer the last rites to a fatally injured workman.** ED COSGROVE

VANCOUVER SUN—Peter Hulbert

Smoke billowing from the forward section of the Norwegian cruise liner *Meteor* portends a grim tale of death. Thirty-two crew members died in the fire which broke out on May 22, 1971, when the ship was cruising in B.C.'s Georgia Strait. A Canadian Coast Guard cutter stands by at bow; passengers are taken to rescue vessels in lifeboats at stern.

Judge Glen McDonald, at work in the field, supervises the removal of the body of a homicide victim from a house on the city's east side in 1957, while curious bystanders look on. During his 26 years as Coroner, McDonald also worked in graveyards, on a mountain top, on Indian reservations, aboard wrecked ships, at airplane crash sites, in hospital wards and in penitentiaries. *VANCOUVER SUN*—George Diack

"Every one of these pills caused an accidental or suicidal death. . .You don't have to know how many there are if you don't take them!" Here is a small sample (275 bottles) of the thousands of death-dealing pills collected over the years by the staff of the Vancouver Coroner's Office and exhibited on the lecture circuit.

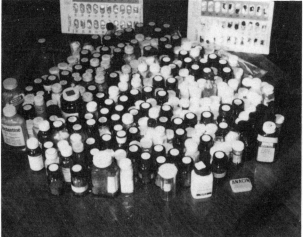

*CORONER'S OFFICE*

Lungs, hearts, livers, kidneys, bladders, skulls, guns, knives, clubs, hammers and dented hard hats were all part of the *Fabulous Traveling Wax Museum and McDonald Candy Cane Show* assembled by the staff of the Vancouver Coroner's Office for educational purposes.

Chief coroner's technician George Marmaduke Shoebotham and the *Fabulous Traveling Wax Museum and McDonald Candy Cane Show,* a comprehensive and graphic exhibit of the causes and tools of death which was popular on the lecture circuit and in British Columbia High schools.                    BART BASTIEN

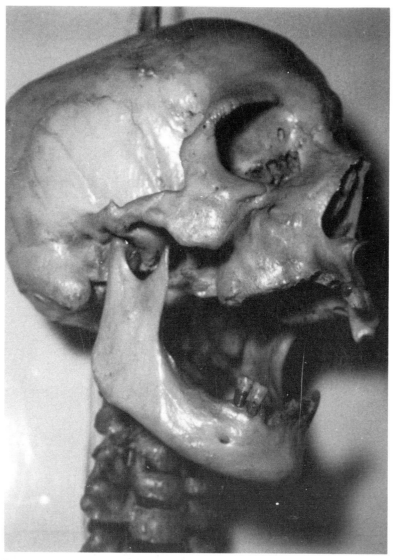

**For many years "Joe" stood as silent guardian to the *Fabulous Traveling Wax Museum and McDonald Candy Cane Show*.** GEORGE SHOEBOTHAM

VANCOUVER SUN—Dave Buchan

Convicted murderer Rene Castellani is escorted from the Vancouver Courthouse by a Royal Canadian Mounted Policeman on November 12, 1966 after being found guilty of poisoning his wife with doses of arsenic. Suspicions in the city analyst's Laboratory and the Coroner's Office set homicide detectives on a tangled trail of investigation that led to the disinterment of Esther Castellani's body and the arrest, trial and conviction of Canada's infamous "Milkshaker Murderer."

Chief coroner's technician George Shoebotham prepares to receive a corpse in the refrigerated area of the morgue. An average of 1,100 bodies a year were admitted over a span of 26 years. There was a homicide victim every two weeks, a traffic death every week and an industrial death every month. Inquests in the adjoining courtroom averaged 1.5 per week.

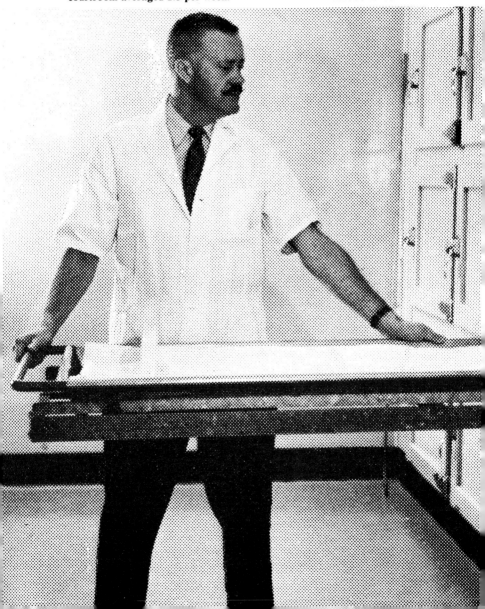

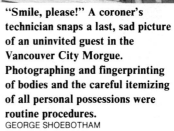

"Smile, please!" A coroner's technician snaps a last, sad picture of an uninvited guest in the Vancouver City Morgue. Photographing and fingerprinting of bodies and the careful itemizing of all personal possessions were routine procedures.
GEORGE SHOEBOTHAM

The legendary David John "Quig" Quigley was the chief coroner's technician at the Vancouver City Morgue for 29 years. He handled more than 20,000 cases and discovered $90,000 hidden on bodies. He also played so many gruesome practical jokes on colleagues and newspaper reporters that he became known as the "ghoul" of 240 East Cordova Street.

doctor qualified to take a stethoscope and come to a professional conclusion that a person is dead.)

By this time I had the police blue sheet in front of me and I said to this union guy, "He died at 12:10 a.m. on Saturday."

He said, "Gee, that's too bad. That's really bloody bad!"

"Well, he died and that's bad, I guess," I said.

And the union guy said, "No, because of the insurance policy—he hadn't paid his premium and it expired at midnight."

"Oh," I said, "I see what you mean. But I can't change the records here or the records at the hospital. It's 12:10 a.m., which is ten minutes after midnight on the Saturday. That is too bad."

He rang off and I pondered the situation. Something was bothering me, something didn't seem quite right. Then I had an idea. In those days we hadn't got the idea of Daylight Saving Time properly organized on the west coast. The state of Washington, to the south, had not opted for Pacific Daylight Saving Time as British Columbia had. It was because of the large farming community there. The cows couldn't understand the change in the hours or something. They were waking up too early, or perhaps, too late.

The answer suddenly dawned on me. I knew what was wrong. I said to myself, "Well, now, if we're on Daylight Saving Time, that means that 12:10 a.m. in British Columbia is 11:10 p.m. in Washington state. That's where this guy's insurance policy is and surely it would be their time that would control the payment."

So I phoned back to the Musicians' Union in Seattle and got hold of the guy who had called me and I said, "Look, do you realize we're an hour ahead of you?"

He said, "No, why?"

"Just think about it," I said. "You said this accordion maestro was covered up to midnight, but not ten minutes after midnight, your time. Right?"

"Right."

"Okay. But, in fact, if we take the timing down to your time, he died at 11:10 p.m."

He said, "Christ, I never thought of that!" I asked him to phone me back.

He got in touch with the general group insurance policy people and they said, "Oh, well, that's different." The guy had been paid up until midnight and the certified time of death—11:10 p.m. Standard Time— was therefore acceptable. The widow would be paid the insurance.

I felt really happy about that outcome. The case was very interesting because it proved the simple point that, internationally, we don't bloody well have a time of death that really means anything. Maybe we should arrange it that people be born and die on Greenwich Mean Time so we cover the whole world. Simple. Too simple.

This sort of insurance situation could apply, for instance, when there's a 10 or 12-hour time difference. The rule of law of an insurance contract is simply that the place where that contract is signed is the place that controls the time. I suppose you'd just have to add or subtract the hours if you expired in China or Russia or England or Timbuktu.

But the case of the accordion-player did have a happy ending. This made me happy.

People are puzzled that an inquest is held into a certain death and not another. Why? Who has the authority to order that inquest? The cops? The Attorney General? A judge? The Coroner?

People also wonder about when an autopsy should be performed and who has the authority to order that. A post mortem.

Let's clear up the mystery.

A bit of history, if you'll bear with me. Under the English Coroners Act, the Coroner goes back so far that he was, among other things, appointed the Crowner. He represented the King. One of his duties was to make sure the sheriff who garnered all the fines and taxes into the treasury was not diverting some of those monies into his own hands or those of his cronies. The Crowner was brought in to look after the treasure trove.

It's also interesting to note in passing that, by tradition, the huge sturgeon caught in British Columbia's Fraser River belong to the Crown. That sturgeon is still under the jurisdiction of the Crowner, or Coroner. He was the fox sent in to look after the other fox to make sure the Crown got its money.

It's also interesting to note that, also by tradition, the only person today who can serve a subpoena or process order on a sheriff, for example, in British Columbia is the Coroner.

He is the only man who can go to the chief law enforcement sheriff and serve that subpoena on him for an offence he may have committed. That's common law.

Now, bearing in mind that background of the Coroner's autonomous responsibility, it is he alone—within the jurisdiction to which he is appointed—who decides to hold or not hold an inquest or an inquiry. He also has the power to order an autopsy. He has all the power. He is, in a way, a God unto himself. It's a demanding and responsible job. You're dealing with lives, frail and fragile.

Every sudden death doesn't require an inquest or an autopsy, of course. Not, for example, if the family doctor has seen the deceased ten days prior to death and is able to say that death was from a condition for which his patient was being treated. And providing that death didn't occur on a bus or in any public situation involving taxpayers' money, like a hot pursuit police chase resulting in a collision.

Often, the decision to hold an inquest is made if an autopsy result shows a cause of death is unnatural. The jury will then have to decide if that death was caused by accident, suicide or homicide. One of these categories must go on the death certificate. Or the jurors can—if they are unable to so classify—say it was death by misadventure, an adventure that backfired. If a man is crazy enough to walk along a narrow plank high up between two buildings and he falls off, that's an adventure that went wrong. He knew he was taking a risk but he sure as hell wasn't planning to fall off and do himself in. Misadventure is sort of a convenient out for a jury but the Coroner will accept that verdict.

Also, if the Coroner finds he has a cause of death which is unnatural and if there's some evidence that a person or persons may have caused this death, or that certain circumstances had contributed to it, it then becomes a matter of public concern. Death costs the taxpayers money. And in such cases the Attorney General becomes involved as well as the Coroner.

In most cases it's up to the Coroner to decide whether to hold an inquest or an inquiry. That decision is his alone and is subject to any person in the general public writing to the Coroner, or visiting the Coroner, and saying, "I want an inquest."

The Coroner is then charged with the decision whether he should convey this request to the Attorney General, the province's chief law enforcement officer, who can order an inquest or an inquiry. The Coroner must comply and if he decides for some reason to waive his jurisdiction and bow out of the case, the Attorney General will simply appoint another Coroner.

An autopsy can be ordered without the permission of the next-of-kin. There have been many cases of resistance—when the deceased is a Christian Scientist or a Jehovah's Witness and the religious thing becomes involved. But such beliefs and arguments must have no control over and no influence on the Coroner's decision.

The Coroner must view the body himself—must have any signs of violence or foul play demonstrated to him. If there are such signs, it's a Coroner's case. The Coroner's decision to have an autopsy performed is a lonely one—an autonomous one and his alone. And it can be met with a hell of a lot of resistance by the next-of-kin or their lawyers.

But, in 26 years on the bench, I can't recall a single case when a person regretted having an autopsy done or successfully resisted an autopsy order. And as soon as the autopsy findings were known and the report received, the next-of-kin always requested a copy. The better they could find out to their complete satisfaction what did cause that death. And we always gave copies to the next-of-kin.

I'm not saying there should be autopsies in all fatalities. That, of course, is impossible. I remember Coroner Turkel in San Francisco telling me that the autopsy index ratio should be 23 to 25 percent. He meant at least 23 to 25 percent of deaths should be autopsied. Not because you're trying, as a Coroner, to keep up your batting average but because there are a lot of cases when doctors will sign a death certificate when they don't actually know the cause of death. That's when you get into the area of which deaths should be autopsied.

The International Association of Coroners and the American Medical Association did get together and did produce this rule: if an attending physician or a family physician has not treated a patient for a period of ten days before death, or if he doesn't know in his professional opinion what caused the death, he should not sign a death certificate.

Simply, if that physician doesn't have a positive cause of death he should not sign the death certificate. But if he does have a cause of death—relevant to an illness the deceased has been treated for ten days prior to death—he should sign the death certificate. If he has any doubt, he should immediately notify the Coroner or Medical Examiner in his area. Everyone should then be satisfied that the proper steps have been taken.

It's awfully hard for a Coroner when he's confronted by a grieving mother who says, "I've just lost my child and you're going to do an autopsy?" She's shocked, she's aggrieved. She doesn't want the body touched, insulted. But, often, that mother will telephone the next day wanting to know the cause of death. It's an anomaly of human nature, perhaps. But I certainly wouldn't want that mother to hear from a neighbor that her husband had come home drunk and thrown the kid across the room and she didn't find out about it until after the body had been buried. The mother, or father, deserves an autopsy and an inquest. Every parent has the right to know.

It isn't an unbending rule of autopsy, but I agree with the late Coroner Turkel that international levels should be established. A Coroner should have the power to subpoena people outside his jurisdiction in cases such as airplane crashes, train accidents or those involving foreign-registered ships. There must be a totally independent investigation of a case in which a police officer is found dead in suspicious circumstances. That's what the Coroner's office is all about.

Here's a thought or two on the subject of three girls—Judy Garland, Marilyn Monroe and Mary Jo Kopechne. They died in different parts of the world—in England, in California, in Massachusetts. Their deaths were all widely publicized.

Judy Garland's pointed out to me that the procedures of the British Coroners Act are the best going. The celebrated singer/actress had died from what seemed at the time to be an overdose of drugs, whether taken accidentally or deliberately nobody knew. The Coroner, a lawyer, said without hesitation, "We'll do an autopsy; we'll do a toxicology; we'll hold an inquest."

The investigators found the level of the barbiturates. The inquest jurors found death due to an accidental overdose of drugs. The case was disposed of in just a few days. The sudden death of an idol of millions had been handled thoroughly, efficiently, decently and with dignity.

Marilyn Monroe. The Los Angeles Coroner decided the movie star's death in 1962 required a "psychological" autopsy. He went to the University of Southern California and hired, at great expense, three psychiatrists to study all the evidence. They went into intricate academic huddles and they went around and around and they did this, that and the other. The Coroner's office had already done a medical autopsy which showed the girl's kidneys hadn't been functioning properly.

But the hired headshrinkers didn't report to the Coroner. They reported to the television and the rest of the media with the Coroner. And they reported that possibly, but not probably, Marilyn Monroe had accidentally taken an overdose of pills deliberately. The jargon was such that only three shrinks could possibly have dreamed it up and then figured out what they had said, if, indeed, they ever did understand what they had said, or if they had said anything at all. And six weeks later they said something else. Nobody understood what that was, either.

Mary Jo Kopechne, the girl who drowned in the Senator Ted Kennedy scandal on Chappaquiddick Island in 1969. Let's think about her. She was in the water for eight hours, something like that. The Coroner was present and a Deputy Sheriff asked him, "What case is that?" The Coroner replied, "Oh, it's a drowning."

A simple drowning. The background and powerful political connections weren't known at that time. So the Coroner signed the death certificate. Asphyxiation due to drowning. Then things started to happen very quickly. The political wheels were turning. Mary Jo Kopechne's body was moved across the Massachusetts state line into New Jersey and buried.

There was no autopsy, no toxicology, nothing. She was merely documented as a drowning victim. I met the Coroner later at a seminar in Chicago, a chap named Smith. He told me straight out that he hadn't known any of the background at the time of the accident. But the fact remains that the Coroner's office is there to find out the background of the circumstances of a death, no matter who is involved. My policy was always: if in doubt, order an autopsy. The next step, if you're still in doubt, is to order an inquest. Then people will come forward and you should get the required answers.

But in the Chappaquiddick case the doubts linger even to this day. Was Mary Jo Kopechne pregnant? Drunk? Drugged? Did she really drown? Or was there another cause of death? And, of course, her parents have consistently refused to permit removal of the body from the grave.

There have been some more recent newsworthy deaths, in California, which pose unanswered questions. William Holden supposedly hit his head on a coffee table while drunk. Natalie Wood supposedly drowned while trying to board a dinghy tied to her husband's yacht. John Belushi. These deaths, to me, haven't been fully explained, mainly because no inquests were held.

But in particular, it's the deaths of those three women that graphically illustrate the different ways in which the Coroner's system works in different areas.

By the way, in some states, such as Maryland, the autopsy index ratio is just three percent. In California, six. London, 18 or 19. In Vancouver it is 23 percent. That is the number of autopsies per 100 deaths. Comparisons are never too satisfactory or foolproof, of course, but those comparisons are interesting.

Comparing the Coroner's system with the largely American Medical Examiner's system (i.e. television's Quincy, et al), we find that the autopsy index ratio in the states of Massachusetts, New York, Virginia and Florida is eight to ten percent. These are their own figures.

People might well wonder why there's such a difference compared with the Coroner's system such as ours in British Columbia. Well, it seems that, where the Medical Examiner system is in effect, the autopsy index ratio is lower by half or even more than half of the rate where the Coroner's system is used.

This is not denied by the Medical Examiners themselves. Some even point to the tax money they're saving by not holding autopsies. Well, one cannot doubt that if no autopsies are done a state's economy would certainly benefit. But the whole point I'm making is that, in the Coroner's system, we use a forensic pathologist, we use a toxicologist or a chemist, and we use the investigators.

The three levels discharge their professional duties and report their findings to the Coroner who then applies them to his decision that he will proceed by way of an inquiry or will put all the evidence to an inquest jury. For example, in the case of Errol Flynn, there was so much public interest I even considered at one stage holding an inquest rather than handling it as an inquiry. As it turned out, we went the inquiry route.

But the facts are still fully out in the open. Under the Medical Examiner's system, the Examiner himself may or may not, and I emphasize the may *not,* ever even see the body in a case, whereas every Coroner is required to have that body identified to him. The Coroner sees that body undressed and he sees if there are any marks or signs of violence thereon and then he considers having an autopsy performed, followed by an inquiry or an inquest.

Sure, the Coroner's system is more cumbersome and it's certainly more expensive. But, on the other hand, if you're going to ascertain a cause of death there's only one way to do it. This is no secret to the Medical Examiners, either. You must look at the bloody body and then call the experts in.

In fact, there was one bizarre case in the United States that absolutely staggered me. A man kissed his wife, went out to the garage, got in his car and was found a while later slumped on the floor beside the driver's seat. A Medical Examiner attended, looked at the body and decided on the spot it was a heart attack death, cardiac arrest.

He signed the death certificate to that effect. Nothing more was done until the Examiner got a phone call from the funeral director, who asked him, "By the way, did you know there was a stab wound in the back of this man's left shoulder that probably went clean through the middle of his heart?"

There had been a history of heart condition in this man's case, certainly, but never a history of a knife plunging into his heart which was ultimately found to be the correct cause of death.

That's an absolutely true story, unbelievable as it may seem. What had happened was that someone had tried to steal the guy's car or his wallet and ended up stabbing him in the back. The Medical Examiner had simply looked at the front of the body. He hadn't even turned it over. Such an oversight could never occur under the Coroner's system. It would be an impossibility.

It's interesting how Medical Examiners came to move into the Coroner's job. Historically, some states—such as Kentucky—didn't even have the equivalent of a Coroners Act or a Medical Examiners Act. In others it was a hit-and-miss arrangement. The Declaration of Independence had completely overlooked the Coroner's system, or a comparable system. So, over the years, each state formed its own concept of what such an Act should be.

Canada had a more orderly situation because most provinces had inherited the British Coroners Act. So we had something in common. In the United States it was a case of every state going about the job differently. I attended many seminars in the U.S. and was intrigued to hear the Americans talking state by state and Coroner by Coroner—from Kentucky to Florida to New York—as to how they were doing things. Their procedures were all completely different, for Chrissake!

The Medical Examiner's system came in because, historically, there had been abuses. By the way, the Coroner's system in the States also involves a Coroner being elected to office every two or four years along with the sheriff and the prosecutor and the dog-catcher. So in that kind of situation, you can just see an inquest being slanted if it involves votes the Coroner might win or lose. It's a possibility. But worse than that was the fact that undertakers used to act as Coroners and always wanted to get on with the job of holding the funeral services so they could get paid instead of holding things up by having an inquest. That made sense from Digger O'Dell's point of view.

So what happened was simply that the Americans finally got the message and said, "Now, look, let's pay a man to be doctor and forensic pathologist and investigator—the whole damn works—and we'll call him Medical Examiner." Along came Quincy.

But don't take Quincy as an example of a typical Medical Examiner. He goes much further than a real M.E. does. He's out in the field all the time and he's always getting slugged or shot at. They don't do that in real life. It's an extreme depiction of the job. Quincy does the job in exactly 60 minutes, with time out for commercials, and as long as people keep writing his scripts he'll discharge his duties. But I kind of like the show. Jack Klugman is a good actor and I've met him. Some of the story lines they've used are very similar to cases I told him about involving the Coroner's office in Vancouver.

Death must be viewed in public far more than in private. That's a concern now in Alberta where they have the Medical Examiners system. The head man has investigators in the field who report back to him. I presume he accepts their reports without viewing the bodies himself. But the trouble with this system is that the M.E. is not tied into the community as closely as are the one hundred and fifty-two Coroners in British Columbia.

We must always remember that death is as much a public concern as birth, marriage or baptism. The Coroner is a part of the community; so was the dead person. So it is incumbent on the Coroner and the witnesses and the jurors within the community to take an interest to obtain all the facts that are available, and then deliver a verdict.

This is absolutely vital if there is to be an answer to that very important question "How come I'm dead?"

# Fire At Sea

In the early morning of Monday, May 24, 1971 the sleek luxury cruise liner *Meteor* limped slowly and sadly into Vancouver harbor from out of the mists of English Bay.

She was assisted by a powerful tug as she passed forlornly under the arching span of the graceful Lions Gate Bridge and headed for Burrard Dry Dock (now Burrard Yarrows Corp.) on the city's North Shore. She listed by 10 degrees to starboard and a vivid red slash of watermark line was visible on her port side, raised out of the water by the list. A plume of smoke trailed thinly from her white funnel.

Standing at the lookout at Prospect Point in Stanley Park, Judge Glen McDonald slipped a coin into the Parks Board viewing binoculars and studied the crippled ship as she passed by.

The sun glinted on *Meteor's* gleaming white hull. The proud red, royal blue and white Norwegian flag at her stern flapped listlessly in the breeze. Only a charred and blackened section of the ship's hull forward of the bridge hinted at the carnage that lay within.

Just two days before, the ship had been cruising serenely in British Columbia's Strait of Georgia on the first of 16 scheduled summer cruises from Vancouver to Alaska.

There were 78 passengers aboard, most of them Americans, who for seven days had enjoyed the elegance, haute cuisine and camaraderie found aboard a European cruise liner. *Meteor* also carried a crew of 91, most Norwegians.

Early in the morning of Saturday, May 22, the 2,856-ton ship was steaming between Texada and Hornby Islands, inbound to Vancouver. The sea was calm, the star-bright sky cloudless, the breeze slight.

The passengers and most of the crew were asleep in their cabins when—at three o'clock and without warning—came the disaster that seafarers fear the most.

Fire at sea.

Some still-awake residents of sleepy Hornby Island, two miles east of *Meteor's* position, had seen the liner's friendly, twinkling lights and had envied the good life being enjoyed by those aboard. When dawn broke they saw the ship stopped dead in the water. A thin grey cloud of wispy smoke lay wreathed around her.

Commercial fishermen had their nets strung three miles away and there were some sports anglers seeking the silver salmon. They, too, looked on with interest.

Initial reports radioed to Vancouver from several ships which sped to the scene said there appeared to be no loss of life; all passengers and crew were apparently safe.

"Everybody's all right as far as we know here," reported an officer aboard the Alaska State ferry *Malaspina,* which was five miles away when *Meteor's* distress call crackled out.

*Malaspina* subsequently took aboard 66 passengers and four crew from *Meteor.*

But it wasn't until the cruise ship was nudged and gentled into the Burrard Dry Dock by a fleet of snub-nosed Cates harbor tugs that the enormity of the tragedy was discovered. Thirty-two bodies lay in the fire-ravaged ruins of the forward section of B deck.

In Stanley Park, Judge McDonald sighed, shook his head and walked slowly to his car. He knew, as he drove through the still-sleeping streets to Skidroad, that another important case had begun.

*     *     *

The first reports we had were very sketchy. All I knew was that she was a Norwegian vessel and was hove to. Then I heard on the radio that all passengers had been transferred by lifeboats to other ships standing by.

We later established that there was a fire in the ship's forward area and there might be loss of life or, at least, injuries. It appeared all passengers were accounted for but there was doubt now about the safety of some of the crew. More news came in: that the ship was stopped dead in the water, with tugs and other vessels surrounding her; that equipment was being put aboard and the crew was fighting the fire with some success.

Eventually, a tug put a line on her and towed her into Vancouver, somewhat under her own power. She was taken to the Burrard Dry Dock and that was when the enormity of the loss of life was discovered, although no doubt it had been anticipated by her Captain, Alf Morner.

The story we had then was that, at about three in the morning, the officer of the watch had seen smoke coming out of the fo'c'sle. Most of the crew's quarters were forward of the bridge on A and B decks. The ship had both watertight and fireproof doors between this area and the passengers' section. The watertight doors were steel and were also fireproof. The fireproof doors were of varnished wood and the lower part of each door had a crash panel which could be quickly broken through in an emergency.

As officers of the Coroner's Court, our job was to go to the dry dock and remove the remains of whoever we found. I took two technicians, Bart Bastien and Ian Marshall. We went aboard and down into A and B decks. It was early on the Monday morning.

What we found was stunning, shocking. It was much worse than we had feared. The enormity of the disaster was immediately obvious to anyone who had seen fire at sea and, as a navy man, I was no stranger to it. We had had absolutely no idea we would have thirty-two fatalities.

Some crew had been transferred to rescue ships, many suffering smoke inhalation. Nor had we known that some of the crew members were women.

Why did the Coroner of the City of Vancouver have jurisdiction to inquire into the deaths of 32 people who were not Canadian citizens and who had died aboard a ship of Norwegian registry sailing, technically, in international waters? The matter properly would come under the jurisdiction of the International Court in The Hague. It was a complex situation, from a legal standpoint.

But again, I went to the Attorney General and said, "Look, we have deceased on a foreign ship. Do you want me to handle it?" In consultation with the Norwegian Consul, the AG said yes. This decision had the consent of the owners, through their Vancouver agents.

There was no place for the ship to go except Vancouver. She had been listing as much as 20 degrees to starboard because of the tons of water poured in by her pumps. It was a tricky situation because, with that much free surface water in her, she might have capsized at any time.

The dockyard workers had cut a big hole in one side so we could climb in and clear some of the debris out. This debris was everywhere in the forward area and yet, curiously, in some of the cabins, particularly in the girls' rooms, there were still clothes hanging up all neat and tidy—dresses, skirts, blouses. They were wet; they hadn't been burned.

And there were the bodies. First thing we did was photograph every position we found. The bodies were piled here, there and everywhere, in the hallways and the cabins. In one case, we found the brother of a surviving member with his head and one arm stuck through a porthole. The port was too small for the rest of the body to go through.

Clearly, a lot of the people had died from carbon monoxide, the gas having sucked the air out of the cabins and hallways. Blood samples we took showed that 1.28 percent carbon monoxide had been in the air.

And I knew from long experience just what carbon monoxide in the air can do. This amount meant that just three lungfulls, three successive breaths, would be fatal. A matter of seconds and it was all over.

What we had was a mixture of what appeared to be 32 bodies—some very badly burned, some in fact reduced to charcoal fragments, and others, oddly enough, we were able to pick up and remove completely intact. In one instance a man had pulled on one sock and was obviously halfway through pulling the other one on when he had collapsed. He looked quite normal, as if he had just suddenly keeled over and died of a heart seizure.

What had happened was that the ship's lookout at the bow had seen the smoke early that morning and rushed down to see what he could do. He found the area full of smoke, went back up on deck and then dashed down to the engine room to tell the engineer to put water to the pumps on deck so he could tackle the flames. "Water on deck" is a standard emergency order to a ship's engine room crew.

Then, struggling as far as he could on B deck, he had banged on the cabin doors as he went. Some of the crew came into the passageway. But by this time the officer of the watch had performed his routine closing of the fire doors throughout the ship. This meant that the crew members were not able to go forward to escape. So they tried to run aft to the passengers' quarters.

But by this time these fire doors were closed too. When a person suffers from a loss of oxygen he becomes very confused. So, obviously, there was a lot of panic that morning. No one, although the crew had been told how to break the crash panels of the fire doors, apparently had thought to do it. Nobody was able to take command and lead the others to safety—or, at least, to some chance of safety. We found eight bodies at the fire doors, within a few feet of safety.

We had 32 bodies—some intact, some in bits and pieces—and we were now faced with the task of identification. I knew it was going to be a hell of a job: one, because of the language problem, and two, because not all crew members were Norwegian. Some were Mexican.

When we had finished aboard ship, the bodies were taken to the morgue and we began this slow process of identification, starting with the badly-burned corpses. In some cases we had identification of at least a kind by listing the cabin numbers where the bodies were found. That was a start—as long, that is, as people had been in their own cabins and not bunking in with others.

The Norwegian and Mexican Consuls had been given all the passports, which had been kept in the ship's safe, by Captain Morner. From these we were able to obtain ages and sexes. In some cases we were able to match the passport pictures with our own photos. All bodies were eventually positively identified.

On the legal front, the already complex situation of the *Meteor* had by now become even more complex. The Provincial Fire Marshal's Office was now involved and the Norwegian government had brought in a seven-member committee from its Justice Department, including the Chief of Police of Oslo, a Judge and the Fire Chief of the city of Stavanger. There was also a serious suspicion that the fire could have been arson so the Royal Canadian Mounted Police were by this time asking a lot of hard and searching questions.

We hadn't taken over jurisdiction in a true legal sense, but for practical reasons the Norwegians were glad to accept any and all assistance they could get, being faced with the sad task of having to go back to Norway and explain how one of their cruise ships could have caught fire with the loss of 32 people of different nationalities. So the cooperation was excellent all the way.

*　*　*

"I can only regret the deaths of 32 of you. I want to thank one and all of you. It shouldn't be in circumstances like this."

Captain Alf Morner, master of the stricken cruise liner, spoke the sad words of tribute at a memorial service in Vancouver for the dead crew members. The service was held just three days after the fire. Among the 200 mourners were many of the victims' shipmates and the passengers who had been taken off safely.

Investigations were continuing by the RCMP and the special government committee flown from Norway to Vancouver, and Vancouver Homicide Squad detectives were helping where they could. Tor Virding, the Norwegian Vice-Consul in Chicago, had flown in to supervise the disposition of the bodies. The *Meteor* lay at the Burrard Dry Dock amid tight security.

The stage was now set for the inquest which opened in the Vancouver Coroner's Court on Wednesday, May 26, 1971, Judge Glen McDonald presiding.

In the drama that unfolded over the next weeks there were stories of heroism, of panic, of drinking parties and burning cigarettes, of flaming bodies, of locked doors, of doors that opened the wrong way, of a possibly faulty fire alarm system, and of possible arson set by a jealous lover.

-Captain John Boden, Canadian pilot aboard the *Meteor,* on the behavior of the surviving crew and crew members of two Canadian Coast Guard vessels on the scene:

"My comments could not be too high. It was through their efforts that the ship was saved. At no time was there a voice raised, or panic, or shouting, or running. Everything was done methodically and in a businesslike way."

-Captain Alf Morner of the *Meteor,* on being told by the ship's doctor that some of the men and women dragged from the blazing crew's quarters were dead:

"I couldn't believe it. . .when I saw them it looked to me like they were asleep."

-First Officer Arne Follnes of the *Meteor* testified that he had first tried the general fire alarm switch on the bridge and then the crew alarm "but nothing happened."

-Willy Larsen, electrician aboard the *Meteor:* The ship's fire alarm system was in perfect working order when he checked it as part of his daily rounds on the day before the fire.

-Deckhand Jose Gutierrez, speaking through an interpreter, told the jury he distinctly heard the fire alarm while racing to get the pumps switched on. "I'm positive it rang, but I can't remember for how long." Gutierrez was the forward lookout who had sounded the first vocal alarm and had run along the passageway, banging on cabin doors and shouting.

And, tearfully, he told the hushed courtroom how he had watched helplessly as his brother, Marco, burned to death in the window of the cabin they shared: "I saw my brother in the window, burning. . .his arm and head were out of the window."

-Captain Morner: the ship's fire alarm was working perfectly a week before the fire and had been successfully tested on May 15 during a lifeboat drill.

-Second Engineer John Clark of the *Meteor:* "I think somebody left a cigarette burning on a side table in a cabin or on a bunk on the lower crew deck. . .setting fire to a piece of paper or some clothing. . .the woodwork aboard the *Meteor* is varnished and, if it's heated up, it will form gas that will lie along the ceiling. If flame hits the gas it will ignite, not only there, but anywhere there is gas. . ."

-Stewardess Esther Roska of the *Meteor:* wooden doors on each side of the crew's B deck quarters were locked every night to prevent the crew from entering the passengers' quarters and this had blocked the escape route during the fire. The doors could be opened only by a key from the passengers' side or by kicking in the crash panels.

"When we were standing in the cabin watching the fire outside, we saw wet spots running down the walls of the corridor. . .they appeared to be spots of water running down. . .it. . .perhaps someone had thrown something on the wall and the fire was jumping to the spots."

-Night Stewardess Carol Beale of the *Meteor,* on seeing Miss Roska running out of the ship's forward section: "She was burned and hysterical. . .she was screaming, 'There's a fire! They're all dying down there!' "

-Bosun Quinton Baiardi of the *Meteor:* "The design of the (fire) door is wrong and the Captain says it is wrong, too. . .it swings the wrong way. . .people were streaming in—boys and girls together—pushing, pushing, pushing, but nobody thought to pull it. . .they had been told about the crash panel but maybe they panicked and didn't think to break it."

Solemnly, Judge McDonald read into the record the pathologist's report on the cause of death of ten of the crew. Four had died of asphyxiation and six from carbon monoxide poisoning; one had a blood alcohol reading of .01 and another a reading of .21.

*   *   *

There were two aspects to that case which really intrigued me, and they were both fully explored at the inquest. One was that the system of fire alarms aboard the ship was wired in series much the same as the old Christmas tree lights we used to have where if one bulb went out, they all went out.

The ship's chief electrician, Mr. Larsen, explained that if the wires in the alarm system were burned through or an alarm bell was burned out, thereby causing a ground, the whole system would be kaput. This was probably why no alarm was heard on the bridge or anywhere else when the First Officer tried to sound the general alarm. The fire had destroyed one circuit and thereby destroyed all circuits. Nothing happened, even though the deckhand swore he heard an alarm.

And, as it turned out, the jury did recommend that henceforth every fire alarm system aboard ship should be on a separate circuit so if fire stops one bell from going off, it won't stop the others.

The other thing that fascinated me was the possibility that the fire might have been set by an arsonist. This was why I purposely asked a lot of questions about a possible lover's quarrel among crew members which may have triggered such an act. The stewardess, Miss Roska, testified she had seen some sort of fluid on the outside of her cabin door and on the wall of the corridor. She said the flames were jumping from one drop of the fluid to another.

One would assume that this must have been an accelerant, or turpentine or gasoline which had been thrown on the walls and doors. There was also an argument put forward—or a suggestion, at least— that one of the dead crew members had been very fond of one of the Norwegian stewardesses.

So, in court, I asked Captain Morner and the ship's doctor if there had been any jealousy between one crew member and another—if one of the girls had maybe jilted a boyfriend or lover, causing him to seek violent revenge.

The doctor, John Crawford, acknowledged that some close relationships existed among the crew when I asked him if crew members indulged in each other's bunks. But he said he had seen no sign of violent jealousies. It was that damn statement about the little drops of fluid and the flames jumping from one to another which really concerned and intrigued me. I was very, very curious.

The opinion of the Norwegian investigators was that the fire was caused by a cigarette in the cabin of the chief baker, Ludwig Huse. Cabin 29 on B deck. It was also of great interest that his blood alcohol level was .21 percent, considerably higher than the legal level of impairment in Canada of .08. Further, Huse was a heavy smoker and, indeed, in the ashtray in his cabin we had found 16 cigarette butts.

So, circumstantial evidence pointed to a dropped cigarette as a possible cause of the fire which, aided by the varnished woodwork, spread rapidly and with ferocious intensity. Yet the baker's body was in fairly good shape when we found it. He had died from carbon monoxide poisoning associated with alcohol in his system. We know that alcohol inhibits the blood from obtaining oxygen when carbon monoxide is around and even accelerates the gas going into the blood.

Then our own Fire Marshal's report came in. The experts had gone into things further and found that the sides of the passageway on B deck had seven or eight coats of varnish spread over a very dry plywood, and that any little flame would have caused the varnish to form droplets—as if the gas inside, or under the varnish, was blowing up little bubbles of varnish. This was what the stewardess had seen. They could now be explained as *not* being caused by something thrown against the wall. The cause of the fire seemed more and more like plain old careless cigarette smoking in bed. I began to feel more satisfied in my mind.

I was also concerned that the shipowners had overlooked a lesson learned by us in Canada as a result of the tragic fire aboard the Great Lakes cruise ship *Noronic* in the Toronto harbor many years ago. After that disaster, the Canada Shipping Act was changed and, amongst other requirements, it now ordered that any bulkhead should be able to withstand a temperature of at least 5,000 degrees Fahrenheit, and that all ships must be equipped with fire extinguishers of a water-spray type that activate automatically when a certain temperature is reached. In other words, an automatic sprinkler system. As a matter of fact, many of Canada's smaller coastal ships went out of business after the *Noronic* fire because the owners just couldn't afford to put in sprinkler systems and bulkheads to comply with the new regulations.

The owners of the *Meteor* had complied with every requirement of the United States Coast Guard, as of the November before the fire. But she was of Norwegian registry and entered Canadian waters only to embark and disembark passengers.

So there was still an international legal question mark left behind when the tragic episode was over—whether or not this procedure was correct. But, throughout the investigation and inquest, I felt enormous empathy and sympathy for Captain Morner and his crew. As a mariner myself, I knew well the terrible ordeal the Master, in particular, had been through.

*    *    *

The inquest jury—having listened to many hours of testimony from more than twenty witnesses, and having even at one stage donned overalls and rubber boots to tramp through the burned-out crew's quarters of the *Meteor*—deliberated for only 40 minutes to reach its decision.

On July 7, 1971 six weeks after the terrible fire at sea, it ruled that the deaths of the 32 crew members were accidental.

Before announcing their verdict, the jurors had heard a fire inspector testify that the fire had probably been started by a cigarette dropped by a drunken crew member.

Provincial Fire Marshal's Office Inspector Ron Pollard told them, in two hours of testimony illustrated with slides and exhibits, that the fire had started in Cabin 29 on B deck, occupied by ship's baker Ludwig Huse.

"We feel in our minds, and this is corroborated by the physical facts, that the fire did originate in Cabin 29 and in the top bunk," Pollard said.

". . .how the fire went up to the ceiling is hard to say. . .it could have been pinups, a calendar, clothing or curtains. Any of these things could have spread the flames to the ceiling. . .

". . .the area filled so quickly with carbon monoxide gas because it isn't a very big area. We're not talking about minutes, we're talking about seconds between the time the fire broke through the ceiling and spread through the rest of the ship. . .panic and the failure of the alarm system also contributed to the deaths. . ."

And the jury recommended strongly in the areas which had severely troubled Judge McDonald during the investigation and inquest.

It urged that automatic sprinklers be made mandatory in all ships' accomodation, that all materials used in the interior construction of a ship be fireproof and that all vessels sailing in Canadian waters should adhere to the safety standards of this country.

In October of 1971 it was announced that the cruise ship *Meteor,* still lying idle at Burrard Dry Dock, had been sold to Greek buyers. She sailed for Europe at the end of that month to start a new life cruising the sun-sparkled waters of the Aegean Sea between the Greek islands. The final chapter in Judge Glen McDonald's association with the ill-starred *Meteor* had been written.

\*    \*    \*

An inquest will be held Oct. 27 into the deaths of three men in a fire and explosions at the Burrard Terminals grain elevator on Oct. 3. . .Federal Labor Minister John Munro said that a full-fledged inquiry commission would be appointed to look into safety in all grain terminal elevators.

News Item, October 16, 1975

\*    \*    \*

On that Friday morning in autumn, when gigantic clouds of ash-laden smoke billowed high over Vancouver's harbor, the massive explosion had ripped apart a huge grain-handling tower on the North Vancouver waterfront, setting off a multi-alarm fire that was battled on land and sea by firemen from three municipalities, including the City of Vancouver.

Three men died in the blast and the flames and two more died of severe burns six weeks later. Sixteen workers were injured, several seriously. Seldom-used disaster plans were swung swiftly into effect at both Lions Gate Hospital in North Vancouver and the Vancouver General, across the harbor.

From the window of his office in Skidroad, Judge Glen McDonald saw the swirling, acrid clouds of black and grey smoke wafting up and over the city. By monitoring radio news reports, he knew there would be fatalities and, subsequently, an inquest.

Just four-and-a-half years after the fire-at-sea disaster of the cruise ship *Meteor,* another of the Coroner's worst fears had been realized. Fire on the waterfront.

*     *     *

This had been a major concern of the Vancouver Fire Department, and those of surrounding municipalities, since Day One. It was a major concern of mine, too, and it still is today.

The problem was never made easier because of the endless arguments as to whether the Vancouver City fireboat could or would work to save endangered properties other than those on the shoreline of the city itself—shoreline properties of neighboring municipalities such as North and West Vancouver, across the harbor. But I'll look at that later.

The volatile dust in a grain elevator is a notorious source of explosions. In this dreadful North Vancouver blast in '75 the cause was overheated material on a conveyor belt. The combination of that and the explosive grain dust killed three people. It was a bad and a sad day on the waterfront. The Vancouver fireboat was able to attend in this case but the explosion was so great that the fire hydrants on shore were ruptured and the elevator totally destroyed.

Also, the terminal had been built in the days before automatic sprinkler systems were required, as they are now. The inquest established to the satisfaction of all parties that the fire could have been prevented had more maintenance been done on the top end of the conveyor belt, where the overheating had occurred. This overheating was apparently caused because a small tap, which had been pouring water on the belt to keep it cool, had stopped working. And the investigations into the fire proved once again that there's nothing you can do with a waterfront fire unless you have complete control right from the beginning. That's why the jurisdiction of the fireboat is vital.

At the government inquiry, one boss said that upgrades were made only for better efficiency and production at the suggestion of regulatory authorities. In other words, not for any considerations of safety. Bosses will blandly say that for years there were no accidents at a particular elevator; that there were such things as warning lights and horns activated in an emergency. But this boss admitted he hadn't heard the horn blow in the four years he worked at the plant. So, who could ever know if it was working? It's like saying, "Well, this gun can't have a bullet in it because I haven't heard it fire for four years!"

* * *

Following a two-day inquest into the deaths of three men in the Burrard Terminals accident, the Coroner's jury said there was a need for better housekeeping at the plant and that the explosion occurred because there was a backup in the conveying of grain through the elevator system, causing a jamming of No. 1 elevator leg.

The verdict said: "The top pulley did not stop rotating and the resultant friction heat built up causing the (conveyor belt) material to ignite in the confined area of the leg, resulting in an explosion...We the jury conclude that these deaths were unnatural and classify them as accidental."

The jury recommended:

-That fire drills involving personnel of grain elevators be held periodically.

-That escape routes be defined and used in the event of a fire.

-That safeguards be installed on all legs (elevating machinery) and conveyor belts that would automatically stop the system in the event of any jamming.

-That all alarm systems have a distinctive warning device to indicate any particular area that may be hit by trouble.

-That elevator dust be kept to a minimum by better housekeeping.

And the jury recommended that the Vancouver City Fireboat be automatically dispatched to any waterfront fire within the limits of Vancouver Harbor, which borders on the North Vancouver shoreline as well as the city proper.

* * *

I remember a notorious case years ago involving a Scandinavian freighter outbound from Vancouver. She had passed under the Lions Gate Bridge into English Bay and was off West Vancouver when there was an explosion in the engine room that killed an engineer. We held an inquest and the main point made by the jury's recommendations was that a fireboat should be made available to all vessels using the harbor and to municipalities *surrounding* the City of Vancouver.

I felt this was so damned important that I saved the recommendation in a special file I kept on safety in our harbor, the busiest seaport on the whole Pacific coast. I'd show the file to jurors whenever we had an inquest as a result of a waterfront accident. And over many years the main recommendation of juries was always that the fireboat should be available for the protection of all vessels and should be used wherever it's able to navigate.

In the case of that Scandinavian ship, there was an absolute refusal by the Vancouver Fire Chief and the Mayor to send the boat outside the limits of the Port of Vancouver. Their reasons were, of course, both political and economic. They felt if they did send the boat outside these limits and then there was another fire inside the port area, the taxpayers who paid for the boat wouldn't get the benefit of it. That's still the situation today. No surrounding municipality—North Vancouver, West Vancouver, Burnaby or Port Moody—has, as yet, agreed to pay a share of the boat's operation.

Then there are those bloody gasoline barges sitting in the middle of Coal Harbor, a hundred yards from the downtown core. These are for fueling pleasure craft and fishing boats. In January of 1974, there was an explosion aboard the Home Oil barge when a 28-foot pleasure boat was refueling alongside it. Three men, the barge attendant, the boat owner and a passenger, were killed in the explosion and fire. The barge, incidentally has never been replaced.

It was the old story of gasoline and oxygen mixing in the hull of the ship. Fortunately, the fireboat is tied up just four or five cables from these fuel barges and is manned 24 hours a day. In this case the crew did a very efficient job of putting the fire out and preventing it from spreading to the other barges and nearby marinas. But, had there been the usual westerly prevailing winds that afternoon, fanning the flames and ashes, there could well have been a major disaster. But for the intervention of that fireboat, it could have been devastating. The enormity of that kind of a blaze is inestimable.

I know of no other seaport on either the west or east coast of North America that allows gas and diesel fuel barges to park smack in the centre of the Goddamn harbor. Vancouver has tanks and barrels of liquid dynamite ready and primed to explode and nobody gives a damn. When you consider the number of boats taking on fuel at these barges, you're just asking for trouble.

It's interesting that Home Oil chose not to put its barge back. Maybe some executive finally realized it's like keeping a can full of gas alongside the fireplace in your living room. Incidentally, it was a coincidence that, just a few days before the barge exploded, some pranksters had put a charge in the Nine O'Clock Gun in Stanley Park and fired a rock through the big letter O in the Home Oil sign. It was funny at the time. But it wasn't long until the barge was blown up by the real thing. That wasn't funny.

We found at the inquest that the fire department had for years been trying to have these gas barges kicked out of the harbor. And, again, I must cite that mother-in-law of ours, the British North America Act, which makes marine matters Ottawa's concern. As a consequence, the City of Vancouver can do nothing to order these floating time bombs removed.

There's also the matter of the railway cars rolling through the downtown Vancouver waterfront near one of the most densely populated residential areas in all of North America. The whole of the West End could go sky-high any day. Frankly, we should all be down on our knees once a day thanking God it hasn't happened yet. So far, this transporting of highly explosive and toxic fuels has gone along safely. But for how much longer? How many near-misses have there been that we don't know about?

Again, this is a federal government matter. It's not the province's concern and it's not Vancouver's concern. Well, I don't know of any death certificate issued yet that says the deceased person was a Canadian from Ottawa or a British Columbian from Victoria or a Vancouverite from Vancouver. They're plain dead is what they are. And needlessly dead.

This lack of control and precaution has never been met head-on by anyone in these three levels of government. They all slough off the responsibilities. Nothing is ever done. It's an absolute bloody miracle that Vancouver has somehow got by without a truly major waterfront disaster since the ship *Greenhill Park* exploded in the harbor in 1945. Many, many inquest juries have made many good, sound and sensible recommendations about the dangers, but maybe we'll have to wait until a few hundred people are blown to bits all at once before we get some action.

There's no question in my mind that the situation will become steadily more and more serious. This eternal hassle about jurisdiction is one we've faced ever since Pierre Berton built the C.P.R. railroad across Canada. When the bureaucrats at the three levels hold a meeting, they go back to their respective bureaucratic offices and come to their respective conclusions that it isn't their respective concern. It's the other guy's concern so let him worry about it.

That North Shore grain elevator accident was a typical example of this sort of fumbling, bungling bureaucracy, because grain elevators come under federal jurisdiction. A bigger and more modern elevator has been built on the site now but it still doesn't comply with the initial requirement that the whole structure be equipped with a sprinkler system.

* * *

In June of 1971 one of Judge McDonald's inquest juries was told that longshoremen on the Vancouver waterfront were "working in a

173

no-man's land when it comes to safety "because of bureaucratic red tape and jurisdictional confusion.

Joe Pennell, chairman of the longshoremen's union safety committee, testifying at an inquest into the death of a worker who fell from a ship and drowned, said the federal government's labor and transport departments and the provincial government's Workers' Compensation Board are all involved in waterfront safety.

"The WCB is being pushed from the waterfront by the Department of Labor which has only three safety inspectors in the whole of British Columbia," he said. "The Department of Labor is thinking along terms that there shouldn't be any accidents and we can't go to the WCB, which has good safety regulations. There is jurisdictional overlapping and this should be changed."

*　*　*

Under the Workers' Compensation Act, we find a simple situation in which WCB officers sit down once a month with employees and employers and others concerned with matters of safety. They have a meeting. And at that meeting all are invited to comment on the everyday things they see on the job and recommend or suggest what they think could be done in the area of safety improvement.

But no way does the WCB have jurisdiction in a case of federal responsibility and there is no such thing as a federally-based workers' compensation board with jurisdiction in areas like grain elevators or the waterfront in general. The anomaly gets even worse. If somebody is killed in an accident, the WCB pays the widow or other next-of-kin, but it has no say about the safety of a grain elevator or the docks or on a ship where an accident has occurred—no control over the safety of the people who work in these areas.

Inquest jurors get frustrated when they learn this. And many jurors worked on the waterfront themselves. They were experts in their fields and over the years made many good recommendations. But they had to go back next day and work under exactly the same conditions they had heard the evidence about.

My simple suggestion—one I've made on many occasions—is that the WCB should take jurisdiction over the waterfront. Nobody else is doing anything to improve safety, that's for damn sure. They might pretend they do, but they don't. So get the WCB beefed up with more inspectors, including marine inspectors, and send these guys out to regularly check safety equipment and the rest of it.

But, oh no. The feds don't want to lose their jurisdiction. I don't really care who is in charge, as long as those people rigidly enforce the regulations and listen to and act on sensible recommendations such as those of inquest juries. But they don't give a tinker's cuss.

It's disgraceful that lives on the waterfront are endangered by politics. The National Harbors Board Police patrol the waterfront. But there's also the Canadian Pacific and Canadian National Police and city police. Here's another collision of jurisdiction when there's crime on the docks. Who's in charge? That dispute has never been really resolved. The city cops quite rightly claim the city is their jurisdiction. But who knows?

(Vancouver harbor is now run by the federally-owned Port of Vancouver Corp., a subsidiary of Canada Ports Corp., which was set up in 1983 as successor to the National Harbors Board. The NHB police force is now called Ports Canada Police.)

I've always taken the position that waters everywhere are international and should fall under international laws such as the International Rules For Prevention Of Collision At Sea which apply to all ships regardless of port of registry or flag.

Here's another example of the jurisdictional squabble. The Vancouver Police used to have scuba divers who searched the harbor for bodies. They pulled out and the Fire Department took the job over. They, of course, were then trespassing on the jurisdiction of the feds and the old NHB which had no hesitation in looking after, not only the docks of Vancouver's Burrard Inlet, but as far down the coast as Roberts Bank—the big coal dock—and the 49th Parallel. They claimed jurisdiction.

So I ask the question: what right of enforcement is being used? Do they have any legal right? They've taken things over and say, "Hey, this is ours—keep out!" All these areas have their own police forces so the whole mess bogs down in yet another mire of a mixture of authority. The bureaucrats have another meeting and then they're right back where they started.

That's the frustrating part of Vancouver. God gave us a beautiful city but, unfortunately, He put people in charge of it.

# I Was Born An Actor

Most people view the Coroner's job as sinister work. They lump the occupation in with those of the pathologist, the undertaker, the embalmer and the gravedigger. Like these practitioners, the Coroner comes to public attention only after a death has occurred. People regard him as a dread, black-gowned symbol of death, a forbidding Grim Reaper's assistant whose duty it is to preside over the nasty business of death.

Usually, nobody likes to think about death. The very word is to be avoided, tucked tidily away in a remote recess of the mind and conveniently forgotten. It is far better, also, to avoid as much as one is able doing business with the pathologist, the undertaker, the embalmer, the gravedigger and the Coroner.

Judge Glen McDonald of the Vancouver Coroner's Court adopted a totally different philosophy from the first day he presided as Deputy Coroner in the cramped Skidroad courtroom in late 1953. The Coroner, he decided, is the Ombudsman of the Dead. His role should always be positive, never negative. His job is to study the cause of death in order to protect the living. The Deputy Coroner developed a unique method of getting this point across to the public.

At the end of every inquest, when he had completed his summing-up and instructions to the jury, Judge McDonald would lean down from the bench and say:

"We have been inquiring to the best of our abilities into the circumstances of someone's death. That person cannot, of course, be with us today in this courtroom. But if he, or she, could be present he would surely want to ask of us one very simple and important question,

'How come I'm dead?' Now, ladies and gentlemen of the jury, when you retire to consider your verdict, I want you to put yourselves in the position of that unfortunate person. Ask that one simple question of yourselves. If you can find an answer, maybe we can prevent a needless death in the future."

* * *

The public has always had a very negative attitude toward the Coroner's Court—what it's there for, what its job is. Well, it sure as hell isn't there to provide happiness or light entertainment. It has a serious job to do in society. It occurred to me at the start that there was a positive side to this business of death. I tried to emphasize that positive side insofar as the philosophical working of the court was concerned— to show that a death *can* be avoided in the future by studying the cause of one before us. I always stressed the positive role.

The study of a death involves a thorough investigation of such factors as time, place and distance in order to better answer the question of when, where and by what means did a person die. The next-of-kin always want to know these answers. And, almost without exception, the next-of-kin also want to make sure that a similar death does not befall somebody else.

Investigation of a death always, in my mind, takes a triangular pattern. One phase is done by the investigating officers, be they RCMP or another police force; two, by the pathologist; three, by the toxicologist. The Coroner receives their reports and decides whether to hold an inquest or an inquiry. This is the positive side in trying to avoid a similar death in the future.

Sometimes it gets very complicated. Just as the three investigatory levels inevitably lead into the Coroner, he also has the authority to order them done again—a re-testing of the toxicology, a pathology re-examination, a re-investigation of what happened at the death scene. Any Coroner who thinks he's running in a popularity contest is dead wrong. He's not popular with any of the investigators and he's not popular with the next-of-kin and their lawyers. But the Coroner's forum—his court—is open to all the public and must always be open to that public.

The people are entitled to make comments, draw their own conclusions, make their own investigations and, indeed, to bring hearsay and hearsay upon hearsay into the courtroom under oath, but always subject to the caution of: "Well, we'll take that but let's try to get the person who actually saw it or did it or knows something about it." the It's Coroner who decides the admissibility of evidence. Then there's another forum, made available by the Crown counsel who may lay a criminal charge as a result of a death. And there's yet another forum called the provincial Attorney General's Office which may order still more investigation of a death. And if such inquiry finds new evidence, then, certainly, further investigation is done, usually by a formal device known as a Judicial Inquiry. The Coroner's Court is not a closure. Rather, it's an Open Sesame court, a public forum where everything should come out in the first instance or, if that can't be done, after a suitable adjournment.

The inquest is usually held a week, two weeks, perhaps a month after the body has been buried or cremated and the memorial service held. The family is still learning to live with the hard fact that there's an empty bed in the home, a pair of lonely carpet slippers by the fireside, a book left open but unread. Little things like that. They have to get used to the fact that there's a vacant place at the dinner table, a son or a son-in-law or a daughter or a grandchild who is no longer there. A widow is slowly learning to realize that her husband will no longer come home from work. A grieving child cannot yet understand why father or mother or brother or sister is no longer around the house. These are haunting experiences. Those left behind are perfectly entitled to come to us and say, "We want to see *everything* you have." And if in everything we have there is something to give comfort and understanding and knowledge, some glimmer of light to illumine the darkness of the tunnel of grief, then it is our duty to help as much as we can. Revelation and discovery can often ease the troubled mind.

The Coroner is never really finished with an inquest. He can reopen it at any time or, if he finds himself dissatisfied with an inquiry, he can turn it into an inquest. If somebody suddenly comes forward with pertinent new information or evidence, if new facts come to light, if a previously missing witness appears, the Coroner's sworn duty is to take up the case again. He has absolutely no choice but to discharge his duty to the full awareness and satisfaction of the public. The truth will out. The truth must out!

The Coroner must also be a person who cares deeply about life, who respects its dignity and values it as the most priceless possession of all. Death is life; life is death. He must have the wisdom and the judgment to use properly the tools and the authority that are vested in him. And he has a lot of authority under the Coroners Act: the power to subpoena jurors and witnesses, the power to order a grave opened and a body exhumed, the power to subpoena *des tucum*—to seize papers and documents from hospitals, doctors' offices, pharmacies.

The Coroner must also work wherever and whenever his duty bids him to. Over twenty-six years I worked in graveyards, on the top of a mountain, on Indian reservations, aboard wrecked ships, at airplane crash sites, in hospital wards, in penitentiaries and at murder scenes. My home number was always listed in the telephone book and I was available twenty-four hours a day, seven days a week. I wanted it that way. It was the only way to go if the job was to be done right. I also had a marine radio-telephone aboard my cabin cruiser so I could be contacted on weekends. That number was listed in the book, too. Many a leisurely salmon fishing trip was ruined by the ringing of that damn thing!

On Saturdays and Sundays, even if I was out on the boat with friends, I'd phone the duty technician at the morgue at eleven in the morning to find out what had come in the night before. I guess that sounds a bit hard and cold-blooded, like asking if the dry-cleaning had come back or if the food for the party had been delivered. But it's a fact. We'd run through what we had and I'd find out when the pathologist had scheduled the autopsies, knowing that the toxicology likely wouldn't be done until Monday morning. But if there was a case with a serious suggestion of foul play, we'd get a toxicologist in right away. It is a fundamental principle of law that justice delayed is justice denied.

I've remarked that a Coroner's duty is to warn the populace of any pestilence in the land. That's terminology from the Middle Ages, of course. By pestilence I mean any form of danger. And with it we must also consider the matters of responsibility and guilt. One of the greatest philosophers of our time, to my mind, was the late Marshall McLuhan, the writer and communications guru at the University of Toronto. McLuhan said we have become a perhaps too permissive society and that perhaps we are too quickly and easily prepared to excuse, or to accomodate responsibility or guilt. We suggest too often that causes and circumstances other than our own—such as Acts of God—have occurred to cause a tragedy. A matter of convenience? A cleansing, a ridding of bothersome conscience?

"We have lost all of our confidence in our right to assign guilt," McLuhan wrote. I often quoted that to jurors when it came time for them to reach a verdict. How can the best friend of the deceased, who was driving the car; how can the best friend of the deceased, who was steering the motor boat; how can the best friend of the deceased who was smoking in the bedroom; how can he or she honestly not be accused or be found without some degree of negligence as to what happened?

"If you find a person or persons to blame, you may name that person," I often advised juries. I never used the words *negligent* or *negligence* because these have legal connotations in the courts implying guilt. But the jurors, in their permissive approach, sometimes couldn't bring themselves to attach blame. They just felt a person had, after all, lost his best friend or a son or a daughter, wife or husband. They thought this was suffering and punishment enough. But a Coroner's jury is not required to consider who suffers; it is required to find out the simple facts of four simple questions: when, where, why and by what means?

The whole strength of the inquest procedure—and of its continuing process—is the fact that an inquisition, with witnesses under oath, is held within a *reasonable* time of death. This is most important.

Testimony is perpetuated against the future, against possible new developments. Witnesses are entitled to look back on what they said years before—should it be a continuing matter—and say, "Yes, if I said that then, it's correct. That's right. Yes, it was twenty feet away, the car was going a lot faster than it should have been." Or they can say maybe they were mistaken. All these matters are kept on record in the Attorney General's office and are available to all members of the public on request.

But we must never lose sight of the most important of all factors— the human element. The Coroner is human, the witnesses are human, the next-of-kin are human, the investigating officers are human, the deceased was human. So the entire spectrum of human emotion comes out at an inquest: grief, conscience, guilt and—but not often—humor. The Coroner must be someone who understands and appreciates all of these things. He must have tolerance and patience. He must have both sympathy and empathy.

There are breakdowns, collapses in the witness box and in the view room. This is routine. There are adjournments, legal arguments, outbursts of anger, accusations, moments of grief and sorrow. All these elements are present. But the duties of the court must always be discharged. I'm not saying within an hour or two after a death but as soon as possible. The sooner the better, for everyone.

*  *  *

Judge Glen McDonald dealt with death every day. It was his job. He woke up to it, drove across the Lions Gate Bridge with it, walked into his office with it and met it head-on in the autopsy room, the view room and his courtroom. Then he took it home with him at night. Files and records and papers in a bulky briefcase. All about death.

*  *  *

People have often asked me about this daily diet of death. How did I handle it? Did I find it depressing and debilitating? Did I become hardened and unfeeling? Did it make me bitter? Cynical? Was I a sort of robot sitting on the bench listening to nothing more than a litany of dry facts and figures, forgetting that life, as well as death, was ever present in my courtroom? Did names become mere numbers? Were human lives and individual personalities no more than statistics? Was I able to stay aloof and detached or did I become emotionally involved?

It was, I suppose, a complex and curious mix of emotion and self-discipline, running a court by the rules, trying to be fair but always trying to be sympathetic and understanding. The fact of death certainly wasn't unknown to me when I started as Deputy Coroner. I had two years and eight months aboard the armed merchant cruiser *HMCS Prince Robert* in the war and we had many deaths. Death was not an unknown visitor. Then, when I was serving on the aircraft carrier *HMS*

*Nabob* we had twenty-three bodies below decks after we were torpedoed off Scapa Flow. I was navigating officer.

We brought the ship back to the Scottish port of Rosyth. The local undertakers adamantly refused to go below and take the bodies out. So I took over and went down with a handy-billy—a block and tackle—and pulled up the arms and the legs and the torsos of the crew members who had by this time been underwater for about three months. It wasn't a pleasant job. But we delivered all the bodies, and bits and pieces of bodies, up on deck and the undertakers took them away. I didn't really blame them for not wanting to climb up and down ladders into the bottom of an aircraft carrier. I wasn't that keen on doing it myself but it was a job that had to be done. So, death was no stranger to me.

As for the Coroner's job, I'll put it this way: some days were clean ashtrays and some were dirty ashtrays. When I came home from the office my wife would ask me if it had been a clean ashtray day or a dirty ashtray day. For me, the dirtiest ashtrays were the deaths of youngsters—three, four, five-year-olds knocked down in traffic, who had probably darted into the street from between parked cars, perhaps chasing an errant tennis or soccer ball. It was always the same old sad story. The kid wasn't looking, the driver had no chance to stop in time and there we were doing an autopsy and holding an inquest into a youngster who never even had a chance at life.

Not only that. Here were a father and a mother who would never know their child again. Or, just as sad, here was a father left with a youngster without a mother. Or a mother with a youngster who would never see his father again. These were the dirty ashtrays. The older citizens, people in their 70s, 80s, 90s—well, I always figured they had probably led pretty full lives and had had a good kick at the cat. These were the clean ashtrays.

Death is the great equalizer, the leveler, the one common denominator in all our lives. I always used the positive approach and so did my staff. We also used the media as much as we could because it was obvious how they could help us in that same positive way. I used the media more than any Coroner in North America. It worked. It seemed a sensible and logical way to go about a job that was vital to the public interest but was often ignored or, at best, treated negatively.

After an inquest, for example, we wouldn't wait for a radio or newspaper reporter to get off his ass and come over to pick up the verdict. We would phone them and give them the verdict. Then, it seemed, they made a point of putting it on the air and getting it into print. It may not have made it, otherwise. And I often heard people say afterwards, "Yeah, I heard that on the news. . .I read about that in the paper. . .you know, he's right. . .what this guy McDonald said. . ." But it wasn't me who was right. It was the jury, for being wise, and it was my staff, for contacting the media to tell them.

There may not be a pestilence in the land but there is a danger—a cause of death—in the land every minute of every day and it's the Coroner's duty to tell the public about this. I did it through the media. In this way people learned of the dangers of letting their kids play on the streets, of wearing dark clothing while walking on rainy nights, of the perils of driving and drinking, of cruising aboard a boat with gasoline slopping in the bilges and scuppers.

I was born an actor. I've always been possessed of more than a little imagination and I never hesitated to bring this into my courtroom. Being an actor is something one must be in connection with death. You must, to a certain extent, act out the facts.

There were many times in court when I knew what a jury's verdict was going to be even while they were out deliberating. So I'd write down something—some comment from the bench—which I knew sure as hell would catch the eye of the media. I'd pass the scrap of paper down to the press table. The reporters would read what I'd written and nod. I knew I had another headline.

I knew what the reporters wanted from the Coroner at an inquest. Like one time I said that the traditional old street lamplighter of bygone days was a hell of a lot more efficient method of lighting the streets than what we have in Vancouver today. That was a pure actor's role. It got the headlines I was after. Plus, of course, an instant denial from the street-lighting people at City Hall. But they did hustle around and they did put in more and better lighting at a corner where there had been a traffic death. That was all I wanted.

I did the same in the years when a lot of old folks, dressed in dark clothing on rainy winter nights, were being knocked down on their way home from Bingo games. My statement that Bingo was the most dangerous sport in the world made headlines all across Canada. That was just fine with me.

I was speaking about serious situations and I wanted the public to read about them and hear about them and think about them instead of passing them over with a shrug. I was quite aware that, usually, the public would rather not know about death. So I used the media for a purpose, not to satisfy my own ego.

I've also been an actor in another sense. I had witnesses physically demonstrate in the courtroom how, for example, gunshot wounds or stab wounds occur, how a strangulation occurs, how a drowning occurs, what happens at the moment of impact when a heavy motor vehicle collides with a frail human body. That sort of graphic thing. But you're only an actor if you've got an audience. My live, immediate audience was usually just the jury, the witnesses and a few people in the public gallery. So I got a much bigger audience by using the media.

I thought that allowing the press and TV cameras into the Coroner's Court would make inquests more graphic, more arresting to the public.

I wasn't trying to turn the Coroner's Court into a music hall or a three-ring circus or a vaudeville act because there's no way that place would ever win a popularity contest.

I simply wanted the public to understand and appreciate what this jury was doing and that jury was doing. I wanted to get away from the old idea that an inquest jury's verdict and recommendations are predicated upon the assumption that ignorance multiplied by six gives intelligence. A great part of being a successful satirical writer or political cartoonist lies in the art of exaggerating the obvious points of a character—the big nose, the big ears, the big mouth. In a sense, this was what I did within the realm of the law to try and get a message across.

* * *

One of the Coroner's hardest tasks was to avoid becoming emotionally involved in a case before him. Like that of any judge, his job was to listen to the evidence, the legal arguments, the pros and the cons, weigh all the facts and instruct the jury. His job was to remain aloof. It was not easy for a humanitarian who was born an actor.

* * *

This is a hard, hard thing. Emotion at an inquest must not come from the Coroner. I've talked to many Coroners all over the world who said they would not sit at certain inquests because they knew they would become emotionally involved; that it couldn't be avoided. I excused myself from some inquests but always for technical or legal reasons.

The Coroner must almost be better than Caesar's wife in order to keep his emotions under control. That doesn't mean he can't have compassion but, after all, he's running the inquest. He's the boss. If a witness is too upset to take the oath or collapses in the witness box, well, that's upsetting and it hurts everybody. The Coroner should care about such things but he shouldn't let it get to him to the point where he, too, becomes emotionally upset. He has a job to do. So he asks the witness to step down for a few minutes, calls for a glass of water, perhaps adjourns the court for fifteen minutes. Then the case continues.

We all have our own reactions to death: anger, sorrow, pity, tears, outrage, numbness, frenzied activity, shouting, silence. Also, reaction seems to vary according to ethnic groups. The Chinese, the Japanese, the East Indians, the native Indians—they seem to accept death as being inevitable; they certainly appear to accept it more easily, more philosophically than the average white person. Religious faith helps, too, of course.

But death favors no one religion and there's no religion in the world that stops people from crying outside with tears or crying inside with tears. I believe there's no Coroner in the world who can let himself join in those outside tears or those inside tears. He must be aloof and as removed from emotion as possible; he must be as fair as possible without fear, favor or affection, hoping that the evidence will be accepted and acted on.

Nobody who has died violently or in suspicious circumstances should leave this world without the dignity of having an inquest. It is a person's right. Words spoken from a pulpit do not examine and explain a cause of death as completely as words spoken at an inquest.

There were many times when I had to steel myself before entering the courtroom because I knew I was going to have a sad case of a child, with everything in the world once ahead of him, who had been knocked down by a car. It would be a dirty ashtray day. The parents would be grieving. The witnesses would still be shocked. And the driver of the car would be upset and depressed. Dirty damn ashtrays!

The Coroner seems to sit before a roomful of more shock patients than you'd find in the average hospital emergency ward. Yet he must keep his proceedings as orderly and as practical as he can. Almost everything at an inquest procedure has a traumatic shock potential. The identification. That's upsetting. Then, in the case, say, of a traffic accident in which a child was killed I'd use a blackboard on which the police chalked the distances in feet, the length in skidmarks, position of the body, pieces of wreckage and so forth. All of this was very upsetting and shocking for those immediately involved with the death.

Frankly, we put all those concerned—the weeping mother and father, the grieving driver, the shocked witnesses—through hell. But they had to go through it. I always wished there was some other way of doing it. But there isn't. This was the only way to get everything right out into the open. In the end, I had the satisfaction of knowing I had at least satisfied the transcript, the court record. But an inquest never really satisfied the parents of the child, you never satisfied the driver of the car. It could never erase guilt and self-blame. Everybody was always agreed on one thing, though: they all wished that terrible day had never happened. So did I. And then I had to sign a death certificate with a date on it showing four, five, six years of living. Period. This part always got to me.

*If only she had used the crosswalk; if only he hadn't been chasing that ball; if she had just looked up for a second; if the driver hadn't been in such a hurry or hadn't lost that argument with his wife this morning...the "but fors" and the "ifs" and the "onlys."* As the old saying goes: if my Aunt had balls she'd be my Uncle! The "ifs" and the "but fors" don't help.

The final diagnosis is death and the cause of that death is in the pathological and toxicological findings. And that's fact.

\* \* \*

Most of us walk swiftly past a building that has MORGUE or CORONER written on it. We quicken our pace. We wish there was another sign saying KEEP OUT! We don't want to think about what goes on inside. We certainly don't want to look. What does go on?

* * *

Every day was a bit different but, just as in any office, we had our set routine. I'd come in at nine, park in the alley in back and go upstairs. My first port of call was always the view room where I'd look at the bodies which had come in overnight. The clothes had been taken off and I'd look for any marks or signs of violence and examine the eyeballs for any breakdown in the pupils, indicating a drug overdose. I'd look at the cubital fossa, the mark between the elbow and the arm, to see if the deceased had been a user. This was routine and, most mornings, I'd run through six or seven stiffs. Then I'd read the police reports. The telephones would start ringing. Was so-and-so in the morgue? Was this person or that person lying there? "He hasn't been home all night and I've checked all the hospitals and I. . .I just wondered if. . ."

I'd tell people we needed positive identification and a technician would have the body prepared and covered with a sheet when the next-of-kin or a friend came in for the viewing. We were, like the Boy Scouts, prepared. We always had lots of strong coffee and ammonia ampules on hand, just in case. It was interesting how people reacted in different ways. Some people looked the strongest but, curiously, they were usually the ones who collapsed. The ones who looked the weakest seemed to have an inner stength that sustained them. It was kind of a crazy contradiction of our image of *Mr. Superman* and *Mrs. Wonderwoman.*

This always fascinated me. But the main worry was that if someone *did* collapse, we had a very hard floor. If a person was to hit his head and suffer a concussion, we'd have another problem on our hands. Perhaps even another body in the morgue. Nobody likes doing this identification thing. It's not pleasant. We always took a gentle approach: perhaps they wouldn't mind coming down to the office, just for few minutes? On that basis most people agreed to come. In various stages of sobriety, I might add. Which was understandable. Some people would come in so completely blotto they couldn't even see the body and we had difficulty even finding out what their names were let alone that of the dead guy. Others would swear they'd never had a drink in their lives but they'd be utterly plastered when they reeled into the morgue.

Death, violence, blood and guts—they're all highly saleable commodities on television. But those deaths are always associated with someone else. When death is associated with you or with someone near and dear to you, it's a different animal altogether. People would stand in the morgue and say, "I don't believe it. I still don't believe it!" They were simply denying the fact to themselves. A person would see a friend he'd known all his life and flatly say, "No, that's not him. Not at all!" Outright denial through self-delusion.

Of course, a person looks different in death. For example, there's a postmortem withdrawing of the skin on the face; a beard will grow and possibly the guy never wore a beard in his life. That sort of thing. We actually shaved the faces of corpses now and again, to help with identification. But if a person says, "No, that's not him," he or she is perfectly entitled to come to that conclusion. They're trying to help us. But what they're really saying to themselves is, "I don't believe what I've seen. I *won't* believe what I've seen."

The telephone was a frequent source of macabre humor. In twenty-six years we changed our number almost as many times and we always seemed to be a step ahead of the current directory. So we got a lot of wrong number calls. We had a standard answering procedure: "Coroner's Office, technician so-and-so on duty. May I help you?"

Invariably, the startled reaction was, "Oh, my God!" Followed by instant disconnection. And if the caller happened to be phoning from a party, he'd yell out to his fellow boozers, "Hey, I've got the bloody Coroner on the line! You know anyone in the morgue?" Or, "Wanna talk to the ol' Grim Reaper?" Or, "Smedley's been passed out under the sofa for two hours. Maybe we should book him in with the stiffs while we've got the guy on the line!"

These were sick jokes, perhaps a natural form of defensive mechanism triggered by being suddenly confronted with someone so closely asociated with the business of death. But the important thing was that we had a number and we were on call twenty-four hours a day, seven days a week.

When you have a death, you've got to find an answer. We could supply it.

\* \* \*

John James Geesell, 46, a navy veteran who lived more and more for his bottle of Bay Rum, probably was murdered for it. A Coroner's jury was told he had borrowed fifty-cents when he left his Skidroad rooming house to buy a drink of Bay Rum and was stabbed to death in the street.

News Item
September, 1969

\* \* \*

The late lamented Ormond Turner, when he was a provocative columnist with *The Province* newspaper, set out vigorously one fine day on a grand tour of Vancouver's Skidroad. In tow he had Judge Glen

McDonald, impeccably attired in blue pin-striped suit, squeaky shiny shoes, white shirt, Royal Canadian Navy Reserve tie and glittering gold watch chain. Their mission: to sample the delights of a flavoring potion called Vanilla Extract and a hair tonic and after-shave lotion called Bay Rum.

They sidled into a Chinese grocery store on Carrall Street and purchased a bottle of each, paying with *Province* expense money loftily carried by Ormond. They noticed a lot of other people in the shop also purchasing bottles of Vanilla Extract and Bay Rum, not for the purposes of cooking or rubbing on hair or face.

Ormond Turner and Judge McDonald sought out a vacant bench, around the corner in Pigeon Park. Amid a gently rolling sea of hoboes, drifters, drunks, guitar players and pigeons, they discreetly sampled their wares. Ormond choked and almost threw up; Judge McDonald blanched and gasped for breath. They traded bottles and swigged again. Judge McDonald choked and almost threw up; Ormond blanched and gasped for breath.

"I have," he declared, "tasted every libation and witch's brew concocted by man and beast in every country in the entire world. Many have been vile. But this—this is DREADFUL!"

"God awful!" gasped Judge McDonald. "God knows how anyone can drink this!"

"Let's try mixing it with Coke," Ormond suggested.

He trotted back to the grocery store and purchased, on *Province* expenses, a small bottle of Coke and two dixie cups.

Coroner and columnist sat among the pigeons and the human wreckage and they mixed the Coke, first with the Vanilla Extract and then with the Bay Rum. Carefully, they sipped their Pigeon Park cocktails.

"DREADFUL!" pronounced Ormond.

"GOD AWFUL!" pronounced Judge McDonald.

And at this point the intrepid adventurers adjourned to the old Commercial Hotel beer parlor, just off Victory Square and known to readers of Ormond's column as The Mahogany Room, to soothe their flaming palates with copious draughts of frosty ale.

* * *

We had been involved in this Vanilla Extract and Bay Rum thing for years. I guess it went all the way back to the years of the Great Depression when drifters and hoboes rode the rods across Canada. A lot of them ended up in the Vancouver railway yards in Skidroad.

Time after time I asked the cops to investigate sudden deaths in the hotels and rooming houses in Skidroad, mostly unemployed guys living on welfare. Just before welfare day, there was always a great run on Vanilla Extract and Bay Rum. It was easy to understand why. The money for the beer and rotgut wine had run out. This habit was causing a lot of deaths.

I studied the federal Food and Drug Act because I felt Bay Rum should come under it so sales could be controlled and policed. That didn't work. Bay Rum was an elixir for use as an after-shave lotion so it couldn't be included in the Act. Sales of Bay Rum bottles were as high as thirty thousand a month in Skidroad alone. Something had to be bloody well done. I approached the suppliers, one of the big soap companies. No, it was no concern of theirs. They were distributing an elixir for use as an after-shave. Why the volume of sales in Skidroad was so high was of absolutely no concern to them. As a matter of fact, the bastards said they thought it was a happy result of their product being appreciated. What a load of BS! Sure, their product was being appreciated. Internally, not externally!

Then I got hold of some provincial government chemists and asked if something could be put into the Bay Rum to make it smell and taste so vile people couldn't possibly drink it. That idea didn't work, either.

The chemists said they *could* add something. But the answer from the manufacturers was that such an additive would cause an ugly stain on the person's face after he'd used Bay Rum as an after-shave, the purpose for which it was intended. Yes, they could put in some kind of ergot which would make people instantly nauseous if they drank the stuff. But if they used the product as it was meant to be used, they'd end up with dark stains and streaks all over them. Obviously, the ergot was out.

Then I went to Stewart McMorran, the Chief City Prosecutor. He took the matter up with the same people and got nowhere fast, too. We couldn't have the stuff taken off the shelves and put under the Food and Drug Act or make it available by prescription only. It seemed there was nothing we could do. I had made some speeches and comments to the press about all this and, of course, the users—the rubbydubs and the winos—got wind of what we were trying to do. "So what?" they said. "If you get rid of this stuff we'll just go back to using shoe polish!" And they laughed.

Shoe polish! Now, that was a beautiful Skidroad cocktail. And you didn't have to go to bartending school to learn how to mix it, either. All you did was put the shoe polish (brown or black, it didn't seem to matter) in an old sock and squeeze. The alcohol came out, you poured it off and drank it. Lovely! Sterno, or canned heat, was another favorite, used particularly by the gentlemen who used to live under the old Georgia Viaduct near the Sun Tower. They set that product alight to get the alcohol out.

The joys of Sterno were obvious. You could cook with it and keep yourself warm and drink it into the bargain. It couldn't be put under the Food and Drug Act, either. And in wintertime these old guys were even into stealing anti-freeze from cars and trucks and drinking that, for God's sake! They'd drink anything they could lay their hands on, providing it contained alcohol. They weren't much into tea or coffee. They were sad, pathetic creatures; men the world had passed by and forgotten about.

But they had their strong independence and their friendships, their sense of humor and perspectives, their loyalties and code of ethics and their camaraderie. They had their freedom. The tragedy was that that freedom was totally ruled by the bottle. Many a corpse was taken from underneath that damned old viaduct. Mostly in the wintertime when the cold and wet were just too great for the survival of the weak. The poor guys just passed out and went into pneumonia. They call it the painless death of the drunk. It's not a bad way to go, I guess.

The crude shelter of the viaduct and the bottle of Bay Rum or can of Sterno were the only comforts they had until death came to take them away. They didn't have a room to go to, even in the cheapest and raunchiest of Skidroad fleabags. Or if they had, they'd usually be too drunk to remember where it was. Sometimes they'd wander vaguely into the street and get run over and end up in my morgue. All of this was very depressing and totally frustrating because there was nothing we could do about it. But I thought a little more publicity wouldn't do any harm.

So, whenever the cops or the ambulance guys took a stiff from a rooming house or from under the viaduct I told them to bring me the evidence. I ended up with a ten by twenty-foot room filled with bloody Bay Rum bottles. But I made my point. I invited the press cameramen to come down and take pictures. The papers gave them big page one play and there was a huge public outcry and song-and-dance about what terrible things were going on in the streets of the city. It was a frustrating end, though, to a reasonably intelligent approach to the problem. Nothing was ever really done. And the sad situation still exists today.

\* \* \*

The eyes of a murdered 19-year-old Vancouver girl are being used in a bid to bring new sight to two partially blind women.

This is believed to be the first time in British Columbia that eyes—or any organs—from a murder victim have been used for transplant purposes. . .

Linda Ann Wood was pronounced dead on arrival at 11 p.m. Monday—25 minutes after the stabbing. Her body was taken to the city morgue where Coroner Glen McDonald was told of her mother's wishes regarding the use of her daughter's eyes for transplant.

McDonald called the Vancouver General Hospital eye department before the autopsy began and the eyes were removed at 2 a.m.

Coroner McDonald praised Mrs. Wood's decision as "a natural and Christian act. . .if people follow Mrs. Wood's example, this might lead to a breakthrough in the use of the Coroner's office as a source of transplant organs. . ."

*The Vancouver Sun*
April 10, 1968

\*     \*     \*

"I want to thank you for the prompt and kind and Christian assistance you gave in providing, from this tragedy, sight for two other people," Coroner Glen McDonald told the grieving parents of a. . .Vancouver girl who was stabbed to death. "Out of this tragedy you have found in your own hearts something which I know you can find of comfort in months and years to come. . ."

Reginald and Evelyn Wood gave permission for the corneas to be taken from their daughter's eyes and transplanted into the blind eyes of two women.

Coroner Glen McDonald publicly thanked the couple in a hushed Coroner's Court moments after he adjourned the inquest into the death of Linda Ann Wood.

*The Vancouver Sun*
April 13, 1968

\*     \*     \*

DELTA—Coroners should be given the right to decide whether organs can be removed from bodies for transplant purposes, the British Columbia Coroners' Association was told Saturday.

Vancouver Coroner McDonald said he is not satisfied that getting permission from next-of-kin is the most satisfactory solution to the problem of removing organs from the dead.

"You can run into a real problem that way," he said. "There can be arguments in the family, or someone in the family can get upset, after the permission has been given. . ."

*The Vancouver Sun*
October 21, 1968

\*    \*    \*

Organ transplants—giving a part of yourself in order to sustain a fellow human being—had intrigued me ever since I was in Russia during the war. We went into Murmansk a couple of times aboard the good ship *Nabob*. The Russians' preoccupation seemed to be to toast us endlessly with vodka and see who could stay up longest without falling asleep under the table. We held our own pretty good.

But it was the medical thing that really interested me. During the war the Russians had lost roughly the equivalent of the population of Canada, something like twenty-three million people. That's an astonishing fact. But how did they keep the millions of wounded alive? I asked about this during the war and on a subsequent trip to the Soviet Union. The answer was simple: transplants of organs and a massive blood bank built up by taking blood from the dead. The Russians had what I can describe only as a "living morgue." This was what sustained the people.

They had absolutely no hesitation in routinely taking blood—providing, of course, there was no infection present—from cadavers. They never had a shortage of blood plasma for transfusions. I was amazed why we didn't do this in North America and I raised the subject one time at an international Coroners' seminar.

"Why is it," I asked, "that we have this resistance to taking cadaver blood for plasma?"

My colleagues were absolutely horrified by the very idea. There was

191

a strong, built-in resistance to it which was echoed by the Canadian and American medical associations. It seems to me a waste not to do this. When we do an autopsy, for example, we drain the blood out of the body and wash it down the pipe. The average body contains four or five pints of blood. Why not use this in a positive way to help another life? If it's refrigerated, blood will keep indefinitely, although it has to be taken within five or six hours of death. It must be done in that time frame. But people resist change.

Do they dread to think they're getting blood from a dead body? Does it matter? We now get blood from the living, through a donor system. Is it morally wrong to take it from the dead?

We have a Red Cross blood donor system in Canada that always seems to be short. Volunteers are always needed. It's basically a damn good program. But, in a catastrophe, where and what is your backup? There's a vast potential blood bank in the dead and it's not being used.

Few people knew about it but my morgue in Skidroad was a pioneer in the field of organ transplants in the sixties and seventies. Transplants, under the table, years ago. About ten percent of our bodies had no known next-of-kin and were buried at public expense. Sad. But we always had calls from the hospitals. Could we supply such and such an organ for a transplant? A cornea, for instance. Or a kidney. We tried our best. It was entirely up to me to say whether something would go or wouldn't go and it was all very hush-hush. But we did it and I've never regretted it.

I was looking at the simple facts. We do amputate legs when we find cancer, we do take off a breast when we find cancer, we do remove many parts of the body. I just took the thing a step further. Perhaps that was the actor in me again. Why not take an organ from the dead, who don't need it anymore, and give it to the living? Today, that's routine medical procedure. It was being done years ago in the Vancouver morgue.

We often had a hospital situation where someone was dying— usually it seemed to be a young lad who had been riding a motorcycle— and was on the Bird Respirator. This meant he was on sustained life-support but there was no more hope of real, normal life. The doctors were keeping the body alive. The brain cells were dead. I had found in Russia they had for many years kept a living morgue of bodies—bodies mechanically kept alive for transplant purposes. Maybe this is going too far. Most people would probably be repelled by such an idea.

But that body grows skin and that body grows blood. It's kept clinically alive for the providing of a supply of blood for transfusions and organs for transplant. This is sort of unreal when you think about it. But when you get over the first shock of thinking about it, it makes one wonder, well, what else can we do? I suppose most people who buy roses don't like to think they're buying roses that have never seen the sun. So it doesn't really matter once you get over that first mental hurdle.

In the Vancouver Coroner's Office we did these things by consent, if we had parents or some other next-of-kin. And if we didn't have that, well, the Coroner just did it all on his own. Under the table.

*    *    *

The very young and the very old.
Honest killings and Junk killings.
The living and the dead.
Dirty ashtrays and clean ashtrays.
All these disparate elements passed before Judge McDonald's bench during his years as City Coroner. He mused upon them.

Old folks' homes and schools make good neighbors, I discovered. I was always interested in the old people of our society and their problems. I love kids, too. And I found that the two groups get along famously together. They complement each other.

When I was living in West Vancouver, I noticed the local Rotary Club people were building an old-age home next to Pauline Johnson Elementary School. Old folks would be living slap by a noisy schoolyard filled with screaming youngsters. This didn't make sense to me. A group of us went to a Municipal Council meeting and I suggested that perhaps it was a poor choice of site. Why should the old gaffers be subjected to all this noise of kids playing and fighting and bawling morning, noon and evening? One Rotarian took me aside and asked if I had talked with any of the old people. No, I hadn't. "Why don't you?" he said. "I think you'll learn something."

So I went to see the old folks and a most charming lady told me most emphatically that the one thing they all didn't want to believe was that in their old age they had lost touch with youngsters.

"Do you mean to say that the kids making all that noise is good for you?" I asked. "Don't you like to lie in late in the morning to rest?"

"No," she said, smiling at me as if I were a dummy. "We get up early. We have our tea and toast and marmalade and we're happy watching the children playing. We enjoy listening to their voices and their laughter."

I'd never thought of it in that light. I went back to our ratepayers' group and said we were on the wrong track. We should support the project. A physician told us, "It's simple. The old people don't want to lose touch, to feel they've been shunted off somewhere to die, and the presence of the youngsters helps a lot. Would you like to be an old person looking at other old people all the time?" It had never occurred to us that that might be less than desirable.

I've seen the same thing in the community of Ocean Park, near my home at Crescent Beach—an old folks' home with a school right next door. It's a happy event when the old people and the young get together and chat and laugh and play little tricks on one another. They all have fun. It's the big event of the day. It's like hearing the birds singing when you wake up in the morning. If you hear them, it's going to be another full day. If they're not singing, you hope it's just because it's raining and they'll be back tomorrow. The school has a holiday today but you know the kids will be back tomorrow.

I always labeled homicides as either "Honest" killings or "Junk" killings. The Junk killings almost always involved drugs, prostitution, sometimes high-roller gambling, often all three. And they were usually the result of jurisdictional disputes between drug pushers, unpaid debts or singing to the cops. Revenge was always the motive. Junky, rotten revenge. Two people shot, tied together, put in a bathtub, gasoline poured into the tub and the bodies set on fire. A drug peddler shot through the window of his car while stopped at a red light in the East End. Car bombings. Cement-boot drownings. That sort of thing.

These killings were always done on a contract basis that started as low as twenty-five dollars for a hit. Really, the only sad part was that the hit-man missed his comeuppance because he was a stranger from out of town, usually from eastern Canada or Seattle. He always made a quick exit with his dough. But his victims didn't represent any loss to society. Their deaths could even be interpreted as a gain for society. A code of honor among thieves. A pestilence in the land had been removed.

Those were the Junk killings. The Honest killings stemmed from the emotions of honest and ordinary people: a domestic argument out of control, a lovers' quarrel, a sudden and uncontrollable mental break-down, crimes of passion caused by surges of anger, pain, grief, frustration. There is a weapon conveniently at hand. There's seldom a real intent in such matters, certainly no motive of revenge or fear. It's just a sudden act of pulling a knife or squeezing a trigger. Then comes death, sorrow and remorse.

Death is what we all think about when we put our heads on the pillow at night. When you're asleep, you're unconscious. Is this what death is? If so, it can't be all that bad. But when you wake up and there's another day there, you want to greet that day and spend that day and spend it as well as you possibly can. The fact of death weighs more heavily on those who are left behind than on the dead. It was to them, after all, that I addressed my remarks from the Coroner's bench. How could this death have been avoided? How might they have prevented this sorrow that was now upon them?

Benjamin Franklin wrote back in 1789, ". . .in this world nothing is certain but death and taxes." Death is inevitable, certainly. We all know that. Yet we all fear it in one way or another. I respect people who believe that death is a rebirth. I envy them that belief because it makes death that little bit easier to accept, your own or that of a loved one.

But, always, those who are left have the harder role. Perhaps they actually want a bit of punishment, a bit of vengeance or retribution. And, too, there's always that self-guilt. Had they done something else, something differently, something more, assisted further along the way, then death might not have happened. This strange and complex mixture of feelings and emotions is always present at an inquest.

I've seen many a parent of a dead child go over to the driver of the car and shake hands and say, "We have no hard feelings, you know." The driver would say, "God, I'm sorry. I just wish it hadn't happened."

Didn't we all?

Death becomes a common bond, as if the dead were introducing people, both to themselves and to one another. It's a black rainstorm with a rainbow shining and a robin singing, all happening at the same time.

The grieving parents and the driver of the car are in that rainstorm but they see the rainbow shining and they hear the robin singing. The child had enjoyed living. The parents had enjoyed living with that child. The driver of the car had enjoyed living until he hit that child. In death everyone suffers.

# *Just Keep Out*
# *Of My Morgue!*

I went down to the St. James Infirm'ry.
  My Baby, there she lay,
Laid out on a cold marble table.
  Well, I looked and I turned away.

  "What is my baby's chances?"
  I asked old Doctor Sharp.
  "Boy, by six o'clock this evenin',
  She'll be playin' her gold harp."

*Traditional Blues Song.*

\*   \*   \*

An 80-year-old pedestrian was killed
Monday night when struck by a car
while crossing 21st Avenue and
Nootka. . .police said it was raining
heavily at the time and visibility was
poor.

News Item, March 2, 1982

\*   \*   \*

In January of 1958 Judge Glen McDonald of the Vancouver

Coroner's Court made a public statement that enraged much of the city's population.

In the furor that followed, newspapers printed bold black headlines, tremblingly irate writers of letters-to-the-editor seized their pens, editorial writers hunched earnestly over their typewriters, and outraged citizens flooded the Coroner's office with indignant telephone calls.

What Judge McDonald had told a meeting of the Vancouver Traffic and Safety Council was simply that Bingo was the most dangerous sport in Canada, that the streets of the city had become the graveyard of senior citizens and that old people should stay home at night.

The Coroner was serious and he was angry. He wanted something done about the increasing number of elderly pedestrians being killed by motor vehicles.

\* \* \*

One of the joys for older people—they used to be called old age pensioners and now they're known, somewhat euphemistically, as senior citizens—is to go out at night, meet their friends and play Bingo.

But they have other things in common: they're over the age of 65 and their reflex actions are just not as quick as they used to be. Their reaction time, in trying to avoid an oncoming motor vehicle, has usually gone from three-fifths of a second or five-eighths of a second down to about two or three seconds.

And they all love to wear black: black are their overcoats; black are their trousers; black are their dresses; black are their stockings; black are their shoes; black are their hats; black are their umbrellas.

This was the popular color with old folk when I was Coroner and it probably still is. It always came about that our traffic fatalities—I'm thinking back to the years of 1958-59-60—involved one pedestrian death a week and that the pedestrian's age averaged over 60 years.

The time of death was always between 9:30 and 11:30 at night; and the night of death always involved rain, darkness, no moon, no light; and the victims were not crossing the street in a marked crosswalk; and they almost always were wearing black clothes.

I was Vice-President of the British Columbia Safety Council in 1958 and I was invited one time to a Vancouver Traffic and Safety Council meeting to talk about anything pertaining to the duties of the Coroner's office. Well, I chose to speak out very bluntly about all the needless traffic deaths involving pedestrians in the City of Vancouver. I had no idea of the trouble it would get me into.

Now, many of the churches and veterans' clubs like the Royal Canadian Legion and the Army Navy and Air Force Vets relied to an extent on attendance at their Bingo functions for a good source of revenue. They also provided entertainment and enjoyment and camaraderie for the old people.

It was a popular night out. You'd go to one church on Wednesday and to a Legion on Thursday and another one on Tuesday and so forth. For the elderly it was a tremendous escape from the routine, from the often sad and lonely business of growing old. The old folks had a few dollars to flutter with and a chance to win some money. Plus, of course, the opportunity to meet friends and buddies. It was, and still is, a nice and warm social thing.

But, like so many other situations, there was the other side of the coin. I had had several traffic fatalities involving these old folks coming home from the Bingo games. Certainly sober, certainly old, and certainly wearing black clothing. I was alarmed by the situation and so were the police, safety groups and church groups.

It was always the same story. The driver of the car was usually sober, and always said something like, "I didn't see her until she was right in front of me." The same sad story over and over. And, of course, if the driver were going 30 miles per hour it would take him 30 feet to get his foot on the brake pedal and stop the car. In the meantime he had, tragically, a body of an old lady or gentleman on the hood of his car or flying over the roof and there it would be, lying on the road behind him by the time he had stopped.

These accidents didn't usually happen in crosswalks. So it was developing into a definite pattern of needless deaths. And I also found out that the average age of the victims was 67 and a half. So I spoke out strongly, both at that Traffic and Safety Council meeting, and at an inquest a few years later that also generated a lot of publicity. I wanted the old people to be educated. I wanted them to live.

But my forthright observations about the city streets being a graveyard for the old didn't go over well at all with some old people. The elderly go in either of two directions. Either they get more confident in their ability to do little things like going out to play Bingo, or they get less confident and so stay home all the time. And the last thing anybody wants to do is to stay home all the time, if they're old and lonely.

*   *   *

Vancouver newspaper copy editors had a field day with their screaming headlines:
CITY STREETS A GRAVEYARD!
AGED "SHOULD STAY HOME"
OLD PEOPLE UP IN ARMS!
"WHY SHOULD WE STAY HOME?"
One outraged old folks' group, the Federated Legislative Committee of Elder Citizens' Association, demanded that Judge McDonald make a public apology and read a letter to that effect to the city's Police Commission.

And, in a letter to *The Vancouver Sun,* an indignant Richard E. Smith—a man of obvious experience in matters of high dudgeon—

wrote: ". . .This is a shameful statement. He goes on to say three pedestrians have been killed so far this year. Their ages were 63, 71, 78. I come under this age class. I am 73 years and 10 months old. I ride my bicycle every day on the busiest streets—during rush hours, too. What does Mr. McDonald think my reactions are?

"For your information, I rode my bicycle in 1957 from Vancouver to Toronto. I rode (pedalling) on the busiest highways covering 3,000 miles. Should aged citizens stay at home? Not me. I shall ride at least 3,500 miles this year. . .To stay home is to die. So, please, Mr. Motorist, respect our aged citizens—don't kill them!"

In 1961, Judge McDonald—still battling to cut the traffic fatality rate among old people—held two inquests into the deaths of elderly pedestrians struck and killed by cars.

What attracted wide media attention was the fact that the juries were made up entirely of senior citizens. *The Province* newspaper even ran a six-column photograph of six jurors sitting in the Coroner's court, captioned "Teach Elderly Pedestrians To Save Themselves." The jurors were aged 82, 71, 72, 71, 81 and 74.

It was all part of the Coroner's ongoing fight for an educational safety plan to be initiated, involving the elderly themselves. And the seniors agreed, recommending in their verdict that such a campaign be conducted through the police, the media, service clubs and senior citizens' organizations.

And in 1963 a Coroner's inquest into the troublesome problem also made headlines when the jury, again composed of senior citizens, recommended that all elderly pedestrians wear white raincoats or carry white umbrellas during Vancouver's long and gloomy rainy season.

This was something Judge McDonald had himself urged in his controversial Bingo speech of 1958 and he earnestly thanked the jurors for agreeing with him. But this inquest came to an unusual and amusing conclusion.

\* \* \*

I held the inquest into the traffic death of an old lady and I thought the best people to have on the jury would be the very people whose peers were being struck down crossing the streets. "The Bingo Victims" I called them. The case involved the death of a lady of 74 who had been hit by a car as she crossed the street during an evening rainstorm.

So I went to the First United Church on the corner of Gore and Hastings and to the St. James Anglican Church on Cordova, both just a couple of blocks from the morgue, and got my elderly jurors from the people there.

And having called the old folks together and having made sure they were all able to see and were able to hear and were able to sit down, they took the oath and we swore them in as jurors and sailed merrily along, running the inquest very straightforwardly.

There were no witnesses except the driver of the car who said, as I well knew he would, "I didn't see anything but black." Typical.

And all the victim's friends who were there said, "Yes, she wore black. It was her favorite color."

I repeated to the jury much of what I had said in the Traffic and Safety Council speech—about the average age being 67 and a half and the slow reaction times and so forth—and I added, "I think the most dangerous sport in this country is Bingo. It has more deaths than any other game: baseball, football, hockey. And this is for a very simple reason."

The verdict could only be one thing—accidental death as a result of multiple injuries, fractured skull, ruptured aorta, or whatever it was, and there could be no blame attached to the driver. There was seldom evidence in these cases of impairment or speeding.

But I thought I was making a hell of a good point for safety and I went on to the matter of the old folks' clothing. I asked the jurors, "Why do you old folk prefer black as a color? Is it because you think I find you more attractive in black? Or is it that you can't afford to buy something in another color?"

Well, they looked sort of sheepish and mumbled something about black being a dignified color for an old person. So then I asked them, "Look, why don't you consider putting on a white armband or carrying a white umbrella or something else white which might warn the motorist, who has 3,000 pounds of metal under his foot, that he should put his brakes on before it's too late? Why don't you make yourselves more visible?"

This message got across to them and, in fact, when they came back with the verdict, one of their strong recommendations was that old people should wear white clothing at night. Great! At last we had some action going.

One juror even said he had heard of a garment-maker somewhere who was actually making white armbands for old people to wear.

"Wonderful," I said. "Come to think of it, ladies and gentlemen, it's interesting that we used to wear black armbands to symbolize death when we went to funerals and now here we are going to wear white armbands to help us stay alive so we don't have to go to our own funerals. I thank you and commend you for your suggestions."

So I excused them, told them to "take your leave, your absence" in the usual winding-up of an inquest, repeated the old business of "having discharged your duties, you may take your leave and now go to your homes." And then, of course, it was "Order in Court" and I walked out. I thought I'd done a hell of a job putting my point across.

I was intrigued by now, so I went back to the jury room and thanked them all in person because they were old people who were concerned and they had done a good job. But, to my utter dismay, everyone was putting on his or her coat and every coat put on was as black as the ace of spades. Everyone had a black hat and everyone had a black umbrella. By this time it was five in the evening of a dark winter's day and it was starting to rain. And here were all these dear old folks going out onto the street dressed like a convention of bloody undertakers. Hell!

I said, "You know, this won't appear in the transcript but it does seem to me that you were talking to yourselves when you said those sensible things about wearing something white. Look at yourselves!"

I made arrangements with the Chief Technician, George Shoebotham to tear up some white sheets we had in the back. I said to the old folks, "Look, do me a favor. We have safety pins here so let's put a white band on each of your arms. That way you'll really live up to your own recommendations."

Well, they happily adjusted one another's armbands as they left. Simply, they were damn proud that they had not only said something worthwhile but had actually done something about it.

I don't know whether they, or others like them, still wear white armbands, but I know I got my point across to them at the time. They had agreed that, while we talked a lot, we hadn't done enough about pedestrian safety in Vancouver or any other city.

These elderly jurors had not just talked. They had done something positive and that made them—and me—happy. I said to myself, "I'm not going to be a cynic. If it works for them just one night even and they all get home safely tonight, that's good. At least it's something."

In my speech to the Traffic and Safety Council, I said I was merely looking at the facts and figures such as dark clothing, slow reactions and the weather. I certainly didn't say anything smart-ass or with tongue in cheek. This was a straight statement that the city streets were the graveyard of Senior Citizens and my suggestion was that the old dears should stay home at night in order to sustain their longevity. I hadn't been looking for headlines but I got them. In spades.

The protests that poured in ranged from accusations of discrimination, interference and of my having adopted a defeatist attitude. If it had happened today I'd probably be accused of being racist, a male chauvinist pig, a pro-abortionist, an anti-Semite and a fan of euthanasia.

Jim Plaskett, who was the Traffic and Safety Council's Executive Secretary, said at the time the calls he got were mostly of an embittered nature. Mine were the same and worse. My approach to the problem was from a Coroner's stance and a humanitarian point of view. If I could find people who were concerned about safety on the streets I didn't give a tinker's damn if others were embittered, or if they were happy as hell as long as they all stayed safe and stayed alive. Just keep out of my morgue!

\* \* \*

For many years the British Columbia Coroners Act—which was, in effect, the English Coroners Act of 1848—stipulated that all inquest jurors must view the body of the deceased in the morgue before the inquest could proceed.

For almost everyone it was an unsettling and stressful experience. For many it was highly traumatic. For some it was terrifying. For others it was physically nauseating.

The jurors, accompanied by court officials, would troop hesitantly and reluctantly into the view room. When they returned they were pale, some were trembling, some even had to be helped to their seats by the stout arm of court officer Corporal Chuck Stuart of the Vancouver City Police. It was not nice.

This unpleasant procedure was the reason that, in the '50s and early '60s Coroner's juries were all-male. It was not considered fitting for a lady to look at a dead body. But Judge Glen McDonald, who also was not happy with the procedure, successfully lobbied the provincial government to amend the out-dated Act.

Now, besides the Coroner, only one person, next-of-kin or a close friend, is required to view the body and that simply for the purpose of identification. As a result of the change, Judge McDonald became the first Coroner in Canada to empanel women jurors.

*   *   *

There was a lot of publicity in the newspapers about the fact that Coroner McDonald had women on the jury for the first time. But I had read through the Coroners Act carefully and, like all those old Acts, it only talked about men. But men meant women as well, in my view, so I interpreted it that way. Until then, nobody had really thought of having women on the juries.

There's no question that this viewing procedure was nasty and distressful. Nobody liked it. Of course, we always had our little ammonia ampules in our hands when we had the viewing and when the next-of-kin came in to identify. Collapses were almost routine. As a matter of fact, you looked twice if people *didn't* keel over. It was a procedure nobody enjoyed.

The procedure was that the jurors would be sworn, then my pathologist would be sworn and then, with the court reporter—usually Walter Gottschau—and the pathologist—usually Dr. Tom Harmon— we would proceed to the view room where the body was lying under a nice, clean, white sheet. This room is a proper and aesthetically pleasing place to be, except it's not the place one would really want to be, given a choice.

Walter would sit down at his table beside the viewing table and we would take the sheet back and there would be the body of, say, a senior citizen who had been struck by a car. The jurors—not too happy with this performance—would duly look at it. Usually, not for long.

I would then ask the next-of-kin, "Can you identify this to be the body of (say) Mrs. Henrietta Smith?"

"Yes, I can."

And then I would say to Dr. Harmon, "Are there any marks or signs of violence on the body you can show to the jury at this time?"

And, of course, he would say, "Yes, there are."

He would then point out such things as a compound fracture of the tibia or the fibula or the femur, or some other injury which not even the cosmetic work of the technicians could conceal. You can't really hide a bone sticking out of a limb.

It was never pleasant and I was happy when we did away with the requirement. Certainly, the Coroner must always view the body. He must do that. And the Coroner must also satisfy himself that it is the body of the person for whom he is going to sign a death registration certificate.

Historically, this procedure goes back three, four, five hundred years to the days when identification of a man found dead in a town or village was very difficult. He may have been wandering from Scotland to England or to Wales and back again and nobody knew who he was if he didn't have relatives in the area where the body was found.

So, identification was very important because he just might be someone who owned a lot of land somewhere and had a lot of money. He might have been murdered in the streets and had his possessions stolen. And he wasn't easy to identify; it wasn't easy to determine who he was because there was no registration and no Department of Vital Statistics in those days. The only knowledge back then of who he was would probably be some little notation in the Family Bible or a letter in his pocket.

The matter of identification remained very important over the years and it most certainly is important now because almost everybody's death is payable with $10,000 or $5,000 in life insurance and insurance companies certainly aren't happy paying out to somebody who says, "I'm the beneficiary," when they're not sure who is dead in the first place.

The fact of evident injuries is very much part of what the jury always has to remember—whether this was a natural death or an unnatural death. You'd think the evidence of injuries such as broken legs or arms or a fractured skull would be sufficient to conclude that a person had died from unnatural causes. Many times the pathologist would show the body and the jurors would look at it and say, "My God, this is a terrible injury!" Broken leg, broken pelvic bones, other damages, massive bruises—particularly visible if the deceased had lived for three or four days and there had been time for the bruising to reveal itself subcutaneously.

But, when we got to the autopsy findings, Dr. Harmon would sometimes state that this person had suffered massive cardiac arrest prior to being hit by the automobile. So the whole thing got thrown back the other way. "My God," the jurors would say, "do you mean that this was a natural death because of a heart attack? I saw those broken legs and those huge bruises."

But, in fact, there had been a heart attack and the trauma of the broken legs and the bruises followed afterwards. This has happened a lot of times when a person has lost control of a car and has hit a lamppost or a telephone pole. We could by autopsy demonstrate that there was a heart attack prior to the injuries sustained in the collision. Although hitting a lamppost can rupture the aorta and all kinds of things can follow therefrom, we could demonstrate, from examining the heart muscle, that there was a dead tissue there and perhaps a blockage in the mitral valve or something else wrong with the ordinary actions of heart function.

The reason for such thoroughness was simple. We never wanted to be accused by anyone of not doing our sworn duty; being placed in a position, say, where it was discovered after the inquest that the deceased had suffered a heart attack which would have occurred had he been driving the car or had he been at home sleeping. That's the double importance of holding autopsies. What the insurance companies do is, of course, a matter of contract between them and the estate of the deceased. But what we were concerned with was determining without doubt what the cause of death was and have all the facts available to both sides if they wanted to go into litigation regarding that death. That's the way it must always be.

We also had the problem of too much time being wasted because of some of the inquest procedures.

One difficulty that arose from the viewing procedure was that we had to round up a jury, swear the members in and have them go through this formality required by law. Often, we weren't ready to go ahead with the inquest because we didn't have all the evidence. Then we had to adjourn to permit the next-of-kin to take the remains away and hold thei funeral service. This all took time.

So, often we had to almost hold two inquests into one situation. We had to adjourn after the hearing and the viewing and this meant doubling the workload. When we had 50 or 60 traffic fatalities a year, it meant we were really doing 120 inquests a year on traffic deaths alone.

And, of course, we always prayed the jurors wouldn't have disappeared or gone on holiday or taken sick or something by the time we were ready to proceed. At an adjournment a person could easily put up his hand and say, "Yes, I'll be back in a month at 10 in the morning." But they couldn't know exactly where they were going to be and, certainly, neither could we. So the Attorney General eventually brought in an amendment to the Coroners Act so that, at the discretion of the Coroner in any community in British Columbia, the viewing of the deceased by the jury could be waived. That way we could open the inquest when we were ready and proceed without interruption. This, mind you, in no way took away the responsibility of the Coroner to satisfy himself about identification.

*   *   *

Vancouver's teeming, colorful and vibrant Chinatown had long fascinated Judge McDonald of the Coroner's Court. His office, after all, was on the fringe of it and, in the company of his staff, detectives, prosecutors and fellow judges, he often enjoyed lunch or dinner in one of its many splendid restaurants.

Usually a bottle of good whisky wrapped in a brown paper bag and stowed out of sight under the round, white-draped table, was brought along. It added a desired bite to the steaming green tea, and stimulated conversation.

As recently as the late '50s and early '60s Chinatown retained a vestige of the mystery of the old days when the first coolies to come to Canada lived there in isolation and there was a wall built around it and the denizens wore pigtails and straw hats and "decent" people stayed away from the streets rumored to abound with sinister opium dens and houses of prostitution and gambling.

There were many private Chinese social clubs where the endless rattle of mah-jongg tiles could be heard, along with snatches of sing-song chatter and laughter, in the streets below. Plus dark and menacing alleys that, to the vivid imagination at least, were fraught with the dangers of butcher-cleaver wars among rival tongs and all the evils of the inscrutable Oriental as so rudely penned in the pages of cheap Sax Rohmer novels. Shades of the twisting, foggy streets of the Pool of London Docks and the infamous Malay Jack's opium house.

There was also a clutch of rundown frame houses which were the last home to many old Chinese men whose time had come to die. These frail men, who had never learned to speak English, slept on narrow bunks in dormitories or tiny private cubicles and played mah-jongg and gambled at fan-tan and smoked their opium and talked softly among themselves and waited patiently for the time when their ancient bones would be taken back across the sea and laid to rest in China, the Middle Kingdom.

It was because of these shabby old houses and the elders who lived in them, waiting to die, that Judge McDonald found himself involved in the confusing matter of the mysterious deaths in Chinatown.

*   *   *

I don't know why but Chinatown had always intrigued me. It was, I suppose, because I'd spent a lot of time in Hong Kong and Shanghai and Tsingtao in my apprentice days in the merchant navy. I admired the work ethic of the Chinese and their respect for the elders of the family, the doyens of the group whose opinions were highly respected. I felt easy and comfortable in Chinese company.

I even started taking Cantonese lessons from the Reverend Ng at the United Church down by the police station. *Everybody's Cantonese* was the name of the text book. For six months I labored mightily with the "ing" and the "ying" and the "yang" and the "ayee" and the "ow?" and the "eee" and found out there were five notes on the piano instead of eight and a few other little things.

Anyhow, that career was pretty short-lived but I could at least say hello and good-bye and thank you and even read a Chinese menu a little. I'd never have made it as an interpreter at the United Nations, though.

My concern at this time was the mystery of the Chinese next-of-kin. Everyone seemed to have five, six or seven uncles and nieces and nephews, but nobody was apparently ever a father or a mother or a brother or a sister. That was the way it seemed to me, at any rate. And what really concerned me was what had happened at several inquests we had held.

There were these rickety old rooming houses on Pender Street and Keefer Street and Gore Avenue where the aged opium-smokers lived. They just lived and smoked and puffed away their last five, 10, 15 years. They almost literally lived in the bunks they slept in. They minded their own business and didn't bother anyone. And, eventually, they died—lying in their bunks.

Little was ever said about this. Except, that is, by the oncoming Chinese, the new Chinese, the younger Chinese. They said it was wrong and the old people should have the same treatment as the white people had, they should go to old-age homes. They should be treated as white people. But curiously, this was only a 50 percent popular idea. Chinese like to die with Chinese, among Chinese. Simple. And I don't suppose I'd particularly want to die speaking only English alongside a bunch of Chinese yapping away in Cantonese.

In turn, they would be faced with a bunch of foreign devils yapping away in English. They wanted to die among themselves, speaking the same language. So they had their happy little mah-jongg games and gambled on a few cards and smoked their opium and life went on. But I got interested when one of these old gents, who was pretty well-off—there never seemed to be a shortage of family funds—died. The family was represented at the inquest by Gordon Cumyow, a Chinese interpreter whom we and the police courts used for many years. He's still working at that job.

What intrigued me was that the deaths of these old boys followed a definite pattern. We'd get a call to pick up somebody who had been taken out of one of these old houses at three, four or five in the afternoon. So, it was up to the hospital, usually Vancouver General, to have the body certified dead and then brought down to the morgue.

Now, it was always reported that these bodies were cold and rigid but coming out of the rigor mortis stage. Rigor mortis sets in, depending on room temperature and other factors, in about four, five, six hours after death and stays for a total of eight or nine hours. Then it goes away as the acids and the blood vessels and tissues soften up. From then on the body is flaccid.

But we were always getting these Chinese bodies in that eight-hour period *after* the four or five hours of rigor mortis. At first it didn't really bother us because the deaths were obviously from natural causes, in most cases bronchial pneumonia or plain senility. They were old, old men. But it occurred to me, and it puzzled me like hell, that the bodies always came into the morgue in that softening condition, indicating there had been some delay in reporting the death. Why so? What the hell was going on?

So I asked Gordon Cumyow to ask questions of some of the Chinese at this particular inquest because there was a suggestion that this nephew or that nephew was going to inherit a fair amount of loot. I wanted to know the answer to my puzzle.

I asked Gordon in court, in English, "Who found the man dead, and when?"

I thought these were pretty simple questions. I was naive.

Gordon asked a witness in Cantonese. The questions and answers then went on between Gordon and the witness for 40 minutes. I thought we'd better adjourn and let them keep talking and we'd go for coffee and get the answers when we came back. In the end, Gordon Cumyow turned to me and said, "He doesn't know."

"There are two questions," I said. "Who and when."

"He doesn't know either who or when."

Holy Christ, I thought to myself. Forty minutes of nattering for that?

But now I was even more intrigued by all this because I had learned enough about forensic medicine and temperatures and chemistry to put me on the track of something here that looked most suspicious.

Incidentally, we always knew the temperature of the room where a body was found, we knew the temperature of the weather outside, we did good research. We judged five degrees Fahrenheit per hour was the loss of body temperature. This procedure lasted six to eight hours.

But these bodies were coming in stiff, yet just going out of the stiffness of the rigor mortis and into that flaccid, floppy-floppy condition of death. This was what told me that something was wrong, that something was rotten in the state of Denmark. Or Chinatown.

So I tried again to find out through Gordon but he said again, "No, he doesn't know who found the body or when the body was found."

Well, I knew a distinctive habit of these elderly, senile Chinese—that they always had to have a pee about two or three in the morning. If they didn't, they died. I don't know the medical reason for this, it was just a little bit of inscrutable knowledge I had picked up somehow and was proud of.

So I asked Gordon about it. He asked the witness. And eventually Gordon said, "I don't know."

The jurors, all Chinese, asked a lot of questions in Cantonese and Gordon was interpreting as we went along and it sounded like rapid-fire machine-gunning. The penny finally dropped when one juror said the old man had died at two in the morning.

I said, "Well, maybe this guy should be a witness and not a juror. How the hell does he know?" It took another thirty minutes to figure that one out. More yak-yak-yak. There were endless questions and answers but in the end, this from Gordon: "He says he lives in the same house and went to have a wee-wee and noticed the man was dead. That was at two in the morning." Now I didn't know what to do. Should we keep this guy on as a juror or swear him in as a witness?

I said, "Anyhow, we have one duty to do right now and that is to go to the view room where we'll examine the body and have him identified."

The jurors stayed in court, chattering, and I took two nephews of the deceased, Gordon Cumyow, court reporter Walter Gottschau and pathologist Dr. Oliver Brammall. We made the formal examination, looked at the deceased's eyes and so forth, and observed there were no signs or evidence of violence or foul play. Now I'm looking at these two nephews and I notice they're not paying much attention to the body at all.

I said, "Mr. Cumyow, will you ask the nephews if they can identify this deceased as Mr. Foo Ching Chow?" So he talks for about twenty minutes and I get the answer back, "Yes."

Great, I thought, we're getting along fine now. "Better ask the other chap," I said. Gordon talks for another fifteen minutes and comes back again, "Yes."

But I noticed that both times these two hadn't bothered even looking at the body. Well, maybe they did but I didn't see them look.

We pulled the white sheet up and went back to the courtroom where we found out in due course that the Chinese owner-manager of the old house had had the death reported to him—we still didn't know by whom—at three or four in the afternoon. Another mystery.

I said, "Mr. Cumyow, would you please ask this gentleman why, if one of my jurors saw the man dead at two in the morning, nothing was done until three or four in the afternoon?"

The cat was among the pigeons. There was a prolonged outburst of

Cantonese sing-song between Gordon and the owner. The answer came back. "He was not notified until four in the afternoon. That's all he knows."

I said, "Well, we've got the ambulance attendants here. They'll tell us when they got the call."

Which they did. They got it at four in the afternoon. It was a routine trip through the old rooming house to the fourth floor, and there was a little bunk with a body on it and they took the body to the hospital where the man was certified dead. They brought the body to the morgue. It was just beginning to come out of rigor mortis. So, to my way of thinking, this two o'clock in the morning bit was beginning to make sense.

I told Gordon, "Look, I'm going to ask the jury in English but you're going to translate what I say. For God's sake let's get this thing straightened out."

The most important thing I said was, "Did this man have a legal passport to be in Canada?" Well, it took 25 minutes to explain that. The answer duly came back after twenty more minutes of yammering and nattering.

"Yes, he did."

"All right," I said, "will somebody please tell me where that passport is now?" It took 35 minutes to explain that to the jury, particularly to my old guy who knew so much that he was a witness, almost.

"No, they don't know."

The answers were coming okay now but it was still damn hard to figure out what the hell was going on. Again, I was getting nowhere fast. Or slow, rather. I knew, however, that the Vancouver Police and the Horsemen were investigating a Vancouver connection with the Golden Triangle drug trade and we had a couple of Chinese on our force for that very purpose. So I asked them to come over and explain to me why I was so bloody stupid. "I just don't know what's going on," I said.

One of them smiled and said, "Well, it's very obvious. What they're doing is selling that dead man's legal passport to some illegal young Chinese who has maybe five or ten thousand dollars. They're making the necessary changes and he's going to walk around with a passport.

"The estate of the deceased will be duly benefited and life will go on. And that's the reason for the delays in reporting these deaths. You're only legitimizing what is illegitimate and what's wrong with this Chinese philosophy? You take an old man's passport and give a new passport to a new life."

"How do I ever *prove* that?"

"You're never going to prove that."

But at least I had solved the mystery of all those dead old men.

I got bogged down in another Chinese connection about that same time. There was this traffic death on Pender Street in the heart of Chinatown. The street was death row back then for Chinese pedestrians who insisted on jaywalking. They were being scattered left and right like tenpins in a Goddamn bowling alley. And I got fed up. I was *really* fed up.

I said to myself, "So now I've got another case of a dead Chinese, hit by a car driven probably by another Chinese. The driver will say he had no way of stopping in time, that the pedestrian just waltzed merrily across the street in the middle of the block and he got clobbered and he was old and frail enough to die and he did die. Same old story."

I said to the jury of Chinese, "Goddamnit, we've all taken this for too long. Chinese people want to come and live in our country—that's great and, sure, we're proud to have the second biggest Chinatown on the west coast and all the rest of it—but, damnit, why can't you guys cross the street like we're all supposed to do or get jaywalking fines for breaking the law?"

This time the jurors really took me seriously. They came back with a verdict of accidental death but they added, "We recommend that two Chinese constables be appointed to the Vancouver Police Force and be on duty at all times on Pender Street in Chinatown."

"Jesus!" I said. "I never thought of that! That's a hell of a good idea!"

I happily took the verdict right over to Chief Constable Ralph Booth, I was so proud of this recommendation. "Hey, Chief this is a hell of an idea!" I said. "City Hall's bound to give you the money and now you've got two Chinese policemen. You'll cut down the pedestrian deaths and get more money in fines into the bargain!"

Booth sighed and said, "Mac, I have a Chinese on the force. Would you like to speak to him?"

"Sure, where is he?"

He phoned around and the guy came in and Ralph said, "What do you think of this verdict Mac has got?"

He said, very solemnly, "Mr. McDonald, I would like that job."

"Well, that's good," I said. "Christ, we're getting progress all over the place. Why would you like it?"

He laughed and said, "Because in six months I'll be the richest man in Chinatown."

"What do you mean?"

"First of all," he said, "the arresting officer won't get the right name. So you're never going to serve the Goddamn jaywalking ticket to a real person, anyhow. But mainly I just have to warn him about giving him that ticket and he'll give me five or ten dollars and I'll put it in my pocket and I don't know what his name is, either."

Chief Booth looked at me, smiling, triumphant.

"The hell with going back and taking any more Cantonese lessons,"

I said. "I think I've got the message—shut up and get out!"

That old Chinese cumshaw was often a very good system as long as everyone involved went along with it. But it can work in reverse, too, and with disastrous consequences, as we discovered. Several years ago a couple of uniformed cops raided an illegal fan-tan game in Chinatown where a lot of money was being thrown around. Nothing was ever officially reported but two nights later this old Chinese man shuffled into the police station at Main and Hastings and told the desk sergeant he wanted to pay the rest of his fine.

"What fine?" the sergeant asked.

"Fan-tan fine," the old man said. "Policeman want twenty dollah and me only have ten. I give he ten and say I pay rest latah. Heah it is, please take!"

And the cagey old bastard even had the officers' badge numbers.

*　*　*

Several years after his run-in with the old folks over his concern for their safety on the streets, Judge Glen McDonald again found himself waist-deep in hot water.

What brought the wrath of the populace down on his head this time was a speech in which he advocated compulsory fingerprinting of everyone in Canada.

He was a redneck! He was a fascist! He was against human rights and civil liberties! He wanted to make every Canadian look and feel like a criminal!

*　*　*

In the fair city of Vancouver it seemed that half the people who came into our morgue had so many aliases that, if they all sang together, they'd have made a massed choir for a Christmas concert. But we always had to make sure whoever it was was who he was. Often, we would go through CPIC, the Canadian Police Identification Commission, and the RCMP and the FBI and Interpol to find out who really was who when they started out on this little plot we call the globe.

Strangely, many jurors would come to me after an inquest and say, "Hey, Coroner, how come we didn't have a look at the body?"

They hadn't realized that by the time they were hearing the evidence the body had long since been buried or cremated. But we had all the information we wanted, namely the identification.

That amendment to the Coroners Act, which did away with everyone having to view the body and permitted identification to be made by just one person, worked well in the urban areas but not so well up-country, in the Interior, where there were many native Indians who didn't have all the identification they should have had. Everybody seemed to be Henry Joe or Henry Smith or Henry something-else and it was a problem finding out just who the deceased was or even who the father was, or the mother.

I had long had this idea about fingerprinting, so I decided to speak up about it. I was then President of the British Columbia Safety Council and I said in a speech that there should be compulsory fingerprinting of all Canadians. We were just then getting into the federal government's Social Insurance Number business so I asked, "What's the difference having a number as opposed to a fingerprint?"

My point was that a fingerprint makes a hell of a lot more sense than a number. A number on a card in your wallet can be lost or stolen. A fingerprint can't. And if a print is badly damaged—burned, for instance—we can raise it by fixing it in formaldehyde and then taking microscopic pictures of it, so it's still useful in positive identification.

I never received more criticism. The reaction was stronger than to anything else I ever said in public. I was a fascist and a redneck and a square! I was trying to make everybody in Canada into an identifiable criminal!

My argument was simple. I said, "Well, what's stupider than the passport I've got in my pocket which has a picture of me taken some years ago? But since then, I've grown a beard. I've lost weight or I've gained weight or I've shaved off my beard. Nowhere does it show my fingerprint."

I was fingerprinted only because I joined the Armed Forces. I wasn't a criminal when I joined the navy. I was fingerprinted for the simple reason that I'd be identifiable when I was dead. And that's exactly what I said in that speech that caused all hell to break loose right across Canada. The same should apply to the driver's licence. The photo taken at the Motor Vehicle Branch is a joke, anyway, because it never looks like you. And, certainly, the police officer who looks at it has not been specially trained in looking at pictures for identification purposes.

But if my fingerprint was on that licence it would be taken down, in the event of my death, by a technician at the morgue and easily checked. But, and it's ironic, the only people who get an honest-to-God technical identification at the morgue are those who have a criminal record and have, therefore, been printed. They're positively identified. There is no doubt. This, in turn, makes the next-of-kin happy.

Often we'd have the police Missing Persons Bureau onto us with claims from people when a body was picked out of Burrard Inlet or English Bay. Who is this person? Who is lost? Was he ever printed? If he wasn't a criminal, of course he wasn't. But we had bodies coming in once or twice a week—floaters—and we'd print them and run them through CPIC and the Mounties and the FBI. But, always, we had only as much information as a citizen would give us or, indeed, as public policy would give us.

I still believe in universal fingerprinting. There are also some apparent disadvantages which could turn into advantages. For instance, with the Chinese people, the skin on their fingers are very, very loose and very thin. As a result, they don't print too well. But this indicates that maybe you've got a Chinese body as opposed to a Caucasian body. Everything gives information to those who require it. That's what is so important. We certainly don't prove guilt or innocence by identification. As a matter of fact, in most cases, we can prove innocence by the process. The trouble is that printing has always had a basic connotation of guilt. If you are charged with assault or murder or some such heinous offence, whether it's under the Criminal Code or under the Common Law, you're fingerprinted.

Fingerprinting in such cases is not so much for identification as it is to match up the prints with those at the scene of the crime. Maybe your prints are on the gun or the knife or the window or the doorknob. Prints can tie an accused into the place where a felony occurred. Fabrication of that link in the total chain of evidence isn't too important, whether the accused is John Doe or Douglas Fairbanks or whoever. The main thing is identification that is linked to the crime.

But everybody who knows about this procedure has taken it on himself, or herself, to come to the conclusion, "If I'm taken to a police station and charged and then fingerprinted, I'm almost guilty, I *am* guilty because they've got my prints." That's the feeling they have and it's an understandable one. And, of course, the police love to brag about how successful they are—that they have stored up all these lovely fingerprints that are available for all time.

In the First World War, the dog tag was the main form of identification for the soldier or sailor or airman. And it was soon found to be worthless. It was often given to a girlfriend as a souvenir. Sometimes it was lost or blown to bits in action. So the military considered the concept of the fingerprint and the boys who went overseas had their prints taken. Not for any purpose while they were living, mind you. It was identification for the next-of-kin when the body was found in Flanders Field or some other grim battleground.

Governments then developed a more sophisticated concept of fingerprinting. This was for security purposes. The authorities would find out if you were qualified to take a responsible and high-profile job in, say, the Prime Minister's Office or some such sensitive area, decreeing that you must have your fingerprints taken. But it was sort of a Big Brother approach and today the average citizen would probably say, "The hell with it! So far as I'm concerned, I haven't done anything wrong and they can't bloody well have my fingerprints!" I suppose it is an invasion of an individual's rights, but surely the discomfiture of your being dead and remaining unidentified seems to me to outweigh that.

Here's another point. What happens if you are arrested, charged, fingerprinted and then subsequently acquitted of that charge? Where are your fingerprints then? Under our present laws you're entitled to write to the Solicitor General of Canada asking that all prints and photographs be destroyed, or that you be at least assured they have been destroyed. All of which is a bunch of hearsay. I don't believe they destroy anything. They're all still there in some big vault in Ottawa.

The government told us when we came out of the Navy, the Army, or the Air Force and picked up our little DVA stipends, that all the prints and pictures they had taken of us would be destroyed. Well, I have subsequently found out they haven't been, but have been microfilmed and are available to anybody who wants to see them.

Here's a personal example. I was arrested on a charge of impaired driving and was acquitted in court. Now, I don't give a damn whether the authorities know who I am or who I am not and I know they can't use that background against me unless I get on the witness stand and testify. But if I do so, then they have at a later date and in another circumstance an opportunity of going back, regardless of the acquittal, and saying, "Is it true that on such and such a day you were arrested for impaired driving and were fingerprinted?" and so on. And all my hotshot peers may be listening to that, and they think, "Oh, my God, he's a bad guy! He's got a record!" I have and I haven't; I'm guilty and I'm not guilty; I'm a victim of circumstance.

The fact of the acquittal gets overlooked. Even if my lawyer stands up and points out to the jury that the previous case ended in an acquittal, the damage has been done. We cannot remove ourselves from that situation. And that is the basic resistance to the idea of fingerprinting.

I can go into the ancient and philosophical Greek and Roman idea that I am a citizen of my state and my state is entitled to know me and I am entitled to know my state. But, unfortunately, in this age of the seeing-eye computer it's too damn easy to pull out that information which is required, conveniently overlooking the nuances and overall background. "This is a bad guy! We got him!" That's not fair and, to that extent, I disagree with the principle of printing.

But we could change the laws of evidence, as we did with juveniles. The biggest difficulty we've always had in trying to identify a juvenile— a dead juvenile, say—is that we've got their prints at the morgue but we can't get prints from the Juvenile Court for a comparison because it's against the law to take them. And, if the authorities did print juveniles all hell would break loose! I've got a young body in my morgue who I know I can identify. But I can't get access to prints because they weren't taken because of the right given to juveniles. And I don't know the difference between a juvenile and an adult who commits an offence.

I know a lot of people will want to straighten me out on that point, but as far as I'm concerned, if you're old enough to pull the trigger, you're old enough to be printed. If you're old enough to stab someone with a knife, you're old enough to be printed. If you're old enough to beat an old man to death with a baseball bat, you're old enough to be printed.

Maybe I am red-necked and square, but I believe it should be done. I'm prepared to let them take my prints. Why aren't you? Have you something to hide?

# The Macabre Murder Of "Lady" Hamilton

## Or The Curious Case Of The China Chamber Pot

For the second time in his career as Vancouver Coroner, Judge Glen McDonald found himself on official business in a graveyard.

It was eight on the morning of Friday, January 21, 1977. The sky was grey and spilling rain from leaden clouds. The Coroner's left shoe was leaking. Crows and seagulls were abundant among the sentinel tombstones and, across the street, schoolchildren waved and cheered and clapped as the somber gravediggers went about their disquieting work.

The Coroner was exhuming another body in yet another case of murder most foul.

The bizarre case involving Marion Hamilton, her aged mother, her cousin and a rambling old house had come to the Coroner's attention a little more than a year before.

Mrs. Hamilton's death was at first thought to be either natural, accidental or, perhaps, suicide. Then, because of suspicion in the Coroner's office, it became a case of murder that eventually worked its way up to the Supreme Court of Canada and the Canadian Minister of Justice.

The strange story began in a dusty and rundown old house in Vancouver's fashionable Shaughnessy Heights district in the early morning of Tuesday, December 2, 1975.

The detective work started when Chief Coroner's Technician

George Shoebotham looked at Marion Hamilton's body in the morgue at 240 East Cordova Street in Skidroad. Something made him suspicious that all was not as it should be.

*　*　*

The Marion Hamilton case was one of the strangest I ever encountered as Coroner. I always refer to it as the "Lady" Hamilton case. That's because a few weeks previously we of the navy had been preparing for the annual Trafalgar Day ball at *HMCS Discovery,* the navy shore station in Vancouver. Lord Nelson and Lady Hamilton were on my mind.

Mrs. Hamilton was brought to the morgue in the afternoon when we were satisfied the day's labors had been about done. We were thinking about knocking off. George Shoebotham came into my office and said, "I think you'd better have a look at this, Mac." We went to the view room.

Shoe was concerned because he had spotted ligature marks around the neck of this old lady. Something had obviously cut into the flesh and left a mark that was consistent with bruising. There was no doubt something mysterious had happened here. What was it?

"Where did this lady come from?" I asked.

She was from a handsome old house in Vancouver's posh Shaughnessy Heights. We found out later she was a widow, 69 years old and a recluse. We suspected she had been strangled or had somehow been hanged. But nothing of this nature had come in by the police reports.

Strangulation usually occurs in one of two ways, it can be homicide or it can be suicide. Or, possibly, it can be an accident, someone perhaps toying with the idea of committing suicide and then doing the damn thing by accident after having had a change of mind. "I don't like this idea much. It's not so hot, after all. It's not nice."

That was, in fact, the argument of the defence at the subsequent murder trial—that the old gal had been sitting on a china chamber pot at the time of death. I wasn't a party to this pot evidence but I assume she was trying to defecate or urinate. The theory was that she'd been sitting on the pot and got restless and kicked it away, or perhaps forgot the string around her neck tied to the doorknob.

But we knew none of this that first day. I asked the cops, "Where did this woman come from? What were the circumstances?"

She had been taken by ambulance from the house in Shaughnessy to hospital where she was examined by a doctor and certified dead from natural causes. There was a delay of several hours from the estimated time of her death and her arrival at the hospital and then the morgue.

The police had been called to the house and found the old lady lying behind the door of the room where she slept. This fact became important in light of the medical and legal arguments that came up at the murder trial eighteen months later: was Marion Hamilton strangled or had she hanged herself with a length of twine attached to the knob of the door? The ambulance attendants had pushed the door open and found her up against the door in a sitting position with a china pot in the neighborhood of her buttocks. Because there was blood on the old gal's face, they called the cops.

The police merely saw an elderly lady who was quite obviously dead. As one ages, folds of flesh appear in the neck so it's perhaps understandable, but certainly not acceptable, that more detailed examination wasn't made at the time by the ambulance attendants and policemen and the doctor who certified her dead.

I went at once to the Homicide Squad and the boys went back to the house to try and find out what had really happened. The autopsy, performed by Tom Harmon, showed this was an unnatural death. Now we had to do more investigation, the results of which would allow us to at least classify the death of Marion Hamilton as accidental, suicide or homicide. But I knew this was definitely not the natural death of a lonely, 69-year-old woman. There was hell of a lot more to it and I wanted to find out what it was.

*   *   *

The inquest was held 17 days after Marion Hamilton was found dead. The star witness was Mrs. Elouise Roads Wilson, a 49-year-old lawyer from the British Columbia capital of Victoria on Vancouver Island.

She was, she told the jury, the late Mrs. Hamilton's cousin, one of her appointed guardians and the only other person staying in the Nanton Avenue house on the night of the death. She also testified that she was the sole beneficiary of Mrs. Hamilton's estate of $175,000. And she explained she had become her guardian after the death of Mrs. Hamilton's aged mother the previous March in the same Shaughnessy home.

The testimony was eerie.

Mrs. Wilson told the jurors that her cousin had developed senile dementia (a psychosis) and had shown signs of not wanting to go on living but wishing to join her dead mother. She sometimes wandered the streets at night and had to be locked in her room.

She said on the night of December 1 she and her husband, Philip, put Mrs. Hamilton to bed about seven o'clock and then Philip returned to Victoria where he worked.

The next morning, she said, she tried to open the door of her cousin's room but found something was up against it. As she pushed the door open "something seemed to fall" and she found Mrs. Hamilton lying on the floor. She called an ambulance.

Detectives and ambulance attendants testified they thought the body had been moved after death and turned face down. Pathologist

Dr. Tom Harmon said he found a deep, narrow groove around Mrs. Hamilton's neck and that, in his opinion, death was caused by strangulation from a thin cord or wire around the neck. He could not say whether death was accidental, self-inflicted or homicide. A length of polypropylene cord was found under a chair in the room.

The inquest lasted two days and the Coroner's Jury deliberated only a few minutes to reach its verdict. On December 22 the jurors decided that Marion Hamilton's death was the result of a homicide.

And on January 16, 1976, Elouise Roads Wilson was arrested in Victoria and, the next day, formally charged wih murdering her cousin.

*  *  *

Her trial was to start in the British Columbia Supreme Court on January 24, 1977, a little more than a year after she had been charged with murdering her cousin.

It looked as if it would be an intriguing affair. It had all the ingredients of a classic mystery novel—the rambling old rundown mansion, the crazy old lady victim, the china chamber pot, the piece of twine found near the body, the family inheritance, the lady lawyer accused of murder, the fact that the victim's mother had died in the same house nine months before but was left lying in bed for two weeks before the death was reported.

The trial was bound to make big headlines and the public was looking forward eagerly to following it. Then something completely unexpected happened which made the whole thing even more intriguing and got me involved in the case again.

*  *  *

Just one week before the trial was to open, the lawyer defending Elouise Wilson obtained an order to exhume the body of the victim's mother, Mrs. Eunice Coote, who had died in the Shaughnessy Heights home, at the age of 92, nine months before her daughter's death.

Robert Gardner, an aggressive and flamboyant young criminal defence counsel, told Mr. Justice A.B. Macfarlane that no inquest had been held and no autopsy performed at the time of Mrs. Coote's death, and that the provincial Attorney General's department had approved a decision by Coroner Glen McDonald to order the exhumation of the old lady's body.

The lawyer explained, "Mrs. Coote died in the same house as the alleged victim; she died while she was in the custody of Mrs. Hamilton, the alleged victim; the circumstances were unusual. It is our position that an inquest should have taken place because of the unusual circumstances of the death, and I shall be applying for such an inquest."

In granting Gardner's application for an adjournment, Mr. Justice Macfarlane commented, "In the interests of justice and of the accused, there ought to be an adjournment."

It was the first time in British Columbia's legal history that the exhumation of a body had been ordered because of a private intervention.

And, armed with picks and shovels, Coroner Glen McDonald and his staff were ready to re-enter the strange and tangled case of the mysterious death of Mrs. Marion Hamilton.

* * *

Why, you may wonder, did Robert Gardner place such extraordinary importance on the death of an old lady? Why did he feel it necessary, in the interests of his client, to have the body of Eunice Coote disinterred from her lonely grave in Mountain View Cemetery?

His argument, of course, was that Marion Hamilton's death wasn't homicide but suicide. Here was a lonely old lady who was very despondent by reason of her elderly mother's death nine months previously.

Gardner's premise, his hypothesis (and any defence counsel is entitled to build such a case of supposition) was that Marion Hamilton had looped a length of twine around her neck and tied it to the handle of her bedroom door. When the door opened, her body had moved and fallen off the china pot. It was only some time later, incidentally, after the ambulance attendants and the detectives had tramped in and out of the room, that this length of twine was found. These were Gardner's allegations, his reconstruction of what had happened.

His argument was simply that the old lady had committed suicide; ergo, his client couldn't possibly have murdered her. Also, "Lady" Hamilton was a bit crazy. Or at least she was unable to appreciate the nature and consequences of her actions.

What Gardner was really trying to prove was that Marion Hamilton had murdered her mother and then, in a fit of remorse and despondency, killed herself. Such an argument could raise a reasonable doubt in the minds of a jury.

In this strange and bewildering case, the Crown had to decide if they had a case or if they didn't have enough evidence. They chose to proceed only after further investigation and after seeing the evidence we had discovered in the morgue the day "Lady" Hamilton arrived.

I'm sure, in fact, that if George Shoebotham hadn't been suspicious about that mark on the old gal's neck, Marion Hamilton's death would have been routinely written off as natural. What would a busy doctor think about the death of a 69-year-old crazy lady living alone in a rambling old house, sitting on a potty? He'd think of something: pneumonia, cardiac arrest, cerebral articulation or some other natural cause. It was very simple and it had almost worked.

Our work at the morgue was always meticulous and we tried never to overlook the smallest and seemingly most unimportant detail. The

Coroner's Office signs a receipt for every body and, in effect, it's a receipt for every secret that body holds. If it's a suspicious case, the body is put in a sealed locker. Nobody, but nobody gets to that body except homicide investigators, defence counsel, Crown counsel and the Coroner. They must attend together and with a Court Reporter who records all that is said. And it is the Coroner's responsibility, and his alone, to order the body released.

\* \* \*

Now, while Mr. Justice Macfarlane, defence counsel Robert Gardner, Crown Prosecutor John Hall, the accused Elouise Roads Wilson and the Vancouver public waited in suspense, the time had come for the solemn disinterment of the body of Mrs. Eunice Coote in Mountain View Cemetery on the south side of the city.

The job was started at eight on the morning of Friday, January 21, 1977 when Judge Glen McDonald tramped into the sodden graveyard accompanied by a squad of Coroner's technicians and policemen. The day was foggy and rain was falling. Lawyer Robert Gardner was present with Dr. John Butt, a forensic pathologist he had brought in from Calgary. Gardner—for reasons known to himself alone—wore a cutaway coat and a top hat. Seagulls looked on with interest.

\* \* \*

The cemetery is across the street from John Oliver Secondary School at Forty-first Avenue and Fraser. The students knew what we were doing and the morning was a bonus holiday for them. They were hanging out the windows cheering us on and laughing and clapping. They didn't get much studying done that morning but they sure as hell learned how to disinter a body, an extra-curricular course. I remember some of them yelling things like "Dracula rises from the grave!" and "Bodysnatchers at work!" Kids! It was only the second time in 26 years I'd been involved in a disinterment. The first time was the case of Esther Castellani, which I talk about elsewhere.

We used shovels and grub hoes to dig the soil away—not to throw it away but to remove it for laboratory examination as to its composition, particularly in the immediate area of the coffin. This is a careful and very important toxicological procedure. The soil samples are specifically tested for traces of heavy metal poisons such as arsenic.

We found the casket four feet down and it was a cheaply-built one, flimsy, and had rotted away and splintered here and there. Also, the grave was unmarked. These things struck me as being a bit odd. Here was a lady who had come from a very expensive residence in a snooty part of town but her own daughter hadn't shown any respect by at least buying a decent casket and putting a plaque on her final resting place. Not much filial love and respect there, it seemed. Indeed, it raised the very question that Gardner had raised—perhaps this *was* more than just

221

a natural death. Maybe Mrs. Coote *had* been done in by her daughter.

We started the job early because I wanted the whole procedure wrapped up in a day: remove the casket and body from the grave, have the body prepared and perform the autopsy. There was also a sense of respect for the dead. We didn't want to linger. People could be thinking, "Why are they giving the old lady this further insult, this further desecration?"

In fact there were some criticisms of what we did. Why was this old, old lady being rudely disturbed in her resting place? So when the job was done, I went to the Reverend C.G.L. Wright at St. James Anglican Church across from the morgue and had him officiate at a reinterment service. I just felt it was the right and proper thing to do. And I also arranged for a plaque of our own to mark the grave. These little things were done out of respect, not for reasons of conscience.

And there was no question but that the disinterment had to be done in public and in daylight. I'd preferred to have gone in at night. But that would have meant using floodlights and would have created even more traffic jams and curiosity. Working at night, we'd probably have been seen as evil and villainous grave robbers and ghouls, body snatchers out of the pages of a ghost story.

*    *    *

The autopsy was performed on the disinterred body of Mrs. Eunice Coote and, three days later, Judge McDonald announced the findings: no evidence of murder; death due to natural causes.

"There was no reason to question this finding as the woman was 92 and had had a heart condition for ten years," Judge McDonald said. "The death certificate was signed without question by her doctor."

Robert Gardner had lost the first round before the trial of his client had even started. And the way was now clear for the opening of the sensational murder trial of Elouise Roads Wilson, stemming from the macabre death of Marion Hamilton.

*    *    *

Dr. Butt, the pathologist from Calgary, was at both the disinterment and the autopsy. But he didn't stay around long. He was obviously satisfied with the results, and he didn't even bother to come back for the inquest we then held into Mrs. Coote's death.

We kept the remains until the inquest was over for a simple reason. In this type of case, you never know if some question will be brought up, the answer to which was overlooked or wasn't sufficiently examined. Meanwhile, the corpse is back in the grave and who the hell wants the embarrassment of having to go back a second time because you goofed the first time?

But as soon as all parties concerned were satisfied, Mrs. Coote was returned to the cemetery by a funeral director and the reinterment service was held. I got signatures from all parties I could think of who would be concerned, including the Court reporter, and that was that. I've been back to the grave a few times to look at it and muse about that whole puzzling case.

One thing that struck me as most unusual about this most unusual case was that the suspicions Gardner had raised were never really pursued. As I said, his own pathologist didn't even bother to attend the inquest to cross-examine. He would have been entitled to cross-examine Oliver Brammall, the pathologist, and even to take sections of the body for his own examination.

Dr. Brammall had examined the spinal cord, the larynx and the thyroid gland. The soil from the grave had been examined and tested for signs of arsenic or other poisons. But none of this became an issue in the subsequent Wilson trial.

The Coote inquest was an open invitation for Robert Gardner to come forward and get from anyone some evidence that hers might have been other than a natural death. My sole desire was to clear the air once and for all. Gardner had said in open court, and I quote, "It is our position that an inquest should have taken place because of the unusual circumstances of the death, and I shall be applying for such an inquest." That's what he told a judge of the Supreme Court. So he got his inquest, I made damn sure of that.

That's what inquests are for: to clear the air, to ask and answer troublesome questions at a public forum to which the deceased is entitled and the last one he or she will have. There's little expense involved for those wishing to testify or ask questions, and experts are often called in to help people in asking those questions. Where else can they get this help? Because after the burial, after cremation or after removal of the body from the province, the body is gone and the evidence with it. People are sometimes just not satisfied. And that's one of the enemies of our judicial system—when people are not satisfied.

It's interesting to note that Gardner asked for the disinterment and inquest only after all the other facts had been made known in Marion Hamilton's death. But there wasn't all that much known. Just what had been going on in that old house all this time? There was even a weird story about a naked man seen running out or into the house on the night of the murder.

So one must credit Mr. Gardner for making his request. The fact that it had negative results is of no consequence. His suspicions were erased; the fact proven. At least we knew that fact now and suspicion would not linger.

There was added intrigue in the case because the accused was a lawyer with considerable status in Victoria. One would presume she wasn't a foolish person. But if she had been bent on homicide or some form of acceleration of death in order to get her hands on that sum of money, would she not have covered her tracks better? Why did she leave evidence lying around? Why didn't she use some other method? Why didn't she fake a break-in by smashing a window or jimmying a door?

The case was what I like to call a real old-fashioned murder mystery, the bizarre kind the English seem to be so skilled at perpetrating and which you read about in *The News Of The World* or *The Daily Mirror*. Most murders these days seem to result from sordid things like jurisdictional disputes between drug peddlers or domestic quarrels. Somebody picks up a knife or pulls a trigger and that's that. These are the Junk killings as opposed to Honest killings.

But the "Lady" Hamilton case had all the required ingredients to satisfy the reading public: a crazed recluse living in an old house filled with dusty furniture; a highly reputable lady lawyer; money to be inherited; a length of cord in the room where the body was found; a strangulation mark on the corpse's neck; a chamber pot; a naked running man; a body dug up and two inquests held. The stuff crime novels are made of. The case had all the elements of intent, planning, method and execution which enter into the area of what is called, legally, *mens rea*—criminal intent. The public loved it.

\* \* \*

The murder trial of Elouise Roads Wilson, Mr. Justice F. Craig Munroe presiding, lasted four days and ended on June 2, 1977. Wilson's new lawyer, James Sutherland, at one stage suggested to the jury that the accused's husband, Philip, may have murdered the old lady. Strangulation, he said, was more of a masculine than a feminine act and there had been no proof that he had returned to Victoria on the night of the murder. In his summation, Crown counsel John Hall said Mrs. Wilson had become obsessed with the idea of obtaining the $175,000 in the estate to which she was the sole beneficiary.

The jury deliberated for two hours and fifteen minutes and found the accused guilty of the second-degree murder of her cousin, Marion Hamilton. Mr. Justice Munroe sentenced Elouise Roads Wilson to life imprisonment with no parole for ten years.

The British Columbia Court of Appeals rejected an appeal against conviction and sentence and the Supreme Court of Canada refused Mrs. Wilson leave to appeal further. A petition for a new trial, made to federal Justice Minister Ron Basford in May of 1978 on the basis of new evidence, was not pursued by the defence.

Elouise Roads Wilson stayed in jail. But she might never have been behind bars at all had it not been for the alertness of a Coroner's Technician named George Shoebotham and the dogged detective work of Judge Glen McDonald and his staff into the macabre murder of Mrs. Marion Hamilton.

# The Fabulous
# Travelling
# Wax Museum

Royal Canadian Mounted Police made 12 arrests and
seized more than 500,000 "hits" of LSD with an
estimated value of $3 million in a raid early Monday.
  RCMP Sgt. Norman Leibel said the seizure, made
after a four-month investigation, is believed to be the
largest ever in Canada.

News Item, February, 1982<br>
The Province

Jeffrey David Cohen had everything going for him. He was young,
he was handsome, he was rich. He was the heir to the vast fortunes of
Vancouver's Army & Navy Department Store empire. But he had a
monkey on his back. He was hooked on heroin. And, in April of 1978, it
killed him. He was 26.

Cohen had tried hard to vanquish the demon which had wasted him
and which eventually took him. He had a four-year history of drug
possession offences and a long history of traffic violations. In January
of 1978 he was convicted of possession of cocaine. But British Columbia
County Court Judge A.A. Macdonell reserved decision on sentence and

ordered Cohen to continue an intensive drug rehabilitation program in California which he had begun the previous autumn.

Cohen, out on a four-day pass from the Pasadena hospital and accompanied by a male nurse, flew to Vancouver that April to attend a family dinner and a meeting of the Army & Navy Store directors, of whom he was one.

Judge Glen McDonald of the Vancouver Coroner's Court subsequently held an inquiry into the squalid death of the young multimillionaire who had everything but happiness.

Jeffrey David Cohen, lying on his back in a bed in one of Vancouver's most opulent hotels, had choked to death on his regurgitated stomach contents. He had made the fatal mistake of mixing alcohol with drugs.

*　　*　　*

Cohen died, according to our toxicologist, from an overdose of alcohol and heroin. His venture into the drug scene was more or less concluded, or so his family and friends thought, by the conviction by the County Court Judge. Mr. Cohen was allowed to go back to California and continue some kind of treatment which, hopefully, would cure his dependency on drugs.

What made this case so interesting to the public, of course, was the fact that Jeffrey Cohen was the heir to the Army & Navy Department Store fortune, a very wealthy young man. He had inherited the family business, a very big one. He didn't want for any of the niceties of life.

He was able to lead his own life, do what he pleased and enjoy a lot of the pleasures which the wealthy have visited upon them. One would say he certainly should not have suffered from any kind of inferiority complex by reasons of life's vicissitudes, which is often the case with others less fortunate.

Now, if you go into the history of drugs in the City of Vancouver, a big and busy seaport, you find many parallels with, say, San Francisco or New York or other big ports where there is a constant flow of illegal drugs. In the old days it was opium; now it's marijuana, heroin and cocaine. There is an international airport and quick access to the producing markets of the drugs of the world. And you always find a higher usage of drugs in any seaport city than in other urban centres.

All this, of course, raises the question of how easily someone like Jeffrey Cohen can buy drugs in Vancouver without having to hold up a bank or rob a store or resorting to any of the usual criminal routines of the drug user such as prostitution or pimping in order to support the habit. So it's sort of a double standard. Obtaining drugs is apparently easy if you're rich.

One might ask, "Why would a rich young man like Cohen get involved in this?" Who knows? I certainly don't know the answer to that. Perhaps it was just part of the lifestyle, the speed of the so-called jet set with which he found himself living. Maybe he just couldn't handle the pace and the stress. Maybe it was just for the vicarious thrills.

Jeffrey had come home to visit his family and attend to company business. He knew, of course, that he was still to be sentenced, or at least put on probation, for the cocaine conviction. But it looked as if he had been making considerable progress toward overcoming his addiction. We learned this from talking with the people at the hospital in Pasadena. He was accompanied by a male nurse and they checked into the Four Seasons Hotel, one of the city's swankiest hostelries. I really don't know why they didn't stay at the family home. The nurse, a Mr. Nobles, was in the room across from Mr. Cohen's. He said later that he had gone to bed that night, leaving Mr. Cohen alone in his room, number 2014.

But Cohen had apparently made some telephone calls or had left his room during the night. The room was checked at eight in the morning because Jeffrey hadn't answered a wakeup call made by his mother. He was found lying dead on the bed, on his back. He had last been seen alive, by the nurse, about 12:30 a.m. on that Monday in April of 1978. There were no visible signs of violence on the body. But there was a dollar bill on a table and it had some white powder on it. The powder turned out to be heroin which, in the body, turns into morphine. Wrapping heroin in a bill, by the way, is a common way of delivering it to a user.

Cohen had had four drinks on the plane flying up to Vancouver, then drank two bottles of champagne at the family reunion dinner and had two more drinks later that evening. His blood alcohol content was .13 percent and there were traces of morphine in the blood when he was found dead. The drug, with the alcohol, had caused what we have learned to know all too frequently in Vancouver as a synergistic effect, the combined action of two or more agents such as alcohol and a drug, be it a barbiturate or heroin or morphine.

The simple mechanics of how this synergistic effect works is a basic situation where, as far as the central nervous system is concerned, it becomes geometrical as opposed to arithmetical. Three plus three equals five or equals seven instead of six because of the depressing effect on the vital centres.

Breathing becomes impaired and there is usually regurgitation of the stomach contents, meaning a person can literally drown in his own fluid. The breathing mechanics have been reduced and impaired by the combined effect of the alcohol and the drugs. If, for example, a man drank eight ounces of whisky and went to sleep he would certainly not die. If he were to take two or three milligrams of barbiturates or heroin—with no alcohol—he would not die. But the combination of the alcohol and the drug would result in severe depression of the central

227

nervous system.

All this goes back a long way in Vancouver history—as far back as the old days of Doridan, which was a simple little tranquilizing pill that was not under prescription in neighboring Washington State but was in British Columbia. So, in the '50s we had the teenagers putting Doridan into Coca-Cola or ginger ale bottles and shaking it all up and getting a high out of drinking the mixture. They did it with Aspirin, too. It was a big thing to put an Aspirin tablet into a bottle of Coke and shake it up. Aspirin is acetylsalicylic acid. Barbiturates are acid and this mixture can produce a high, followed usually by a depression.

I used to wander around to the beer parlors on the Skidroad near the Coroner's Court, and talk to the managers who would save me the various types of barbiturates, stuff like Sodium Seconal and other sleep-inducing agents, which the patrons would mix with their beer. These drugs were just picked up off the floor, they were so prevalent. Everyone, it seemed, was mixing them with their beer and there seemed no difficulty at all in obtaining them from dealers on the street.

I just asked the managers or the owners to pick up and save what drugs they were finding on the floor. Deaths caused by this synergistic effect were becoming more and more frequent and I was very concerned about the deteriorating situation, especially when it involved young people. In each case we sent the blood and liver and urine to the toxicologist, who had them tested to see what we could find. And, always, we found a certain level of alcohol. Not a lethal level—certainly nothing as high as .30 percent. He also found a level of barbiturates but, again, nothing as high as eight or nine milligrams. But an admixture of a half of each, of booze and drugs, could be fatal. And that was what the toxicologist always found.

One concern was to find out which of the drugs were being used the most. Hence the scheme of picking up what we could in the beer parlors. It was just a matter of putting them in a bag behind the bar and I'd come around and pick them up and stay for a couple of beers as well. We found that most were just the popular type of sleeping pill. We put them through toxicological tests and they were properly composed of barbiturate acid and weren't contaminated. So there was no explanation for all these deaths other than the mixing of a drug with alcohol. Similar deaths were occurring in New York and Seattle and San Francisco but their numbers weren't as high as ours in Vancouver.

We then started recording just where these deaths were happening and, after an investigation over three years and covering 937 deaths, we found them all to have occurred in the Skidroad area, near the waterfront and, perhaps ironically, near the Coroner's Court. We knew, of course, that this sort of thing happens also in suburban, residential areas of the city when a wife or husband can't sleep, gets up, takes a sleeping pill and then says, "Well, now I'm up I may as well have a drink, too,"

Accidentally, they're into a synergistic effect situation, the lethal mixture of two things which should never be combined. And 90 percent of the deaths we studied were accidental. They were just not meant to happen. It wasn't as if someone had deliberately consumed a bottle of scotch or gin or rye and a bottle of barbiturates into the bargain. In most cases there was no suicidal intent at all.

In my experience, the suicidal person would never, never waste good whisky. I wouldn't. The usual method would be simply to get rid of a bottle of pills and leave a note. Hopefully, they'd leave a note. But even this was not always the case. The tragedy in these deaths was that people just couldn't take that next vital breath to stay alive. Physically, they couldn't. So they died. And that's what happened to Jeffrey David Cohen. There was no inquest in his case simply because we felt there was no explanation for the tragedy other than accidental death. So the inquiry result was written up that way.

\* \* \*

Judge McDonald's official *Opinion of the Coroner* into the death of Jeffrey David Cohen, dated April 19th, 1978, said an autopsy performed by Dr. Eric Robertson, plus toxicological tests, disclosed: terminal aspiration of the gastric contents; general visceral congestion; probable overdose of alcohol and narcotics.

The Coroner concluded, "I am therefore of the opinion that this young man, who had a history of being in possession of narcotics on two occasions, May 2nd, 1974 and August 14th, 1976, came into possession of narcotics on a third occasion. Investigation by members of the Vancouver Police Homicide Division confirms my opinion that there is no evidence of violence or foul play and I am therefore concluding this Inquiry by finding in my opinion that the deceased came to his death as a result of the synergistic effect of alcohol and morphine, causing terminal aspiration of gastric contents, and that this death should, therefore, there being no evidence of suicidal intent, be classified as accidental."

\* \* \*

There was some criticism of this finding. Critics argued that cocaine (which Cohen had previously possessed) was not necessarily a fatal tranquilizer or drug, and that heroin was not necessarily fatal and nor was its turning into morphine in the body fatal. No one will argue with that. Cocaine, as a matter of fact, has been of value in anesthesia for treatment of ear and nose disorders. So none of these drugs, *per se,* is necessarily fatal. It's that damn mixture of the two, drugs and alcohol, that results in an utterly disastrous opposite effect to what was intended.

Although there was this criticism of Cohen's death being classified as accidental, I honestly feel, in reflection and retrospect, his death *was* accidental. There was no reason to believe that Jeffrey Cohen didn't have the best of all possible worlds ahead of him. Even his drug-related troubles invoked the sympathy of people. He hadn't harmed anyone but himself. He was on his way to a cure, perhaps. So it was more than a pity that he died. The tragedy for us all to see was that he had foolishly mixed alcohol and drugs.

LSD was a type of acid we became very familiar with at the morgue when it became a rage in Vancouver in the '60s. It was a hallucinatory drug, a fearful thing. I had two journalist pals who got involved with it. Ben Metcalfe, of *The Province,* took it in a hospital under clinical supervision and wrote an excellent series for his newspaper. Marie Moreau, of *The Vancouver Sun,* took it for medical treatment and by all accounts it had a considerable effect in ridding tension, stress, insomnia and so forth. But these instances were ones of controlled supervision.

However, any chemistry student with a bit of talent could make a similar type of drug which could then be sold on a market nobody in those days really understood. Just a point the size of the head of a pin was all that was needed to send a person on a wild trip. Put the stuff on a postage stamp and you had a hundred doses. That was how little of the damn stuff was needed to send people on their way. It was frightening. And, of course, this always begged the awful question: what would happen to an entire community should someone put even a small amount into a town's fresh water supply?

The tragedies caused by the use of LSD came truly home to us at the morgue when we suddenly had two deaths involving young people. Their parents, as a result, formed an association called Parents Anonymous. Simply, they wanted to find out what was going on among the school kids of the day. These kids weren't using the pure Lysergic Acid which for years had been manufactured by a Swiss pharmaceutical house and used by physicians under strict clinical and legal controls. They were experimenting with the crude stuff. And it was going on in affluent homes, mainly. Some of the effects were truly stupendous: a person could honestly believe he could fly, so he jumped off a roof; a person honestly believed he could stop a train in its tracks, so he challenged a train. Quite obviously, it didn't work that way.

Our difficulty, the same facing the International Association of Coroners and Toxicologists, was that the amount of Lysergic Acid needed for a trip was so small it couldn't be found by a chemist and by the use of gas chromatography and electro-spectro-photography in order to prove that, yes, there is acid here. We've had the same difficulty for marijuana, cannabis—finding traces sufficient for one to conclude that something was there and was it a lethal dosage?

Really, the only evidence we had concerning the use of acid was from people who were with the deceased when he or she took the acid or bought it in the first place. There was a huge criminal element involved in all this and it was a totally different drug scene to the beer parlor barbiturate situation. Wherever and whenever there is a market or a demand, the pushers are there, like vultures hovering over a corpse.

But the legal use of LSD today is strictly controlled, used in institutions where other, more routine methods of curing alcoholism or treating prescription drug-prone people have failed. It's used as a last resort, I suppose. Well, maybe it isn't an alternative but, at the same time, it has been used and, often successfully used, although it's still controversial. But as far as the illegal use is concerned, the user never knows if he's getting good quality acid or bad acid and he's going to have to take that risk if he wants to keep using the stuff.

\* \* \*

In October of 1974 Judge Glen McDonald journeyed to Toronto to address the Ontario Association of Coroners. His topic was "The Drug Scene in British Columbia" and his speech set the audience on its collective ear. This pleased him.

There had been, he said, more than 1,000 hard-drug-related deaths in Vancouver from 1970 to 1974. British Columbia was left virtually on its own to deal with 65 percent of Canada's drug problem. It was important that the federal government take over the fight on a national and international scale to take the profit out of heroin trafficking.

"So long as the price of a kilo of heroin goes from $5,000 to $280,000 with six levels of dealers making big profits along the way, there is no possible solution," he said.

And, using the argot of the underworld, the Vancouver Coroner explained exactly what was happening in the enormously profitable business of importing and selling heroin in Canada's third largest city:

-The importer arranges to buy a kilo (2.2 pounds) from Turkey, Thailand or Mexico for $5,000.

-Reduced to 80 percent heroin, the stuff is sold to a "kilo connection" at a 300 percent profit.

-The "kilo connection" reduces the concentration of the heroin—or cuts it—by half, and sells it to a "connection" at a 140 percent profit.

-The "connection" cuts this mixture to a one-part-in-four ratio and sells to a "weight-dealer" at a 120 percent profit.

-The "weight-dealer" reduces this on a one-to-12 ratio and then sells to a "street-dealer" at 130 percent profit.

-The now heavily-diluted mixture is cut to only 1-24 its former strength and is peddled mostly to "jugglers", dealers who have addicts as regular customers. The kilo of heroin has now become 9000 caps that are selling on Vancouver's market for between $30 and $40 apiece.

Judge McDonald told his audience, "If a problem of this magnitude existed in Toronto or Ottawa or Montreal, I'm sure something would be done about it—by taking the profit out of the heroin trade. Serious consideration should be given to a federally controlled drug maintenance system for addicts in both Canada and the United States. Either that or set up strict continental enforcement of drug laws right out to the territorial limits."

He ended by telling a fairy tale: "Once upon a time, a fair and modern city nestled on the shores of the blue Pacific. Every prospect pleased and, in the eyes of a certain political columnist prominent in that city, only politics was vile. He made an excellent living, stamping his tiny Gucci shoes on the foreheads of his victims when they incurred his severe displeasure. And it didn't take much to incur his wrath."

"Nobody denied that he was a shrewd little man who kept his principles (if any) well below his vest. Some believed him to be a closet Tory because he had attacked, albeit unsuccessfully, the regime of the Liberal Philosopher-King. Some believed him to be a secret agent of the Kremlin because he had a continuing public love affair with a lesser king—David, a Socialist. But the little people knew that his carefully-honed newspaper attacks could, when he wished, destroy the careers of those unwise enough not to cover their tracks."

"But the man in the Gucci shoes, for all his sophistication, had a blind spot. Tunnel-vision, wiser men called it. Growing in his beloved city, about which he boasted far and wide, was a rotting cancer. He couldn't bear to look upon it or talk about it. He didn't want mud on his shoes or dirt under his fingernails."

"This was a sickness which afflicted thousands of creatures of lesser fiber. They sat in corners all around his domain and poked syringes into their bodies, then drifted into Wonderland for a few hours. These people didn't read anybody's column. They didn't snicker at the Gucci Man's cleverness. They were addicted to something other than smart-aleck remarks and political infighting."

"These outcasts of all ages (from 14 to 50) lived in the city only as leeches. They stole. They robbed. They prostituted. And, somehow, they always got the money to buy their drugs which were delivered regularly from Hong Kong, Thailand, France, and Turkey. Nobody could stop the horrible stuff from being delivered and making them sicker. Many of them died. And were better off dead. Maybe they were the lucky ones."

"And, all the time, the political Wise Men counted their votes, sipped their martinis, and, like the Gucci Man, turned their faces away. They didn't care about the cancer. They chose not to know of the shattered families. They didn't care that some men in authority were being bribed and corrupted."

"And no wonder. Millions of dollars of dirty money flowed through the city. Time and again, fortunes were seized by the police only to be ordered returned to the masterminds behind the sickness because of something quaintly called lack of evidence. It was dirty money, everybody knew it. But it went back to the profiteers."

"Lawyers in fancy offices, with big retainers in their pockets, stood by night and day to rush to the aid of any of the evil men caught. Every assistance was given to those who made the people sick and soon they were free again to distribute more drugs and kill more people."

"And some policemen, good and decent men who knew all about this evil cancer, stayed in uniform but gave up the fight and said to each other, 'Why should we bother to try and stop this? Nobody else cares. Why should we spend our time being demeaned and insulted and treated like dirt, especially when powerful men like the Gucci Man ignore it?'"

"And throughout this fair city walked the ghosts of the dead, many of them mere youngsters trapped in the net. How did they die? They were shot, tortured, hot-capped and overdosed. One cynical old man mused that, had all their tragic bodies been mummified over the past ten years, they could have been resurrected as a gruesome exhibit at the opening of the city's Granville Mall. The lines of mummified bodies would have occupied all the space between the trees. Only the innocents would have been surprised."

"None of this was secret. Most of it was kept from the ordinary people by those who controlled the newspapers and wrote the columns. And it was ironic that everyone in this happy city went home at night and watched fantasies on foreign television networks about the never-ending battle against crime. In these Hollywood fantasies the police always won. And so the people slept easier, not knowing that the same battles were being fought in their own fair city and were being lost every time."

"Little did they know that sentences of death were being planned by callous men in Montreal and Vancouver. Cold-blooded decisions to kill those who cheated the Big Boys. Nor did the little people ever suspect that a succession of police informers had been strangely murdered on their suburban doorsteps. But, had they seen this as a plot on the Yankee television, they would have said, 'Thank God it doesn't happen here!' But it did. And it does."

"The people of the fair city had just been dragged through a long election campaign to choose a new Philosopher-King (the old one in different dress) and nobody ever talked of the cancer. It was too nasty to think about."

"There were those in the city who would have fought this evil, who would have isolated those with an infectious disease from the rest of society, and given them their damn drugs until they died. But they were labeled Rednecks, and reviled and despised by the tennis-playing sophisticates who sneered at them as being out of touch with the New

Society."

"And those who wanted to fight were powerless against the vast disinterest of the politicians and the nitpickers in the Ivory Towers.

"And nobody lived happily ever after, not even the Man In The Gucci Shoes!"

So ended Judge McDonald's fairy tale.

\* \* \*

Disgustingly, Vancouver was the heroin capital of North America. Hardly an honor for the City Fathers and the residents. Life went on with the use of heroin by mainliners, as they're called, in their late forties or fifties and who had usually done twenty or so years in jail.

An interesting thing about the heroin problem is that the criminal offence is for being in possession of it or for trafficking in it. If it's in one's system, that doesn't count. In the hundreds of autopsies we did on mainliners, we found that death was never caused by organ failure. The heart was sound, lungs were sound, diaphragm, bowel and so on were all sound. The one thing these people didn't do was eat. They always had that in common and that was almost always the cause of death. They had spent all their money on heroin and couldn't afford to eat. They died of malnutrition. Starvation.

For a mainliner, the idea of dying from an overdose was an insult. He could handle four, five, six, as many as twelve caps a day. These people were on a constant high and they had gotten along reasonably well. But in the end they died of malnutrition. They lacked protein. Those were the oldtimers; first-time users often die of bad stuff or take inadvertent overdoses.

When I spoke to the Coroners in Toronto I chose dope as the topic because it seems everybody in Canada is always asking about the terrible drug problem in Vancouver. It wasn't nice but I told the damn truth. I said I had evidence of 1,000 hard-drug-related deaths in Vancouver from 1970 to 1974. My point was that British Columbians were being left almost on their own to deal with 65 percent of the nation's drug problem. And I said that unless we were prepared on all our shores and in all our air space—of the United States, Canada and Mexico—to keep the stuff out, it would continue to come in. It's still bloody well coming in. Nobody has done a damn thing.

My argument was very simple. When the price of a kilo of heroin goes from $5,000 to $280,000—with the six levels of dealers making enormous profits along the way—there is no possible solution. This suggests almost that I've become the Devil's Advocate saying, "Look, why don't we legalize the stuff and sell it and get rid of the underworld scene, thereby saving society all the costs associated with dealing with the criminals and users?"

The underworld drug scene was something I could talk about a lot. I knew it and I also knew that the common denominator was, and still is, that we were never able to find Mr. Big. It was the pusher on the street and the user who went to jail. They would come out and, of course, Mr Big would still be in business. That's the awfulness, the shoddiness of it all.

Let's consider two cases. A heroin-user was released from Oakalla Prison in Burnaby. That afternoon he was lying in the morgue, dead from an overdose. He had thought he could take a score but it proved too much for his system. He was dead. Now, had he been kept on the drug and maintained his drug habit in jail, perhaps he wouldn't have died. Interesting?

Case number two: A Vancouver heroin addict moved to London where he studied diligently for two years and became a cabdriver, no small accomplishment in one of the world's biggest and busiest cities. But all the time he maintained his drug habit by legal prescription. He did his demanding job at the same time and he did it well.

So, it can go that way, it has been known to work that way. The difficulty is enforcement. That's where the system breaks down—too many people on prescription drugs and inadequate control. Too-busy doctors, too few policemen. So the seller gets back into the market and the user gets what he (or she) thinks is better service. That's the unfortunate part of the scenario because the average heroin-user isn't a criminally-inclined or violent person. He's happy to go through life without harming anyone, as long as the habit can be maintained. And, again, it's the poor who suffer the most because they can't afford the habit without turning to crime. There are lots of well-heeled lawyers, physicians, accountants who are on heroin or other drugs. They seldom get into trouble because they can afford it. So, what's so wrong with controlled drug usage? Right now we have a law for the rich and a law for the poor.

It's stunning to think of the huge arsenal of drugs that are legally available today. I got some figures, back in 1955, at a Coroners' seminar, which said that in that year 350 pounds of sodium barbiturates were produced in the United States. Five years later the figure was 350 tons! The consumption had gone up so much that the habit was irreversible. Everyone in the country seemed to be taking drugs of one kind or another.

Should we have marijuana under prescription? That's another problem. One theory is that it's a sort of chain reaction thing, marijuana to heroin to cocaine and other hard stuff. The usage really depends entirely on the self-discipline and willpower of the user as to how far he's going to go, how long he's going to live.

So, perhaps I'm a square when I suggest that any use is abuse. The old Presbyterian syndrome if you like. When you have such shocking figures as a thousand drug deaths in a city in four years, something has to be done. And it's that dilution at the various levels that's the real killer. The user just never knows what strength he's getting. And if he realizes he's had an overdose, it's too damn late. It's a dose he's not able to control because, either by accident or design, he's been given something too strong. But if heroin were legalized, it would be controlled by the government's Consumer Affairs Ministry. Dosages would be safe.

Simplistically, perhaps, there is really only one of two ways to go: drugs should be made legal in order to wipe out all profits made on the street; or the present law should be vigorously enforced. Enforcement is doubtless too expensive; the other route is, perhaps, too permissive. But education is vital. I can't stress that enough. My staff and I used to visit schools trying to educate the kids, and the teachers, about marijuana, about heroin, about hashish. The kids were always interested and concerned, particularly when we showed them facts and figures proving that the deaths of many youngsters of high school age were from drug overdoses. We showed them what we called the Candy Cane, a portable display of the drugs we had found on corpses. It was graphic; it was a real hit. We'd go for an hour's talk and often stayed for two hours. Sometimes three.

I usually took Bart Bastien, a Coroner's Technician who specialized in the extrusion and examination of teeth. It was what we fondly called the *Fabulous Traveling Wax Museum and McDonald Candy Cane Show*.

I really don't know if we accomplished a great deal. I certainly hope we did, but I've never quite made up my mind about that. But, I reasoned, if the students, after having been shown the dangers of drugs, went ahead and took them, at least our conscience was clear. We had tried our best. That was all we could do.

Graduation time was the worst. This was when we told the kids, "If you're going to have a graduation party and whoop it up, please, for God's sake, don't go overboard! Don't make it an all-night party! Don't drive a car if you're on booze or marijuana or other drugs or, worst of all, a mixture of both! For God's sake, never mix drugs and booze! Your next stop will be our morgue and we don't want you there. Stay the hell out!"

Maybe we helped, but there was always the old game of Chicken. If you're with a gang and someone in that gang has got dope, you're going to join him. If you don't, you're a square.

\*　　\*　　\*

The invitation to the Vancouver Board of Trade Luncheon at the Devonshire Hotel on April 10, 1978 said:
"GLEN McDONALD, LL.B. SUPERVISING CORONER
OF THE PROVINCE OF BRITISH COLUMBIA
The Coroner's name is well known to most British Columbians,

although most of us are fortunate and have not made his acquaintance professionally. This luncheon is a rare chance to meet him ALIVE AND OUT OF COURT. We promise you a frightening insight into what goes on in the daily life of a busy Coroner. You may be horrified—you will not be bored! Mr. McDonald has entitled his address *The Final Diagnosis* and that seems to say it all. PLAN to come early and view his exhibits!"

*The Fabulous Traveling Wax Museum and Candy Cane Show* of Judge Glen McDonald and his staff was on the road again.

The *Wax Museum* was a portable display of macabre artifacts dedicated to the worthwhile, but often unpopular, proposition that the dead can educate the living. Every body has a story to tell.

Judge McDonald was, and still is, immensely proud of the exhibits put together over the years. In 1979 he told a magazine interviewer, "No other Coroner's office has it. It's unique in North America."

The exhibits included a one-inch-thick steel pin which passed through a man's heart; the glove worn by a man electrocuted by a high-voltage wire while walking his dog, plus the dog's leash, part of the wire and a photograph of the body; a model of a fishing boat and government documents telling the story of the disastrous 1975 herring fishing season in British Columbia; part of a lower denture embedded in a larynx; a stab wound to a heart; gunshot wounds to a heart and a brain; a cancer of the bladder; sections of smokers' lungs.

And in the morgue autopsy room, the *Wax Museum* was always faithfully guarded by Joe, a hanging skeleton constructed of bones from many contributors who over the years had passed, albeit unwillingly, through the doors.

Both the *Wax Museum* and the *Candy Cane* were the brainstorms of Judge McDonald. But the genius who turned the ideas into reality was George Marmaduke Shoebotham, the moustachioed Chief Coroner's Technician who retired in 1981.

\* \* \*

These were two of the most innovative things I did. I was proud as hell of them and still am. It all started back in 1956. The Coroner's Court satisfied the requirements of the British Columbia Coroners Act, but I wasn't satisfied with just that. I felt we needed something physical, with visual impact. I felt there were stories to be told and messages to be given to the public. So, with the help of the *Wax Museum* and the *Candy Cane,* I delivered these graphic and ghoulish messages on the Rubber Chicken and Hand-Painted Green Pea luncheon circuit. The impact was great and the reactions rewarding. We struck home.

When the guy in charge of getting speakers for meetings of service clubs or the Board of Trade or the Chamber of Commerce or the Jaycees ran low on ideas, he picked the Coroner. I'd start with, "Well, I don't know why you've invited me here to speak to you. It reminds me of when Zsa Zsa Gabor's umpteenth husband was asked what he thought about marriage and he said, 'I know what to do, I know how to do it, but I don't know how to make it interesting!' That's my concern with you, gentlemen. But, moving from the jocular to the factual, death nobody wants, death nobody likes, death everybody would like *not* to hear about and, certainly, not be connected with."

The causes of death were what I tried to get across. How could I do this without showing people the actual visual exhibits? My thought was that if we took, for example, the belt worn by a window cleaner who had fallen from the fifth floor of a building and showed how the soap had caused the buckle to slip, we had proved a point. We could show how, when a pin was put into a tractor, a piece of metal had flown off 20 feet into the heart of a man, killing him instantly. The simple answer was don't use a steel hammer, use a wooden one.

I knew pictures speak louder than words so I inspired in George Shoebotham an interest in plastics. We made plastic cupolas, nine inches in diameter and attached them to plastic plates. Then came the anatomy lesson. We fixed a rotted liver in formaldehyde, put it in the plastic and sealed it. We did the same thing to illustrate other causes of death, such as myocardial infarction, with the actual veins and vessels of the heart in plastic. The object was to show people what is inside their own bodies, the things they don't see when they look in the mirror, and what these organs look like when they're abused. So began the *Fabulous Traveling Wax Museum and McDonald's Candy Cane Show.* The exhibits got more and more sophisticated over the years. At first I just carried them around in a box but, as the display grew, we put them on folding doors and hung them up like Venetian blinds. It grew so big that in the end we had to drive the bloody thing around in the morgue wagon.

We were always adding to it as we went along and we put in displays of grass, heroin and cocaine. We almost needed a drug squad man with us when we traveled, it was so bloody big. We were afraid of being busted by the Mounties.

We ended up with four hundred exhibits, from a toenail to the top of a head, showing every cause of death there could be, including fetuses from abortions. We didn't hide anything. It was the Coroner's Office in the field. We were damn proud of it! And our crowning glory came when we had it all on display one year at The Pacific National Exhibition, alongside the Vancouver Police Show.

We got rave reviews. It's a fascinating thing. People will look at gory details about death, but they don't like to read about it or listen to some guy mouthing at them about it. When they actually see what you're talking about, they say, "Yes, there is a point there. I can see it now." The visual presentation made all the difference.

Curiously, there was a resistance among Coroners and Medical

Examiners all over North America. But my argument was always that the Coroner's Court is the openest court in the land, with still and television cameras allowed and all media in attendance. We're doing the last thing we can do for the deceased. We're trying to satisfy that question which the dead will never ask or hear the answer to.

That's what it was all about. From the start, everything fell into place. When the ambulance people picked up a body, they would take everything out of the bathroom or kitchen medicine cabinet. We put this dope in a turkey bag and signed for it. Now we could see just what he or she might have taken.

The turkey bag was okay for a while but after a few years we needed a Goddamn warehouse for the pills we'd found. I couldn't figure out how to get this story across to the public so it would have drama and impact. Well, I could say I have three million pills, two million pills. Or I could say nothing. Who cared? It didn't matter. But if I could show people a visual exhibit, the message might get across.

That's what we did. I got Shoebotham and Bart and said, "Is there some way we can put all these pills into a pipe—like a gas pipe—six inches in diameter, made of plastic, like a candy stick? Put all the red pills in and then the white pills in and then the pink pills and all the others? The Tuenols, the Seconals, all the barbiturates."

Shoe went to someone who made plastic things. He said he could do it. I got a pole ten feet long. That was the longest we could put into the morgue wagon. We put some pills in the bottom of the pipe and slowly built up layers of all the different colors. When you turned it around, the damn thing looked just like a candy cane.

The *Candy Cane* stirred a hell of a lot of interest wherever it traveled in the province. It proved its point. It got the message across. Then, being possessed for once by a bright idea, I said, "Let's have a contest. We'll ask people to guess how many pills are in the *Candy Cane*." We never did award a prize because we didn't know the answer ourselves. But the numbers were incidental to the important question raised:

"Ladies and gentlemen, every one of those pills in that pipe caused an accidental death. You don't have to know the number if you don't take them." That was my answer to my own gratuitous question. It was a visual presentation that put across the positive side of what the Coroner's work is all about. Hopefully.

It seemed odd to me that our splendid display was always resisted by other Coroners and Medical Examiners. Perhaps people don't like to be reminded that they're in the business of death. But death has to be faced. Religion belongs in the church, death in the morgue. But death also belongs in the church and religion in the morgue. Who can say?

A thing that always bothered and deeply concerned me was suicide, particularly amongst juveniles. We tried over the years and with the cooperation of the press, to minimize publicizing jumpings from bridges and buildings. We had found that if one kid jumped and the story was given a big headline it triggered something in another teenager. Then we'd have a second jump and a third jump. We kept quiet as hell about that stuff.

I made a point of not talking about suicide to university or high school students. I was scared some young newspaper reporter would take the thing out of context and magnify it to be the biggest thing I had said. I couldn't know who was in a state of dementia, or contemplating suicide. "That's it—I'm going!"

There are people in the next world I want to ask, "Did you really commit suicide or was it an accident?" One person knows the answer to that question. Accident? Suicide? Homicide? Misadventure? Those are the jurors' options. I was 10 to 18 percent wrong in my classification of accident as against suicide, and that was always in favor of the deceased. But, like any other chicken, I reserved the penultimate decision to the insurance company. And I've always reserved the ultimate decision to the time I meet my Maker and also meet that person and can ask, "Look, did you deliberately intend that which we have found to have happened?"

# *The Wardroom*

*Those were the days, my friend—we*
*thought they'd nev—er end—we'd sing*
*and dance forev—er and a day*

Christ, I'd been Coroner for twenty-one years and I always thought we were using the Bible to swear in witnesses at inquests. I was wrong.

One day I asked my court reporter, Walter Gottschau, to check if it was dirty or tattered—maybe we should get a new one.

He handed it up to me on the bench and I opened it and—be damned—the bloody thing was all written in Arabic or something. It was the Koran. Well, they're both black, aren't they? It was a black book!

There didn't seem to be much sense changing it after twenty-one years. It had done its job. It had scared the pants off witnesses for all those years so they told the truth, the whole truth and nothing but the truth.

So we kept it and didn't tell anyone.

> *Judge Glen McDonald*

\* \* \*

We hire only people with a sense of humor. You need a sense of humor to work here.

> George Marmaduke Shoebotham
> Chief Coroner's Technician
> Vancouver

\* \* \*

In late 1953 a young lawyer named Glen McDonald arrived at the Vancouver Coroner's Court in Skidroad to sit in for the ailing Dr. John Whitbread. A child had died in a dentist's chair; a Coroner's jury was charged with finding out why.

Dr. Whitbread had run a stiff and formal court. But McDonald soon learned that, around the corner, the door to the police station press room was always open, even though one risked getting a dart in the forehead since the board was on the inside of the door which opened outwards.

The new Coroner was welcome in the pigsty press room; the exuberant members of the Fourth Estate were welcome in the Coroner's office, the courtroom and the morgue. And they all met for drinks in the West Coast Central Club next to the police station or the Empress Hotel beer parlor across the alley or the Wardroom in the morgue.

During the next 26 years Judge McDonald was to work with staff members and associates such as the puckish and ghoulishly eccentric David John Quigley, the flamboyant George Marmaduke Shoebotham, Bart Bastien, Tom Harmon, Chuck Stuart, Ted Fennell, Walter Gottschau.

The Coroner, a former naval officer, tried to run a happy ship but the niceties of protocol were observed. He was Mister McDonald to the junior staff and Mister Mac or Mac to the more senior members. Likewise, Chief Pathologist Tom Harmon was Doctor Harmon and, sometimes, just Doc. Technicians Dave Quigley and George Shoebotham became Quig and Shoe. It was an easygoing ship but the formalities of the court were strictly observed and hats and caps always removed in the Wardroom at the back of the morgue.

In the cramped and cluttered press room, always piled knee-deep with old newspapers and empty whisky bottles, Judge McDonald was to meet, besides the legendary Ray Munro, such reporters, broadcasters and photographers as Jack Webster, Jack Wasserman, Eddie Moyer, Hugh Watson, Simma Holt, Barry Broadfoot, Paul St. Pierre, Ben Metcalfe and Gordon Sedawie. There were many more.

News reporters in the '50s and '60s—unlike those of today who grimly approach their video display terminals wearing three-piece suits and bearing lofty doctorates in political science—prided themselves on being individualists. Characters. They acted their self-appointed roles to the hilt and revelled in the drama, humor and pathos they found every day in both life and death. Judge McDonald was an individualist, as well. He, too, was a born actor who relished the limelight. And an era was born.

\* \* \*

I was lost. I'd had a marriage breakup and my three daughters were living in England. I looked long and hard at myself and saw three options: I could go back to sea, I could take to the bottle or I could get my nose into this Coroner's job and see if I could make it smell. This was the course I steered. It worked.

It smelled like a job nobody wanted to hear about or have anything to do with. Would I just end up in a cul-de-sac, doing a job everybody regarded as negative if they bothered to think about it at all? I wanted it to be positive and meaningful. I wanted the word *coroner* spelled with a big *C*.

I had read occasionally about inquiries and inquests and I knew the verdicts and recommendations all went to the Attorney General's Department in Victoria. Then I found out they were buried in a vault in a warehouse somewhere and forgotten about. This was no damn use to anyone.

I was determined to change the situation and I unhesitatingly used the media as my ally. It was a big change in the life of a guy who had thought of becoming a shipping lawyer. It was a big change for the public, too. People learned that Coroner was finally spelled with a big C. There was a lot of work to be done, particularly in areas like safety in industry, traffic, the waters and the home. Positive and preventive work, in the same way preventive medicine and preventive dentistry are practiced today.

For instance, my very first inquest was into the death of a child who had a tooth extracted in a dentist's office under nitrous oxide, or laughing gas. It wasn't an easy inquest to start one's Coroner's career with. Anesthesia is always a tricky medico-legal subject and there was a lot of complicated medical testimony. But the only expert who was really needed was somebody who could restore the life of this young lad. No such person was in court but—right at this first inquest—I tried my damnedest to give the grieving parents an answer to their son's silent question, "How come I'm dead?" And maybe we did come up with something positive because major tooth extractions are today done under strict medical procedures with little risk involved.

Right from the start I saw the opportunity to ham things up a bit to attract attention, to get the Coroner's Court into the spotlight. That was where the media came in. I felt the Coroner's office should deal with a lot more than just death. It should deal with life. After all, there was no point in the pathologists and toxicologists and investigators and technicians coming up with answers to why this guy or that guy was dead if we didn't get that message back to the public. So I turned to the press.

The reporters would sniff around the office every morning but they didn't seem too interested in getting a story or covering inquests. I guess they were too busy covering the police beat or playing darts in the press room or drinking whisky donated by shyster lawyers. But I wanted them interested so I made it clear that all the press people were always welcome at all inquests. In fact, if we had an unusual or particularly interesting one coming up, I'd have George Shoebotham or someone phone up *The Sun* and *The Province* and the old *News-Herald,* the radio stations and, in later years, the television stations to make sure they all knew about it.

And if they didn't come, I made sure they were notified of the jury's findings and recommendations so at least these would get some ink and air time. What the hell, the coverage cost us nothing and—news being a competitive business—if one station or paper had an exclusive story, the other stations or papers would then want to get more information so they could develop it for later editions and broadcasts. So we had them all in competition with one another, fighting to get all the information they could from the Coroner's office. This was just what I wanted, to get the public involved through the media.

The reporters in those days were very different from today's breed. They were colorful and individualistic and cared intensely, not only about a good scoop, but about other people, about life and about death. Some—like Gar Macpherson of *The Sun*—packed revolvers with them and went on raids with the cops. That's how closely involved they were with the crime beat. They lived with it day and night.

So I didn't have to force myself to make friends with people like Jack Webster or Jack Wasserman or Eddie Moyer or Gar or dear old Jack Nilan. It was a natural rapport. It was my pleasure, when the day's work was done, to join them and hoist a few beers. It was good fellowship. There was always a feeling of mutual trust and respect but I also knew they'd be making their notes under the table. I loved that because it meant I was proving my point, the very thing I had set out to do. I was selling that nagging question the dead had left behind and the reporters were listening.

Then I got a new insight into the job. I discovered that reporters would sometimes know certain things about a case that even the Coroner's office or the Homicide Squad didn't know. They could feed *me* information which I could in turn feed to my investigators and pathologists, background things like if a person had suffered from diabetes or had a history of alcoholism or mental illness or had lived in Asia or Africa. Such knowledge was often very useful. So it was a two-way street, this flow of information, and as a result the public was better informed about what we were doing. Whether that information actually meant anything to them didn't really matter to me. I just felt they should know, that they had the right to know. Now they had that knowledge. They could use it or not as they wished but at least they had it.

This close and easy relationship with the press was not only justifiable but necessary. It was also fun. I'd stroll over to the old press room in the alley behind the police station every morning. My God, if ever a place should have been declared an historic site, that was it! There would always be four or five empty or half-empty bottles of rye or scotch on the floor, even at nine in the morning. The floor itself was never to be seen because it was covered with old newspapers up to the desk tops. There was usually a poker game or a craps game in full swing at any given hour, involving the reporters, lawyers and policemen. It was a friendly, cheerful place to be.

I dropped in to chat and find out what was going on in the city, what crimes were on the overnight police blotter. I'd often pick up a lot more grapevine information from the guys in the press room than from what was on the official blue sheets. I'd tell them who had been brought into the morgue overnight. It was a give-and-take and a take-and-give relationship.

Then the camera came into my life and I spotted another opportunity for play-acting for a positive purpose. Press photographers started turning up at inquests with new high-speed cameras and said they could take pictures without upsetting anybody or interfering with the decorum of the court. "Okay," I said. "Why not? Go ahead."

Cameras are not allowed in other courts in Canada. That's why we see artists' sketches of court proceedings in newspapers and on television. But I'd just attended an International Coroners' Seminar in Chicago where the subject of cameras in court had been discussed. The question was, "If the Coroner's Court is truly the most open court in all the land where anybody can stand up and ask questions or call witnesses to testify, why should the Coroner not allow people to take pictures in the courtroom?" Good question.

The flash camera was definitely out. It would upset people already under strain and we'd have ended up with the foreman of the jury and every other juror tripping over themselves to get their pictures in the paper. We'd probably have had defence counsel primping and preening and posturing and posing for the benefit of the cameras they knew were in court. There isn't a lawyer in the world who doesn't want free publicity. I was never exactly shy about having my picture in the paper, either.

But I felt there was room for compromise and that some photos should be allowed if the court was, indeed, as open as we boasted. Back in 1961, when I was inquiring into the needless traffic deaths of so many elderly pedestrians, *The Province* newspaper ran a six-column picture of the inquest jurors, all of whom were elderly. Now, that had the sort of impact I was after. People looked at that photo and it led them into reading about the inquest. The end clearly justified the means.

But many of the Coroners and Medical Examiners at that Chicago seminar disagreed with me, saying "Glen, you're getting into politics, you're getting into pandering to the press and the rest of the media. All you want is your own picture in the paper!" All I had to tell them in reply was that in Canada Coroners don't run for election every two or four years the way they do in the United States. I wanted pictures for the public's benefit, not my own. So I got into the photography thing and never regretted it.

I did make a rule in which I stipulated that photography would be permitted in court providing it didn't conflict with the procedures of an inquest. I didn't want people being disturbed. It was fair. It was my ruling. It was my court.

Then the television cameraman arrived on the scene. He could sit quietly with his fast film and almost silent camera and sometimes nobody even knew he was there. But the same rule applied. The fact remained that it was my courtroom, nobody else's, and only I could say, "Everybody out or everybody in!"

I had established a principle: *that an inquest is the last hearing a deceased is going to have and that all should be allowed to assemble and be present and all others will be duly informed by the media.*

So why not allow pictures of what was taking place? Maybe it's true that one picture is worth a thousand words. They certainly helped get the message across.

I wasn't abrogating the rules or hamming the act up and turning the Coroner's Court into a circus. I was accused of that many times. But my answer was always that a circus is supposed to provide entertainment and delight. And if anyone calls a Coroner's inquest entertainment, I know bloody well the next-of-kin most definitely do not! The facts and records of a cause of death are of vital concern to the public. That is why that public should have access to them without hindrance, fear or favor.

\*   \*   \*

Judge McDonald inherited his staff from Dr. Whitbread, including people like Dave Quigley, whose vast experience with the grim business of death encompassed such disasters as the Halifax harbor explosion in the First World War and the explosion of the munitions ship *Greenhill Park* in Vancouver harbor in the second. Quig's official title was Chief Morgue Attendant, but only because he was the only morgue attendant.

His job was to cut bodies open, sew them up again and generally assist the pathologists. He also washed the windows and swept the floors and, with an Irish twinkle, kept everyone in good humor. When the magnificently moustachioed George Shoebotham arrived to become his assistant, they decided the title Morgue Attendant was undignified. So, with official permission, they retitled themselves Coroner's Technicians. The name had, they decided, a nice ring to it. When Quig retired in 1960, Shoe became Chief Coroner's Technician. He was subsequently joined by people like Bart Bastien, who came from an ambulance service, and Graham Cowley, a wandering actor from the north of England.

Ted Fennell, the City Analyst, worked in the laboratory downstairs, assisted by Eldon Rideout and Mel Yip, and for many years the all-important liaison between the Coroner's office and the police was supplied by Sergeant Stan Laycock and Corporal Chuck Stuart of the Vancouver City Police. The tireless Walter Gottschau scribbled short-hand notes at some 2,000 inquests from 1954 to 1980. Win Davis took over from Lil Macpherson and, until her retirement in 1978, served unflaggingly as Judge McDonald's secretary, taking dictation, typing letters, cutting swiftly through government red tape, consoling the bereaved, arranging staff birthday and retirement parties and compiling an impressive library of eleven bulky scrapbooks crammed with news clippings and photographs.

Strangely, perhaps, the morgue was always the most cheerful place in the whole police station complex in Skidroad. It always attracted caring people to work among the dead who could no longer speak for themselves. It was also a magnet for the reporters sniffing out the news in the police station halls and corridors. They hit it off with the Coroner's staff and the staff got along well with them. Besides, the press always knew there was a cold beer in the fridge of what was called the Wardroom or a bottle of booze snuggled under a corpse in a slab in Quigley's morgue. The Coroner's Court was peopled by a big, happy and slightly loony family. There were some wicked jokes played.

*   *   *

That remark Shoebotham made about needing to have a sense of humor was right on. Over twenty-six years, I can't think of a single member of the staff who didn't have a great sense of humor. It was a qualification for the job, a condition of employment. Without it the grimness of the job would get to you, depress you, and you'd probably end up lying in the damn morgue yourself. For this reason the morgue was always a friendly and cheerful place, even though it was a place so closely related to death. That seems contradictory. But there was a joke and a giggle every day. The need for humor came into the job all the time.

There is a positive philosophy but one also has to realize it's nothing to be ashamed of if you can't work among the dead. Some people just can't do it. And if you're not able to always bear in mind that you're constantly trying to prevent accidents and deaths—by education—if you can't look at it that way, you shouldn't be there. Look for another job!

But the job can be depressing. Several of our morgue attendants became morbid and depressed over the years. Dealing with death every day was getting to them. The Coroner's staff also had the reputation of being a hard-drinking crew. This was absolutely correct. The nature of the job had a lot to do with that, too. A release, an escape valve. That's what the booze was there for, tucked away in our wardroom.

The sting of death was always with us but the victory was in trying to keep the atmosphere reasonably humorous and convincing the staff not to concern themselves solely with the fact they were working in a morgue but were really working on behalf of the living. I wanted them to think positively and remember they were trying to help the bereaved. They, after all, were the most important people we dealt with.

The dead were beyond our reach but the cause of death wasn't. That was what mattered and I wanted the next-of-kin and friends left behind to understand that. In the context of all this, we always had a joke and a laugh every day. The therapy bit, to escape from the dangers of morbidity. As a matter of fact, I sometimes thought perhaps that laugh was a little artificial, the joke was a bit forced simply because of the depressing surroundings we found ourselves in every day. But we played some good gags on each other over the years.

As Boss, I was the butt of many.

Soon after I started in the job I became known as the "Landlord of 240 East Cordova Street." I grew fond of the old brick building and, being a bit of a gardener, took an interest in the little garden out in front. It was really just a bunch of shrubs and hedges which had been well fertilized over the years by the empty whisky and beer bottles tossed into them and passing drunks urinating over them.

I decided one day, having nothing better to do, that the garden needed tidying up. I suggested to Shoe we should do some spading and weeding and planting. George and a few others sallied forth with shovels and hoes. It became a standing joke among the cops passing by that Shoe had finally been promoted and was doing the job he was best suited for. Then a reporter loomed into the office and asked if I'd heard about all the bones that had been found.

"Bones? Found where?" I asked.

"In your front yard," he said. "In that little garden you're digging up."

I ran down and there were four or five cops standing around, Shoebotham with his bloody old shovel and a Jesus great pile of bones at his feet. Then the press photographers arrived.

"My God, somebody's been using this as a cemetery!" I said. "Maybe it's an old Indian burial ground! Maybe someone has been chopped into little bits and buried! Let's get these the hell out of here!" I couldn't figure out what was going on, but I told George, "Let's treat them as human remains before we do anything else!"

We found a stretcher in the Number One Firehall next door and carried the bones into the back of the morgue. We had an expert right there in the form of Tom Harmon, the Chief Pathologist. By this time the reporters were buzzing around trying to get interviews.

"Had there been a murder and the body buried in the front yard of the Coroner's office? What a sensational story!"

All Tom could do was laugh, "Do you know what you've got there, Mac?"

"No, I don't know what I've got there!"

"Well, they're either old cows' bones or dogs' bones or a mixture of both, but they're sure as hell not human!"

"Thank God for that! But can someone please tell me just what the hell's going on?"

I learned later that some imaginative cops had buried the bones one night when nobody was looking and then called the newspapers when they spotted Shoebotham digging them up. They were telling me that if I wanted a garden, they wanted a laugh out of it. They got their laugh. But I got the last one. The pictures looked great in print and the publicity didn't do the Coroner's office any harm. But I never did get over the fact that we had enough damn bodies and old bones in the back of the building without finding more in the front!

*   *   *

David John Quigley, the Chief Coroner's Technician at the Vancouver Morgue for 29 years, has died at the age of 68.

Quigley, who retired in 1960, was a native of Halifax, N.S., and an army veteran who enlisted in the First World War as a drummer boy. He worked in the aftermath of both the Halifax harbor explosion of 1917 and the *Greenhill Park explosion* in Vancouver harbor in 1945.

He served under four coroners and five pathologists during his career and in his 29 years at the City Morgue handled more than 20,000 cases.

And in those years he found more than $90,000, all of which was turned over either to next-of-kin or the City. In one celebrated case he discovered $73,000 in cash sewn into the coat lining of a dead man who was believed to be destitute. He found $5,000 hidden on another corpse and $12,000 in an old tin trunk in a Skidroad rooming house, each bill carefully wrapped in a sheet of old newspaper.

News Item, *The Vancouver Sun*
April, 1964

\*   \*   \*

Dave Quigley, or Quig as he was fondly known, was a dedicated worker possessed of a lively, bizarre and ghoulish sense of humor. The police reporters all liked Quig but found they could never trust him. They never knew what macabre joke he would play on them next.

In a *Vancouver Magazine* article in 1979, writer Sean Rossiter recorded that Quig would often eat lunch with the reporters in the press room or the West Coast Central Club. If he spotted a green young reporter, the veteran would quietly zero in on the easy mark. His favorite trick was to take a sandwich out of his lunchbucket, place it on the table in everyone's view and say, "Well, let's see what I've got for lunch today." He would then remove the top slice of bread and carefully examine the contents, feigning surprise when a human finger rolled from off the bed of lettuce and bologna.

"Jesus!" Quig would exclaim. "Not again!"

The laughter was always a little strained.

But Dave Quigley was popular with the low-paid reporters because he kept at least a few of them in high-quality, slightly used sports jackets, slacks and shoes. They didn't have to guess where they came from. Hugh Watson, who for many years covered the police beat for *The Province,* remembers the time Quig came to his rescue in a moment of need.

"I had this heavy date with a student nurse from St. Paul's Hospital. It was her grad night and we were going to a dance at the Palomar Supper Club. I'd even rented a tux but had no black shoes to go with it. All I had were my scuffed old brown loafers. I was also broke, as usual.

"I was standing around in the press room wondering what the hell to do when Quigley wandered in. 'Let's see, you're about a nine-and-a-half,' he said. 'I think you're in luck.'

"He disappeared back into the morgue with my shoes and came back with a pair of smart black ones. 'You can borrow these but be sure and have them back by nine in the morning. The widow's coming to pick the body up,' he said.

"It turned out they belonged to a guy who had been decapitated by a freight elevator that morning. But they fit perfectly. I gave them back to Quig next morning and got my loafers back. I've often wondered what that nurse would have thought if I'd told her whose shoes I was standing in."

George Marmaduke Shoebotham, who eventually succeeded the legendary Dave Quigley as Chief Technician, vividly remembers his very first day on the job.

"Quig told me something was leaking in the refrigerated area of the morgue. Would I go in with a can of putty and see if I could fix it up? I did. Next thing I knew the door was slammed behind me.

"I was freezing in the middle of a bunch of corpses. Sod this, I said, I'm going back to the ambulance service! I heard Quig making loud footsteps outside and then I heard him shout, 'Oh, my God, it's my heart!' This was followed by the sound of a body falling. Had Quig died, leaving me locked up for the night with the stiffs? No. He opened the door, chuckling. It was just another of Quig's gags."

\* \* \*

Quigley was a great practical joker, although he was dedicated to his job all through his career. His jokes and tricks were legendary, if gruesome. And nobody was invulnerable. Not even the Boss. I'd sit down at my desk some mornings and be confronted by a severed hand curled around my pen. I'd open an official-looking envelope, thinking it was from some government department, and a couple of fingers would fall out. Quig seemed to have a thing about fingers.

But it was a two-way street. We were always being badgered by reporters who would drift in from the press room. The first thing a reporter would do in the morning would be to tramp into the morgue and bother Quigley who was busy admitting bodies and counting noses. The reporter would poke around and try to get a lead on who had died overnight, if there was a body in the morgue of somebody important, if there had been a homicide or a sensational suicide that none of the other press guys knew about. It was their job but Quig sometimes got fed up with all the questions and thought, "Okay, if you guys are going to bother me, I'm going to bother you right back! I'll get even with you!"

There was a famous occasion when he'd had a row with Barney McKinley of the old *News-Herald.* Tempers were simmering. Quig got his revenge. We had had an amputation case. Dave got the hand and tucked it up into the right sleeve of his jacket. He marched into the press room. Sure enough, Barney was sitting at his desk eating his lunch. Quig approached him with all deference. "I'm sorry I was tough on you, Barney," he said. "Let's shake hands on it."

Whereupon he stuck out his right arm and Barney McKinley was left shaking a hand that had no body attached. He fell off his chair and lost his lunch at the same time.

Quig also pulled a marvelous trick on Clem Russell of *The Sun.* This, too, involved a tuxedo but at least Clem had bought a pair of black shoes to go with it. Clem was a lifelong bachelor and a fussbudget, always worrying about how he was dressed and if he looked natty enough.

Quig met him in the press room late one afternoon and was amazed to find Clem decked-out in a tuxedo. He was going, Clem announced, to a dance at the Commodore Ballroom and had rented the tux in order to impress a young lady. I guess she was impressed. Not the way Clem had planned, though.

Quig had a devilish idea. "Just a minute," he said. "There's something missing. You don't have a white hankie in your pocket. I'll get you one."

Quigley vanished into the morgue, came back with a clean white handkerchief and tucked it neatly into the breast pocket of Clem's jacket. Poor old Clem told me later he was waltzing merrily away and casually pulled out the handkerchief to wipe his brow. Two fingers fell onto the polished floor of the Commodore Ballroom. The evening was ruined. Dave Quigley had struck again.

But I felt sometimes Quig carried his practical jokes too far and I had to tell him maybe this wasn't the way to do things. One case concerned a severed head and the other a crab.

Dave had had another tiff with the press, this time with Doug Glasgow of *The Sun*. So he sneaked into the press room when he knew Doug was out looking at the police blue sheets, opened the desk drawer where he kept his lunch and replaced Doug's brown paper bag with one of his own. When Doug went to eat his sandwiches he pulled out the severed head. Quig had scurried back to the morgue. It was Doug's turn to fall off his chair.

"Floaters," they're called. Decomposed bodies found floating in the harbor or washed up on the beaches. They're not nice to look at and sure as hell not pleasant to smell. The cops hate fishing them out of the water because they fall to pieces. Even the pathologists and morgue technicians never become hardened to their awfulness.

Vancouver is a big seaport and we get a lot of floaters and did autopsies and inquests on them over the years. It was never a job I looked forward to. The trick was to try not to get too close to the corpse. But even if you stayed ten or twelve feet away you'd be overwhelmed by a sickening odor from the cadaver. You might suddenly lose the expensive steak you had for lunch. That was nothing to be ashamed of. It was only the loss of a steak; you could always buy another.

We'd wear surgical masks on these jobs but they didn't help much. We used strong disinfectants but I thought they smelled even worse than the body. There were the maggots. That was a truly disgusting sight and I've seen even technicians and pathologists blanch and turn away. But it was a job that had to be done.

The maggots inside a floater would be so much alive that the body would literally move around on the autopsy table. It was eerie. That's what happens when you drown in the sea around Vancouver or anywhere else. Crabs, fish, eels, sharks—all the species of marine life get into the act. That's the way of life. It's a law of what we might call the

Marine Jungle. All creatures are living and surviving and prevailing around death.

Some years ago there was concern that longshoremen working the Vancouver docks refused to wear life jackets on the job. Some had drowned as a result. It was a serious situation. I zeroed in on a case when a worker, not wearing a life jacket, fell into the harbor, hit his head on a log and drowned. His body wasn't recovered for three weeks and by that time the ravages of marine life had taken their toll. When the body came into the morgue we had everything—crabs, little fish, maggots, limbs gnawed away, the eyes eaten out. It was a disgusting sight.

I decided right then we would have an inquest because this was a case involving a needless death and the important matter of industrial safety. An inquest could perhaps lead to badly-needed education. I wanted to teach the longshoremen a lesson so I purposely empaneled jury members from the union who were opposed to the wearing of life jackets on the job. I simply wanted to show them the grim consequences of not doing so. Show them I did!

"And now, Mister Foreman and jurors, I will proceed with you to the view room where the deceased will be identified to you and any marks or signs of violence thereon shown you." They didn't know what they were in for. Dr. Harmon and I led the way and, dramatically, we ripped off the white sheet. There lay this awful spectacle of what had once been a human being; of what the sea life had ravaged and insulted. No eyes left. Lice. Maggots. Moving, quivering flesh. Flesh eaten away and bones bared. A strong stench of powerful disinfectants which left no mystery as to why they were present. One of the big longshoremen collapsed on the spot, fainted dead away. The others, I could see, were aching to leave that grim room and dash across the alley to the Empress beer parlor. But we had a job to do.

I asked, "Are there any marks or signs of violence on the body of the deceased?"

Doc Harmon said, no, there were not. Death, in his opinion, was from drowning and the condition of the body was due to the normal activities of marine life in the harbor of Vancouver.

Back in the courtroom, I asked the jury if they thought this man would have suffered these terrible insults and indignities if he had been wearing a life jacket. The jurors got the message. They returned a verdict of accidental death due to drowning but they also strongly recommended that henceforth, longshoremen wear life jackets when working on the docks and ships. I had proved a point. I had taught them by dramatic and gruesome tactics. Some lessons are taken best by way of insult.

But the end to that awful story involved dear old Dave Quigley and his macabre sense of humor. Several weeks later I heard, via the grapevine, that Quig had taken a crab from the longshoreman's chest cavity and given it to a reporter to take home for dinner. I pray to this day that the unsuspecting reporter never found out where the succulent seafood feast had come from. That was when I told Quig that enough was enough!

* * *

It seemed odd that David John Quigley, a man who dealt with other people's deaths every day of his life, should become so preoccupied with the approach of his own. So much so, in fact, that Judge McDonald and his staff discovered it had become an all-embracing obsession. Quigley's agony became a Coroner's Court legend. It came about this way.

* * *

When he was in sight of retirement, Quig had to make a decision regarding his forthcoming pension from the City. Should he sign it over to Mrs. Quigley or keep it in his own name?

This dreadful decision really bothered him and he kept coming to me, asking for advice. I knew his will was in order because I'd looked after it. It was simply a question of who was going to die first.

"Quig, only He knows. Up there," I told him.

But I did add that, usually, the husband goes before the wife and every life insurance company in the world would tell him that. This news seemed to get Quig even more upset so I arranged for Tom Harmon to examine him and, also, Dr. Maurice Fox, one of the ablest physicians in the city, to give a second opinion.

The unanimous opinion was that Mrs. Quigley would definitely live longer than Mister Q. The appropriate forms were filled out, signing the pension over to Sadie, and we had our farewell party for Quig when he retired in 1960. It was a great party. The only fingers in evidence were live ones.

But Sadie had the last laugh. Four months later, sitting with some friends in the Empress beer parlor, she dropped dead of a heart attack. She was trundled across the alley into the morgue. Quig was distraught, not only about Sadie's demise but about his beloved bloody pension plan. He blamed us and the learned doctors for their confident prediction of Sadie's longevity. It wasn't until we convinced him that the pension would automatically revert to him that he spoke to any of us again. Quig died four years later. I was gratified to know he had forgiven us our imperfections.

* * *

Another legend of the Vancouver Coroner's Court involved Ray Munro and the gangland murder of a bartender named Danny Brent. Brent was an obscure figure involved in the underworld drug trade; Munro, by contrast, was extremely high profile.

A tall, handsome, charming reporter-photographer with Vancouver's *Province* newspaper, Ray Munro looked always as if he had just stepped from the set of Ben Hecht's play *The Front Page,* brown fedora jauntily set on the back of his head, even bearing a Press card stuck in the band. He lived the role to the hilt in real life, mesmerizing, bedeviling and bedazzling editors, judges, policemen, promoters, women and big C Coroners along his merry way.

Ray Munro raced about the city in a grey Ford coupe equipped with siren and red flashing lights. He conned Ken Stauffer, co-owner of the Cave night club, into believing he was a Cossack dancer and performed, wearing fake moustachios and high boots, to sellout crowds for two weeks.

He captured a rapist in Vancouver's Stanley Park with the help of Don McLean, a *Province* reporter dressed as a woman. He accused members of the radical Sons of Freedom Doukhobor sect of shooting down his rented airplane in the British Columbia Interior, later confessing that he had himself shot bullets through the wings with a revolver.

He toured Canada as a hypnotist and it was said that, while practising the trade, he put a *Province* copyboy to sleep and was unable to wake him up for two days. He was the first person to parachute to the North Pole. And, on September 15, 1954 Ray Munro and Danny Brent met on the tenth hole of Vancouver's University Golf Course. Or was it the 13th?

\* \* \*

Danny Brent was head bartender at the Press Club, the joint owned by John Hickey just up the street from the old Sun Tower. It was a popular watering hole for newspapermen and cops and lawyers. John always graciously extended credit. I dropped in for the occasional drink and got to know Danny.

The next stop in Danny Brent's life was that he was found dead on the University Golf Course, shot through the head. He was lying near the green of the tenth hole and had obviously been shot with his jaw right on the grass. We found a bit of gold filling from a tooth embedded in the grass. It was clearly a gangland killing and a cache of heroin was later found in a locker in the Vancouver Bus Depot. The key was in a pocket of Danny Brent's jacket. But what really puzzled me was when I saw a copy of *The Province* newspaper later that day. There, splashed across page one, was a photo of Danny Brent's body lying on the grass with the number thirteen flag flying behind it.

"My God! Maybe I'd been at the wrong golf course or looking at the wrong Danny Brent!" So I chased down Ray Munro, who I found sitting over a gin and tonic in the West Coast Central Club. He was grinning like a Cheshire cat, as usual. I'm sure he was expecting me to show.

"How come," I said, "you got a picture of flag number thirteen on the green and here I'm going into an inquiry or an inquest with all my reports saying this man died on the tenth green?"

"Simple, Mac," Ray said, completely unruffled. "It was easy just to switch the flagsticks. The tenth green seemed so dull. Now, number thirteen—what artistry—what poetry!" He even bought me a drink. That was Ray Munro.

\* \* \*

There were the legends of the refrigerator that *nobody* owned and the Wardroom that *everybody* owned.

\* \* \*

One of our technicians moved from his house to an apartment and bequeathed us an old fridge. We hefted it into the back room of the morgue. This was what I, as a navy man, christened the Wardroom. It was a cozy place to sit and have a friendly chat and a drink. We had a place to keep the beer and the tonic cold. Everyone was welcome to come and have a snort and a chin in the Wardroom. A lot of people came.

It was our private place. It was our philosophy that we saw enough of death and depression each and every day, so why not enjoy a quiet and contemplative drink when the day's labors were done? Many a thoughtful moment was enjoyed in the Wardroom.

One day the fridge broke down. We couldn't fix it. We arbitrarily decided it was up to the City of Vancouver to foot the bill. After all, along with the beer, the fridge contained an overflow of forensic samples and specimens pickled in formaldehyde from the morgue and the analyst's office. Hearts and kidneys and livers and so forth. It seemed only fair that the City should pay to have the thing repaired. We invented an official serial number and submitted a bill for repairs. The City Fathers weren't the least impressed.

"Not on our list," they said. "We don't own this."

We tried again and again for twenty years, always using different code numbers. But we never did get a dishonest dime out of the City for that damned old fridge.

\* \* \*

There was the legend of the Coroner's annual Christmas party, a joyous occasion enthusiastically attended by the staff, judges, prosecutors, policemen, reporters, photographers, lawyers, funeral directors, ambulance drivers, the firemen from Number One Hall and the occasional stray drunk who wandered in to seek shelter and solace from cruel wintertime Skidroad.

Everyone was welcome at Judge McDonald's celebration of Christmas. The sole stipulations were that each guest bring a present, preferably of the liquid variety, to put under the tree and everyone must have a good time. Attendance was so great the party overflowed from the courtroom into McDonald's tiny office, where the merchant navy red ensign hung on one wall, and downstairs to the cluttered lab shared by Dave Quigley and George Shoebotham. Some guests found themselves drinking amid the corpses in the morgue itself.

It was a time of camaraderie and of good fellowship and of coming together. Dave Quigley sang; the Coroner pumped his shiny-toothed accordion; everyone joined in. There were drinks and carols and more drinks and roast turkey with the trimmings. There was storytelling and there were jokes. There was laughter. There was a star on the top of the tree.

*  *  *

Christmas was always a special occasion at two-forty East Cordova Street. I insisted we have a party every year. It was a standing order. Nobody ever objected. We held it in the courtroom and the bar was set up on the table used by legal counsel. But sometimes the room got so crowded the party would spill over into the morgue, among the white sheets and the slabs and the bodies. For some reason the witness box and the bench were always popular spots for the taking of a drink.

I insisted that everyone should contribute something to the bar and nobody objected to that either. There wasn't a funeral director in the city who failed over the years to contribute a bottle of scotch or rye or gin. And, of course, we always had a tree, decorated by the staff and with presents underneath, covered with fairy lights and with a star on the top.

We shut up shop at one in the afternoon of Christmas Eve and the guests would troop in clutching their gaily-wrapped bottles. People really had nowhere else to go. Well, you couldn't very well hold a party in the middle of the police station, you couldn't hold one in the police courts, and the press room was too damn small. Our courtroom was the obvious place and I always made sure it was never booked for an inquest on the day of Christmas Eve.

The biggest funeral parlor in the city in those years was run by Simmons & McBride and they played a very important role in the party. A few days before Christmas I'd get a card from them wishing me the compliments of the season. But there was always another message on it, too. So I'd trot up to the James Inglis Reid butcher shop on Granville Street and pick up an enormous free turkey. I'd give it to Shoebotham and, somehow, he'd find room for it in the old fridge in the Wardroom or in one of the freezers in the morgue, alongside bits and pieces of bodies and specimen jars. It was just another carcass.

The day before the party we'd take the bird across to Henry at the Ovaltine Cafe on Hastings, around the corner from the police station, and the Chinese chefs would look after the cooking department with all due care and attention. At one-thirty, two waiters would appear with the turkey and all the trimmings and place it ceremoniously on the counsel table. The party was now officially underway.

This was when Quig always played one of his typical bloody pranks. He'd rush out of the morgue wearing a bloodstained smock, carrying a surgical saw and a huge knife and hand them to me as I was about to carve the turkey.

"You can only have these for a few minutes, Mister Mac," he'd say in a loud voice. "I'm busy doing a job in the back!"

They were glorious times, full of song and drink and good cheer, an assembly of caring people with a common bond. They enjoyed life to the fullest because they all knew and understood death. They got a bit wild and exuberant at times but there was never any unpleasantness. No fights, no lost tempers, no heavy and heated arguments. We were all there to have fun. And everybody left, as best they could navigate, when they were told the party was over.

I always brought the old accordion down and played extensively. Perhaps too extensively in the eyes of some people but what the hell, I had a captive audience and if they didn't like my music they could always leave. Providing, that is, they'd already contributed their bottles. Nobody left. Everyone joined in the singing, as well as they could depending on their state of sobriety.

*By the Sea, By the Sea, By the Bee-yoot-ee-ful Sea!*
*Roll Out the Barrel.*
*Mademoiselle From Armentieres.*
*The North Atlantic Squadron.*
*Knees Up Mother Brown.*

Great old songs with a good beat to them. I always maintained that I was truly destined to be a whorehouse piano-player or a second-rate beer parlor musician with a squeezebox. So I'd never start playing until everybody—including me—had at least three drinks in them. Then I was bound to be a success. I couldn't miss. Naturally, we'd end up with carols—*Silent Night, Good King Wenceslas, O Come All Ye Faithful.*

I thought at first that Dave Quigley, being a sort of rough-cut diamond of Irish ancestry who had worked amid death all his life and seen many terrible things, wouldn't fit in with this somewhat maudlin outpouring. But the mood always got to him and there were many Christmas parties when I saw old Quig with tears streaming down his cheeks.

It was unreal, somehow. Here was a man who had been eyewitness to so much of the destruction of life, who had opened up and sutured twenty or thirty thousand corpses, and who had lived all these years in the constant company of tragedy and death. Now he was weeping among the living. Somehow, with our Christmas tree with that lonely little star of Bethlehem twinkling on the top, we had got through to his warm Irish heart. And there he was, with tears in his eyes and a sob in his throat, trying to sing that stupid song, *I'll Take You Home Again, Kathleen.*

Well, I never did find out who Kathleen was or if she ever got home again but I managed to play it with him on the squeezebox. And that was when—well, when Quigley sang we all knew somehow that he was our mentor.

* * *

The era ended, as inconspicuously as it had begun, in 1979. The British Columbia government took over the Vancouver Coroner's Office. Some staff, like Judge McDonald himself, took early retirement and fled the strangling red tape of bureaucracy. Some were transferred to other offices and others quit.

The old pile of beige bricks at 240 East Cordova Street, built in 1932, was declared a Heritage Building and will never be torn down. On one side, the superannuated Number One Firehall is now a theatre and actors' workshop. On the other is an addition to the police station, known now as the Public Safety Building.

The morgue was left to stand empty, alone with its silent memories and, perhaps, ghosts.

The party was over.

> *La la la la la la—la la la*
> *la la la—those were the days,*
> *oh yes, those were the days.*

### END

# *Addendum*

The era of the fiercely independent and individualistic Vancouver Coroner's Court ended on a note tinged with sadness. But there are many fond memories, many laughs still shared. Some members of a staff that spanned more than two decades have been mentioned in this book.

Others who contributed to the court's unique sense of family included: Dr. Oliver Brammall, Dr. Eric Robertson, Andre Filion, Ed Langille, Ian Marshall, Richard Sloan, Chuck Standish, Hal Murphy, John Tillett, Joe Carpenter, Doug Jack, Diane Messier, Val Steggles, Hana Zita.

And among the many denizens of the infamous old police station press room were to be found: Barney McKinley, Gordon Dickson, Ormond Turner, Norman Hacking, Ron Thornfer, Tony Eberts, Tom Ardies, Dick Beddoes, Mark Raines, Doug Glasgow, Frank Meade, Gar Macpherson, Jack Nilan, Malcolm Baber, Toddy Beatty, Georgia Lane, Al Hartin, Thelma Roote, Jack King, Ted Greenslade, John Kirkwood, Clem Russell, Wilbur Bryan, Harold Guilfoyle, Gordon Purver, Ed Simons, Patrick Nagle, Jack "Snuffy" De Long, Stan Shillington, Yorke Vickers, Frank Walden, Ron Haggart, Ron Rose, Terence "Tooth Fairy" Ross, Bruce Ramsey, Scoop McKeevie, Tom Jarvis, Jim Billingsley, Bryce Williams, John Olding, Tom Gould, Ed Cosgrove, Don Matheson, Chuck Jones, Dave Buchan, Ray Allan, George Diack, Danny Scott, Charlie Warner, Byron Scott, Ralph Bower, Rex Ellis, Ross Kenward and two Bill Cunninghams.

Some names may have been missed in print but are not forgotten in memory.

# INDEX